PAT SILVER–LASKY

SCREENWRITING
for the 21st century

BATSFORD

For Peter
My Mythic Mentor
And tireless researcher
For his love and support
In the long journey that is a book.

A CIP record for this book is available from the British Library

First published 2004 by B T Batsford
The Chrysalis Building, Bramley Road, London W10 6SP
www.batsford.com

ISBN 0 7134 8833 6

An imprint of Chrysalis Books Group

Distributed in the United States and Canada by Sterling Publishing Co., 387 Park Avenue South, New York, NY 10016, USA

Printed in Great Britain by
Creative, Print and Design (Wales), Ebbw Vale

Illustrations:
Pat Silver-Lasky (p. v)
Jesse L Lasky and Cecil B deMille (p. vii)
DeMille's note on Samson's Character (p. 36)
Mainstream Structure for a Feature Film (p. 43)

Using the Card System (p. 46)
Action versus Dialogue (p. 59)
Mythic: The Hero's Journey (p. 78)

Cartoon by Peeby (p. 98)
Reader's Report (p. 112)

| CONTENTS

| SOME QUOTES FROM FORMER STUDENTS:

obsessed with dialogue, now I'm obsessed with structure, and I'm a much better writer because of it.' Anthony Alleyne, writer, director – currently preparing a series for the BBC

'Pat Silver-Lasky is without doubt one of the most sharp, remarkable and uniquely talented creative writers and consultants that I have had the pleasure and privilege to work with. She has both a magnificent knowledge and a unique vision to suggest always the perfect solutions. I can't think of any future screenwriters that wouldn't enormously benefit of her unique skills.' **Edmon Roch, Associate Director to Whit Stillman:** *Barcelona, The Last Days of Disco*

'Whilst at the London International Film School, Pat single-handedly nurtured, supported and developed my script writing ability. She was objective and critical, but in a way that made you enthusiastic and eager to better yourself. Without Pat's great support, encouragement and knowledge I would not have had the understanding of structure, dialogue and story telling for the visual medium that I find so vital now that I am an independent filmmaker. Pat is still a constant source of support and information and I know that without her, my films would be far less worthy of recognition. She still remains a great friend.'* Alex Tweddle, producer, writer, director 'Jack' short film for TV 2002

'The wonderful thing about Pat Silver-Lasky is that she is both a great writer and a great lecturer. This means that you are getting taught by someone who is writing now, not someone who has read the manuals. As Pat has written for both the States and the UK you get the broad picture. I always found her lectures enjoyable, informative and concise. Bang on the money.'* Martin Carr, producer, Destiny Films. 2002 BAFTA nomination for one of his BBC films

'The thing about Pat is she takes your writing to a whole new level. She makes you think outside the box and fully understand the story you are trying to convey. Before I met her I was

'Pat has been my tutor, mentor and friend since we met at The London International Film School in 1994. In that time I have seen her in her many hats! Whether lecturing to an audience of students, advising on a one to one basis in her capacity as a script doctor, collaborating on projects as a co-writer or simply chatting over a cup of tea, her guidance, teachings and insights are always readily available. Pat is an invaluable asset to anyone wishing to survive, as she certainly has, this most challenging of professions. The tales and stories she can recount from her amazing career are an education in themselves.'* **Andrew James, playwright/actor** A Masterclass with Michael Caine

'Pat became my friend and tutor who not only quenched my thirst for knowledge but gave me a passion for more. It's always frustrating as a novice writer to have great ideas but lack the know-how in turning them into readable and professionally structured scripts. I spent many priceless hours with Pat shaping my ideas, absorbing her vast knowledge and being enlightened by her writing techniques which can turn a good idea into a cracking idea. Her ethos and way of working are a perfect mix of creativity and commercialism without cliché or the banal. I know I will be drawing on the invaluable guidance Pat has given me throughout the rest of my career.'* Max Barber, freelance writer/director for BBC, Channel 4, Discovery Europe, Carlton Television, UKTV

| INTRODUCTION

In 1914 my father-in-law produced the first full-length feature film in Hollywood, *The Squaw Man*. He and his company, The Jesse Lasky Feature Play Company (which later became Paramount Studios), founded an industry that has grown beyond the wildest dreams of those long-dead film pioneers. My late husband, Jesse Lasky Jr, carried on the cinematic tradition, writing more than 50 films including *Samson and Delilah* (1949) and *The Ten Commandments* (1956). Their films had one purpose: to entertain. If they informed in the process, it was a plus. Cecil B DeMille's mantra was, 'If you want to send a message, use Western Union' (occasionally incorrectly attributed to Sam Goldwyn).

In the days of silent films, movies could easily travel around the world and, with appropriate subtitles, be seen and understood anywhere. They did carry a message: it was a way of life. Perhaps not actual life – but life in an idealized world. The real world responded, taking up the celluloid vista of style, make-up and dress, of home furnishings and etiquette, of romance and social graces, and making them their own. Hollywood movies were selling the American Dream. Sound and colour added to the appeal of the good life with a happy Hollywood ending. Everyone wanted to get into the movies, if not as a movie star, then as a director or maybe even a writer – although this last profession is perhaps the least understood aspect of filmmaking.

This book is about writing screenplays for the 21st century. I've been a novelist and scriptwriter for television and films for over thirty years. I've learned that for every method of writing a screenplay, there is an alternative that also works. So what can be taught? Not talent. You either have that or you don't and I can't give it to you in this book. Scriptwriting is a highly specialized craft and requires the use of technical skills. Yet there are no hard and fast rules. It's not enough to have a good idea for a character or a great story premise. That's only the starting point.

I can explain the writing process and analyze the available techniques of form, structure, and content; the framework with which you must begin. I can clarify such

terminology as cliffhangers and imagery and show you how to ask yourself the right questions (a vital tool). I can illustrate the different approaches to writing the novel/stage play/television drama/feature film; teach you how to use the card system, steplines (a step-by-step breakdown of the story), outlines, and treatments; and how to understand the genres. This book will guide you in analyzing elements of your screenplay – such as what percent should be dialogue and what visual description – and what subjects are not filmic in the first place. You will not find terminology like 'quasi-antiplot' or 'didactic ideational structure'. You will be learning new words that are normal film terminology, finding new terms and understanding old ones in a new light. A glossary of these terms can also be found at the back of the book in appendix 1.

Some techniques qualify as being essential tools for the scriptwriter. Even those writers who claim just to sit down and write with no rules and no end in sight, unconsciously follow simple guidelines because they are essential. In understanding these guidelines and discovering why they work (and why some don't) you should be able to put your own individual voice to practical use.

It's just as important to learn what not to do. The old admonitions – don't flashback within a flashback, don't squeeze all your exposition into voiceovers, do get your initial turning point into the first fifteen minutes, don't dump all your back story into one scene, do get conflict into all your scenes, don't kill off your hero in act one (yes, there are acts, even though it's not on stage and there's no curtain) – these are all trusty rules for good drama. But all rules are made to be broken if there is justification. It's how you break them that makes the difference.

The would-be screenwriter with some natural talent and an open mind can learn the basic procedures – concepts that will make it easier for you to use your own vision, to analyze your own work, and especially to spur your imagination to churn up those ideas, hopefully fresh and original. You will learn how to develop a simple idea into a story told through a visual medium. This book can help

talent find a voice by giving it a direction and the tools with which to create a saleable screenplay. You've heard of writer's block? The prevention lies in some simple ABCs and a possible D – and not in a bottle of whisky or a few Es!

Scriptwriting is an art as well as a craft. Shakespeare is said to have said (in fact it was the French literary theorist, Georges Polti, in 1895) that there are only 36 dramatic situations in the world, but just think how many thousands of stories have been told! What made each one individual? What twist can you put in your 'tale'? What is different about your story? Does it lie in the nature of the character? The type of story? The structure? Is your approach to the material comic, ironic, or serious? Is your aim to frighten, to mystify, or to arouse high emotion?

In investigating the essential qualities of a screenplay, as compared to a stage play or novel, you will discover how to manipulate the creative process to produce successful scripts for film and television. This book concentrates on the writer's role in learning the craft in a professional way and presenting work that professionals will respect. You'll learn how to pitch a 'logline' (one sentence that sums up the entire movie) and get your project read.

Today, if you surf the Internet you'll discover some 57,000 sites that deal with aspects of screenwriting. I can't tell you which ones would be helpful because I haven't seen them all. There are dozens of 'how-to' books on the subject and a number of gurus who will dissect films for you, starting with *Casablanca*. My students at the London International Film School (where I was script consultant and lecturer for eight years) had read a few of those books and were still mystified.

So with both my professional and my teacher's hats firmly in place, I feel qualified to set out this practical, professional guide for the serious beginner. You've got to love movies – even crap movies – because it's not going to be an easy road. If you're ready, read on. There are opportunities in the marketplace for good scriptwriters today.

Chapter 1 | WHAT'S IT ALL ABOUT?

What are the defining images of the 21st century? Is it American culture: New York cops and car chases, Chicago hoods and drugs, LA palm trees and sex? Quentin Tarantino rode this wave, making films that were both artistically respected and part of the American pop culture. In Britain, *Lock, Stock, and Two Smoking Barrels* investigated an English version of the 'slice of low-life' genre. Is London the 51st state – as the Barbican's 'Year of American Culture' claimed? How do sex, violence, animated comic strips and the cultural imperative of America affect the British and European screenwriter?

Movies are essentially a business: the business of entertainment. Entertainment can be characterized as escapism, but it should be something more than an aid to digestion for the middle classes. In the wake of world terrorism and war, what subject matter will draw in the public? Is it fantasy, such as *Harry Potter* or *Lord of the Rings*? Science fiction or comedies? Films analysing the horrors of war or political polemics?

So how do the major film companies choose their subjects? The truth is, nobody knows what's going to work until the film plays before an audience. That's why they have preview screenings, where the first cuts of films are shown to a randomly selected audience. Tastes and rules of censorship have changed. Cecil B DeMille said that 'you can show any amount of decadence and debauchery as long as you show that it is morally incorrect and it's punished'. That may have been true in the 1940s but it is not true today when the criminal is often the hero and gets away with the girl and the money.

But how far can you go? If you want to sell your screenplay, you must be aware of the distributor's problems. A producer won't buy your script if he thinks he can't get it distributed. And he will have difficulty getting a film distributed with a rating more restricted than 'Parental Guidance' (PG). Even though the rulings in the UK have recently been relaxed, a film must get no more than a PG rating to make a lot of money.

The Story-Tellers

The idea of presenting stories dramatically in front of an audience began, as far as we know, in ancient Greece some 2,500 years ago, and a small number of those plays have come down to us today. To relate the difficult or 'action' parts of the story the Greeks used a chorus of voices behind the central characters. (Playwrights were not allowed to depict violence on stage; it could only be described by the chorus). The chorus worked a bit like the voiceover narrations in many modern-day films (Woody Allen, who uses a lot of narration, put a real Greek chorus into *Mighty Aphrodite*). The Greek plays had beginnings, middles, and ends – and suddenly the format was born.

In the Middle Ages came the English mystery plays, which had a religious story-line (usually a retelling of well-known Bible stories) and were presented as a pageant in churches and village squares. Many are still performed today in Britain and on the Continent.

Theatrically dramatic story-telling as we know it was finally crystallized in 16th century Italy with the Commedia dell'Arte and was further developed into comedy drama by Molière in 17th century France. In the 19th century Alexandre Dumas (père) and his son (Dumas fils) formulated a structure for their plays and wrote what were known as Boulevard Comedies. They kept some 12 writers working for them in an early version of a think-tank (an approach used today by most American TV sit-com producers). These comedy dramas became the hit of 19th century Paris.

Norway's great author and playwright, Henrik Ibsen (1828–1906), was influenced by their success and further developed the dramatic form. August Strindberg (1849–1912) took up the gauntlet in Sweden, and in Russia, Anton Chekhov (1860–1904) followed suit with some heavy drama, each developing the formula and structure a little bit more.

Until the mid-20th century most plays were

formatted into three acts. Then someone decided that the audience might walk out if there were two intervals and the stage play began to be presented in two acts. But by this time the movies had begun to try their hand at visual story-telling. Filming in New York, D W Griffith made *The Musketeers of Pig Alley* (1912) which ran for 17 minutes. In 1913, Jesse L Lasky Sr, who believed in the story first and foremost, bought a hit stage play and went out to an area of orange groves called Hollywoodland in sunny California with his new partner, Cecil B DeMille, to film it[1]. It was the job of the third member of the company, Sam Goldwyn (Goldfish back then), to sell *The Squaw Man*. That was the beginning of Hollywood as we know it[2].

Bums on Seats

If a filmmaker wants to stay in the game of commercial movies he must make films that audiences will pay to see – films that will put 'bums on seats'. That may sound obvious, but many filmmaking writer/directors discount it from their thinking in order to bring their personal view of the world, however narrow, to the screen with the aid of some intrepid backer's money. While their concept may be fascinating, and, if they're lucky, find art-house distribution (increasingly difficult as independent cinemas are muscled out of the market by multiplexes), the project is sometimes too idiosyncratic to appeal to a wide audience or – worse for their backers – to get a distribution deal and recoup its costs.

Experimental filmmakers should in the first instance keep a close eye on their budgets. If an experimental film gets great critical reviews, the filmmaker may be able to raise the money to make another film. You can risk a bit of experimentation if your budget is under £50,000, and a few successful films have fit into that financial bracket. *Clerks* (1994) – budget $25,000 – won a prize at the Sundance Festival and the makers got a contract from a major studio to make a feature for $5m. *The Blair Witch Project* (1999), written and directed by Daniel Myrick and Eduardo Sánchez, was made for peanuts. Both did their makers a lot of good.

Studios promote successful independent filmmakers so that they can copy their trend-setting ideas to make commercial films: for

instance, *Bhaji on the Beach* (1993) written by Gurinder Chadha and Meera Syal, and directed by Chadha, gave rise to further comedies about growing up in multi-ethnic societies. Chadha moved to Hollywood to make the successful *What's Cooking?* (2000), while her wonderful British film *Bend it Like Beckham* (2002) achieved her first major theatre distribution to become a box-office hit.

Many would-be filmmakers today care nothing about any films made before the days of Quentin Tarantino, yet there is much to learn from the work of the past, if only how tastes have changed. There are many places to see classic films, including on television (though they are increasingly hard to find on the free-to-air channels). In London the National Film Theatre regularly screens film classics. Film clubs can be found in most major cities around the world. if you are trying to write for the cinema you should become acquainted with the work of such international masters as Fellini, Godard, Rohmer, Antonioni, Rivette, Zanussi, Ingmar Bergman, Kurosawa, Mizoguchi, and Hitchcock (who qualifies as both British and American). Of the Americans, John Ford, Howard Hawks, Billy Wilder, Anthony Mann, Preston Sturges, and Orson Welles are a few of the names with which to familiarize yourself. Many, but not all, were auteur/directors – writing as well as directing their films.

It won't help for a screenwriter to think of him/herself as sitting in a candlelit garret writing immortal prose. He (from now on I will use 'he' to stand for both 'he' and 'she') is part of a vast industry and must know something about the business if he wants to succeed. You need more than an idea. You have to have a good script to open the door. You can learn much about the structure and shape, the mood and imagery of film making, the precision of dialogue, the ebb and flow of story, how to set a plot-point, and many other nuances from these masters – and most of all, in my view, from Hitchcock.

A would-be screenwriter should have a perception of all the allied problems of filmmaking. Ideally one could benefit by working as a 3rd Assistant Director or even doing props or being a 'gofer' (the dogsbody, doing odd jobs on a film) just to get the feel of the medium and what it's like to actually shoot a film. You must also have a working understanding of the producer's problems. In terms of investment, to be a success a film must simply make more money than an equal investment in the money market – even if it is only 1 per cent more. On a first film it's particularly important to be sure your backers get their money back. If they do, you can call on them again – and for more money the next time. That means lowering the level of risks in a very risky business.

'Business' is the operative word in English-language commercial cinema. Hollywood is a 'company' town and the product they export is an image of American culture. When you give a screenplay for a major film to a Hollywood producer, you are actually writing a prospectus for a $200 million stock option – so high are their costs due to the fees of major stars, their huge marketing budgets and so on. Through the weight of American business dominance in the entertainment industry, that outlook has spread increasingly around the world, and the situation is not much different now in Britain and many parts of Europe in the 21st century.

The Process

Once a film story is purchased it goes through development, pre-production, production, post-production, marketing, and distribution. Although the writer is not directly involved in all these steps, it is helpful to be aware of them. We will look at them insofar as they apply to the writer.

Around 60,000 scripts are registered with the Writers' Guild of America each year. Few actually get optioned by a film company. Only about 400 are made annually. But while the situation is improving in the UK, where several hundred scripts are submitted each year, there are still very few British films being made.

The crucial thing that determines which films do get made is not talent or genre, but a calculation of the money that can be made from it (though of course talent and genre are two of the factors taken into account in that calculation). Getting access to money takes inventiveness – or a rich and willing parent!

Producers can get important pre-finance (money at the development stage) if they can attract 'A list' actors and directors – and it is the script that attracts those major players.

Many agents today are packagers, putting together several 'elements' from among their own clients, such as star and director. If you, as a writer, can interest an agent in your script for a star or a name director they represent, you might open a door. If you write a star role, you have a better chance of opening that door.

Lower the risks by studying your craft and presenting a marketable product. American screenwriter Kurt Luedtke, who started his career as a journalist, bought a book on scriptwriting and wrote his first screenplay. He wrote characters' speeches that lasted fifteen pages without a break. He recalled sadly that 'most of what I was doing could not be done'. But he learned quickly and went on to write the screenplays for *Absence of Malice* (1981), *Out of Africa* (1985), and many other fine films.[3]

By November 2001 the national box office in the United States for that year topped $8 billion for the first time. In 1998 ticket admissions in the US stood at 1.45 billion – the largest figure since 1959; but 2001 topped that figure (as did 2002 in its turn). The fear of terrorism after 11 September and the subsequent anthrax scare, and war in Afghanistan and then Iraq kept Americans out of aeroplanes for a while but it did not keep them away from the cinema. In fact, the BO (box office) was $580 million higher by November. The highest grosser of 2001 to that point in the year was the Dreamworks' film *Shrek* ($266.7 million) followed by New Line's *Rush Hour 2* ($224 million) and Universal's *The Mummy Returns* ($202.1 million)[4]. These statistics say a lot for the popularity of comedy and action genres. The more frightening the world becomes, the more many people seem to crave escapism.

Jesse Lasky Jr said, 'The human condition is the basis of all drama. From it stems all men's hopes, passions, suffering and search for meaning. That's what men call truth.'

Now, let's find out how to write a screenplay that could get made – and not land on the shelf when it does.

Chapter 2 | FILMS – ARE WE COMMUNICATING? (AND IF SO, WITH WHOM?)

Mike Figgis's Timecode

Too often, it seems, a little early success can go to a filmmaker's head and somebody else's pocketbook. A recent example may be of particular interest to potential scriptwriters.

In 2000 the film *Timecode* was made by the highly praised and talented British director Mike Figgis (screenwriter/director/musician/composer. Figgis's films include: *Stormy Monday*, 1988; *The Browning Version*, 1994; *Leaving Las Vegas*, 1995; and *Miss Julie*, 1999).

Figgis was quite understandably fascinated by the move into the digital revolution in filmmaking. In a seminar at BAFTA[1] he called it 'the most exciting period in the movie media since the beginning of sound'. Figgis decided the technology would work well to tell four stories at the same time and was keen to make such a film. But he realized that the project he had in mind would cost a lot of money and he would have to interest a studio in the idea.

'Unfortunately America is the place that we do have to consider', he told the BAFTA audience, and since he had what he called a 'housekeeping deal' with Sony, he pitched them his idea off the top of his head with no script, although he pointed out that the studio system normally wants to start a project with a solid script. 'The evolution of controlling scripts makes the studio system workable because controlling the script controls the money.'

In fact, he wrote his four story-lines on sheets of music paper, calling it '... a 93-bar film – a scene to a bar'. His plots were to be interactive; and yet with such a complicated story structure, the director felt it unnecessary to have any script. 'I had no blueprint for the film,' he said (referring to a *stepline* and *treatment* – see chapter 7), 'and when I went into Sony to try to sell the idea, I had f***all to talk about.' Instead, Figgis brought Sony a short tape of his idea for the four plot lines. Since he generally writes and scores his films

as well as directs them, he was confident he could convince the studio to spend the millions required.

The boss of Sony, John Kelly, liked the idea of moving into the digital field and the other members of the board went along with him. Perhaps a tad worried, Kelly told Figgis, 'I hope you know what you're doing, because clearly from this tape, no one else does.'

Despite his lack of preparation, and largely based on his success with *Leaving Las Vegas*, Figgis confidently began filming. Juggling the story-lines in his head each day as he shot with four Sony cameras, he rightly complained that he had been asked to rent the cameras at a fixed price and Sony would not modify them to his specifications. (If they were moving into the digital field, Sony should have given him his modifications and complete technical support.)

It is not surprising that the story structure became unworkable. Until the final day of shooting, Figgis admitted he had no endings for his four stories. He wrote the ending on the last day and commented, 'the stories came to an end when I ran out of film.'

Timecode opened in twelve cinemas and had the highest BO average for that first week. 'We've got a winner here!' said Kelly and Sony moved it to 60 cinemas – where it promptly bombed. Figgis blamed its failure on *Hannibal* (2001) opening that same week. Anyone in marketing will tell you that after the first week, word of mouth can make or break a picture and the word seemed to be that *Timecode* was a non-starter. Quantity of plots does not always add up to quality screen time.

After selling only 351,929 tickets in its first 17 weeks, Figgis's experimental *Timecode* was shelved for further theatrical release for the foreseeable future although the director pointed out that it was available on the Internet. It has since been screened on TV. Not much return on Sony's investment there, though nothing to compare to the losses on *Battlefield Earth*, said to be over $50m. If the admonition of estate agents is 'location, location, location', the admonition of filmmakers should be 'preparation, preparation, preparation'.

Mike Figgis complained that the press are happily 'in bed with the studios and their films – even crap product – get highlighted by the press'. In this case the press were not in bed with Sony, who had to swallow their losses.

Did this fiasco hurt Figgis? With two other films in 2001 – *Hotel* (called improvised and plotless by one critic) and *The Battle of Orgreave* (part documentary) Figgis, admitting that he was now 'hurting in the pocket', he accepted an assignment from Walt Disney Studios to make *Cold Creek Manor* (2003). One can assume that they will keep a tight control on the screenplay. They always do.

What's Wrong with the British Film Industry?

Lots, according to former British Film and Tourism minister Kim Howells. He urged UK moviemakers to make less costume drama and go more for realism – subjects such as the foot and mouth crisis.

He insisted that moviemakers needed to look more at society today and political issues in the widest sense. Howells commented that 'heritage' films were the easy option. Films such as *Howard's End* (1992), *Sense and Sensibility* (1995) and *Mrs Brown* (1997), all of which won or were nominated for Oscars and made a lot of money for the British film industry. Neither was Howells a fan of *The Full Monty* (1997), which he called 'cliché-ridden', *Four Weddings and a Funeral* (1994), or *Notting Hill* (1999) – the three most financially successful British films of recent years. He also complained of what he called 'arty farty' films and that film writers had literary pretensions and constituted a 'Cambridge Footlights and RADA school of filmmakers'.

Why should we care what he said? Why is it relevant today? Because he was not a lone voice in the wind. This is the kind of thinking that has marginalized British filmmakers' progress.

On the brighter side, he proposed that money should be directed towards better scripts (presumably with no literary pretensions but a lot of polemics) and mini-Hollywood style companies. Howells also said, 'I once went to Hollywood ... and was hugely impressed with the way that their writers forgot about their egos and just wrote, rewrote, rewrote and rewrote again until it was right. What I admired was the factory idea.'[2]

There is no doubt that from the days of the first silent films the Hollywood factory system has developed the art of structuring screenplays, and mainstream cinema today takes full advantage of this. But there is a newer-than-New Wave of independent young filmmakers in North America and in Europe who get lower and lower-budget films made with handheld and video cameras and thereby establish a toehold in the business. Festivals have given young filmmakers a helping hand. These people cover the festivals to network, as much as to show off their films and view the work of others. In the United States, Sundance is the most famous festival and has certainly done its bit for a harvest of beginning filmmakers. The Nantucket Festival focuses on the screenplay and the writing.

But back to Mr Howells's comments. Is entertainment only entertaining and nothing more? After all, film is a form of communication – communicating ideas (despite DeMille's comment), stories, feelings, emotions. Yet what is the main reason that audiences pay to sit in a darkened cinema with several hundred strangers and watch a story unfold about somebody else? What is their need? The newspapers and television will keep us abreast of what Howells sees as film fodder: foot and mouth, rail crashes, hospital disasters, kidnappings, plane hijackings, wars, political spin and the like. While there are obviously many fine, indeed great, films about those subjects, most of the public most of the time prefer to see a movie that will take them out of their own lives and their real world with all its problems for 90 minutes or more. Going to the movies offers a person the opportunity to experience excitement, fear, adventure, mystery, cops and robbers, disasters, a love affair, a good laugh, even a good cry – the gamut of human emotions without fear of human contact. They can enjoy or suffer vicariously with the hero and other characters as the tale unfolds. This qualifies as entertainment.

Who provides the most important element in a film? The star actor will tell you, 'Without my performance and charisma, nobody would come to see the movie.' The editor would say, 'If only you'd seen the rubbish on my cutting room floor.' The director is certain that 'without my creative guidance we wouldn't have a film.' The producer will say, 'Without the money I raised nobody would be working.' The composer will tell you his music created the mood and held the whole thing together. Of course the writer will assure you, 'Without my screenplay, there'll be no film' – and it did all start with the script.

They are all correct – and all are missing the point because the truth is, a movie is produced by the co-operation of many talents. Each person's creative effort is part of the whole, and all are interdependent. The script is only a kick-off point, a blueprint for the 'house' that is to be 'built'. Often the writer is made to feel that his script is merely a point of departure as he sees his lines changed and other writers are brought in for the second, third, fourth and maybe fifth drafts. Behind his back he's sometimes called a hack and a necessary nuisance. For example, *Shrek*, nominated for Best Screenplay Adaptation in 2002, was from an original book by William Steig, adapted by Ted Elliot and four others, with additional dialogue by three more writers.

The script *is* the starting point, and it is no doubt true that the writer's place often gets trivialized. In fact, 'the screenwriter as victim' is a favourite theme of script writers: in Billy Wilder's 1950s satire *Sunset Boulevard*, the film opens with the writer/hero dead, floating in a swimming pool. The story is narrated by him and unfolds in flashback.

Author/screenwriter Budd Schulberg, who won an Oscar for his film *On The Waterfront* (1954), when recently interviewed by the Writers' Guild of America, had an angry comment on the invisibility of the screenwriter: 'The next battle is this ridiculous possessive credit that the director takes ... It seems to me just logical that it would only be "a film by John Smith" if John Smith wrote it and directed it. I think it's just totally self-indulgent on the part of directors [who take such a credit without being the author] and I think it's outrageous ... there are all of these public opinion polls and people are asked who they would choose for Best Actor, Best Director, Best Picture, but the public has not a clue that somebody *wrote* the picture ... And how many times have we seen these actors get up there and thank everybody in the goddamn world except the writer ... and they never get around to saying, "I'd like to thank the writer for writing this role, without which I would have no character to play and nothing to say or do"... I'm still waiting.' Elia Kazan directed *On the Waterfront*, and it was shot in 37 days on a budget of $800,000 because Hollywood had just discovered Cinemascope with widescreen colour and Darryl Zanuck didn't want to spend a lot of money making a black-and-white movie at that time.

Some writers, when they get sufficient clout, turn their hand to being part of the producing team. Screenwriter Horton Foote, when asked the difference between just being a writer and a writer/producer replied, 'I think if you're just a writer, then you have no way of being part of the mechanism. I mean it's, again, writer for hire. And they soon let you know that they own the rights. Which I think is the most tragic thing about a screenwriter in that situation.'

Today's filmmakers wear many hats: director/writer and sometimes additionally the star/producer. The French call this multi-talented person an *auteur* (literally, 'author'). The true auteur conceives the film, writes the script, develops the style, the concept, and the characters – and then directs it. American films were generally opposed to the auteur concept until recent years, but Quentin Tarantino is certainly an auteur and today many American actors are trying their hand. Sometimes – particularly it seems with actors – their effort to control everything can turn a film into an ego trip.

The producer generally acts in an advisory capacity and oversees the work of the writer, casting director, director, and so on. He may be to some extent an auteur although his talent lies in keeping all the *elements* in harmony. In Hollywood the original moguls such as Goldwyn, Lasky, Mayer, Warner, Cohn, and Selznick were in total control of everything in their films. Spielberg is a director but puts his stamp on the whole film through his company Dreamworks, and works closely with his writers.

Films Should Make You Think

A film should involve the audience and lead them to an understanding of the motivations and conflicts that the characters endure. Film is an art form as well as entertainment, but how do we define art? Should a film strive for the same aesthetic qualities as a painting? Art, it is said, should be a stimulant to society. Films do not generally work when they attempt to preach at us or to propagandize us into the ideology of the writer or his cause – although in war times many of them have tried to do so. If you walk out of the cinema and find yourself evaluating the problems and decisions the characters have made or the ideas that the story has put forward, you could say the film has made you think. That counts as a stimulant.

Screenwriting is its own art form, part of which is a technique of structuring. Proper preparation before writing the actual script can make all the difference in creating a successful screenplay. It's easy to make a film that isn't audience-friendly if you simply don't take a viewer's responses into account. It's more difficult to bring an idiosyncratic vision to bear while still making a commercially saleable product. You are not making your film for a select audience of one. But can a film be both a commercial success and art at the same time? Look no further than the works of Alfred Hitchcock – the most successful money-making filmmaker of his day, who is now considered a true artist. A screenwriter can learn much from studying his films, and other classics. See why they hold up (or do not) even years later. It all comes back to story-telling.

What is the scriptwriter's part in all this? As a blueprint for a film, a script has no intrinsic value (other than your pay packet) until it's brought to life on the screen. Film companies have, historically, felt safer adapting books or stage plays to the screen, and the reason is not hard to guess. From a marketing viewpoint, the property already has built-in audience acceptance (or at least recognition) since some percentage of the public will be aware of the play or book's title (may even have read it) and might come to see the film because of that.

Mushrooming costs mean that production companies take fewer risks that may not pay off. That's why Hollywood so often copies former successes – including the most obvious kind in the form of sequels – and why it is more difficult to sell an idea that's too original. Writer Kurt Luedtke said, 'Writing screenplays is a relatively easy thing to do but I think that writing them well is as difficult a thing to do as you can imagine.' In television, the BBC keeps producing adaptations of the classics, partly because the Brontés and Jane Austen are marketable in the United States because the Americans are able to understand the upper-class British accents that they feature better than modern films that feature strong regional British accents.

Form Dictates Content

Technical advances change the way we do things. The coming of sound in the late 1920s completely altered the writer's place in the film industry. While the need was still there for a rip-roaring good story, instead of writing merely a story-line which told what his characters were to do and adding titles to spell out what they were occasionally meant to be saying, the writer had to give his characters dialogue. Because we (the audience) could now hear what the characters were saying, they had to do less with their facial expressions and body language. And of course, the actors had to have trained voices. It changed the method of acting as well as that of writing.

The invention of non-inflammable film stock meant that movies could have a wider distribution, and even that affected the writing because the market place was growing. The advent of colour brought the filmmaker a chance to explore stories in a more realistic, visual way but also to create fantasy images that black and white could not hope to achieve. Think of filming *The Wizard of Oz* (1939) totally in black and white, or *Harry Potter and the Philosopher's [Sorcerer's] Stone* or *Lord of the Rings* or *Moulin Rouge* (all 2001) without the use of colour.

Computerization has allowed the filmmaker complete freedom to create anything he or his writer could imagine. *Crouching Tiger, Hidden Dragon* (2001) blended reality and fantasy into a minor masterpiece. Animated films have moved from children's cartoons to mainstream story-telling. When *Shrek* can be nominated for best screenplay (as it was at the 2002 Academy Awards), you can get an idea where things are heading and what the future may hold – perhaps in the future there won't be any actors (only kidding!). However, *Shrek* was a valid choice because it is a well-told fairy tale with enchanting characters, lots of suspense and lots of laughs; a thoroughly satisfying story that appeals to adults as well as kids.

File Your Ideas

Where do stories come from and what source material does a writer draw upon? It pays to keep a file of your ideas – even scraps of an idea. Write them down. If you have a computer, keep a file of them where you can review them from time to time. Sometimes you come across an article about an event, a happening, a person, a crime, a natural disaster, something of human interest, anything in the newspapers that has an interesting twist or setting and captures your imagination. Cut it out and file it. Your file might give you the basis of an idea around which you could later (even years later) build a story. When I was writing a lot of crime series for TV,[3] I found ideas from years before in my files that turned themselves into the core of plots. If it's a period story you want to tell, you can look forward to researching your subject historically to give it authenticity. If you begin such research keep a file of where each item or idea came from. You may write a book to go with the film and you'll need it.

Keep One Idea Dominant

Whatever the action of your story, ask yourself, 'what if the opposite were the case?' – for instance, 'is he really guilty?' versus 'he's innocent'. In a mainstream story one idea should be dominant at the climax, although different characters might see the truth differently. Akira Kurosawa's award-winning film *Rashomon* (1950) is a great example of this concept. The device he uses – taken directly from the original short story by Ryunosuke Akutagawa – presents four equally believable eyewitness accounts of a murder, but each identifying a different culprit. If you build the force of your premise and then shatter it to make the opposite view the only

convincing one, you will put your audience off balance and will have heightened the suspense of your story. *The Usual Suspects* (1995) is another good example. But no matter how many twists and turns your story may take, when the climax arrives it must be valid and believable. A good story, well-told, should not leave gaps in logic.

Research

This also means inventing your characters and discovering the magnitude of their lives. Your sources can come from 'field' research, or from an adaptation of a book or story (with permission, of course – you must be very clear about avoiding plagiarism). A story could come from your own experiences or those of someone you know, but beware of writing as a therapy for your hang-ups. Having said that, you might come up with some interesting stuff depending on your experiences, as long as you remember that realism and truth do not necessarily make good drama, and such ideas may be more suited to documentary. A documentary can focus on an event or a world condition or on the life-styles of animals or humans, but it does not necessarily reach a dramatic conclusion – unless the lion eats the filmmaker. Documentaries can be episodic based on an *umbrella theme* (covering related topics). Even commercials have story-lines of sorts.

Good writers research the territory of their stories and meet the types of people they will write about. They pick up expressions, phrases of real speech, attitudes, and character traits, and work them into the mouths of their characters. For *On The Waterfront*, Bud Schulberg went down to the docks and befriended the longshoremen (dockers), absorbing ideas that embellished his story-line. This is a traditional writer's tool.

Writers of crime shows quite often work with the police (as I did). Sometimes research can be a trap because it can turn you into an investigative reporter instead of a writer of dramatic material. Don't get so swamped by the reality that it leads you from your story. Research is there to embellish and round out your characters.

Ask Questions: The Five Big Ws and one H

The most important questions you can ask yourself when you begin are who, what, when, where, why and how? The questions never change, but the answers do. Remember that there aren't many 'whys' without 'becauses'. Know your created world thoroughly: this will ensure the essential truth of your story-telling.

It is important to identify the point of conflict in your story. All drama needs a structural design, and conflict is at heart of any story-telling. How can you find this? You must look for unusual human relationships between your characters and where their desires are in opposition in order to discover where the conflict lies. But is conflict simply a matter of a punch up, a car chase, a violent argument, or a gun battle?

Conflict can be as small as two characters with different beliefs and attitudes who are striving to achieve something in a relationship, or despite each other. A scene is about two (or more) people who want different things. Two men battling over a chessboard is conflict, although from a camera's point of view the board action must not become bored action. Two dancers trying to outshine each other or one man fighting the elements, or winning a race, are conflict. Love triangles – whether two men and a woman, or two women and a man – are an aspect of sexual politics and always involve conflict. It's all about human behaviour under stress.

The Technique of Structuring

For a story to have shape in a mainstream commercial film, something has to happen to alter the ordinary everyday life of the protagonist (the main character, whether male, female or even an animal, either real or animated) with whom the audience must have empathy. It is important to understand that 'empathy' means mentally identifying with and understanding the character, not merely feeling sorry for him. Without a strong protagonist that an audience can relate to, your story becomes no more than a series of events.

The *story-line* is the plot. The protagonist wants something. He has a goal. The audience experiences the story through the actions of the protagonist and his struggle to achieve that goal – or not to achieve it, if that is the way your story develops. If the protagonist doesn't want anything, you've got *minimalism* (which we'll discuss in Chapter 4).

And where is the opposition? What is it that keeps him from attaining his goal? Is your protagonist being blocked by the forces of nature, by society, or by a particular antagonist (an opponent or adversary) or group of antagonists? Any story must hook the audience in the first five or ten minutes. It must hold them, and keep them asking 'what next?' Something happens that changes the protagonist's ordinary life and forces him to make a decision. This is the *initial turning point* (sometimes referred to as the inciting incident) in the story – the moment when the protagonist's life (which was going along fairly smoothly for no more than ten or fifteen minutes into your plot) has suddenly changed and he is forced to make a choice about what to do next. Your story must have a series of events and payoffs – a series of climaxes. How the protagonist will react and what decisions he makes at every new obstacle will form the steps of the main plot story-line and define the resolution of the story.

Initially, in setting down your story idea (a first step) you should create much more material than you will ultimately need. Put down everything you think of. You will discard and refine later, but at least you will have choices: writing is rewriting. Don't cling to things when rewriting unless they are totally justifiable by the criteria *to move plot or to develop character* (this is something I'll be emphasizing throughout).

Visual Versus the Verbal

Obviously, film scripts are written for a visual medium. A script is composed of two elements: the story (the structure or steps of the plot) and the dialogue. Perhaps three-quarters of the work up to the final draft is in structuring your story – creating the action events and establishing a group of characters who can bring the story to life – and only one quarter is in creating the dialogue. Converting a written idea (from a book, for example) into a visual idea means the audience should not need to rely entirely on dialogue to understand the story. If you were adapting a book, there might be pages or even a chapter that could be distilled into one or two exchanges of dialogue that would suffice to make the point. Remember, we are watching faces on a screen. The lift of an eyebrow can tell us a whole paragraph. *See, don't Say should be your guideline* in bringing a story to the screen.

Putting the protagonist and the plot under some pressure makes a story more immediate and suspenseful. Compressing time helps to escalate the excitement of the 'will he, won't he?' question the audience is waiting to discover. That's why so often in stories, the protagonist (such as a cop or a newspaperman) is told, 'You've got [x] hours to … [do whatever it is he has to do].' The pressure of time hots things up. The TV series *24* is based on this time pressure – being filmed in 24 'real time' episodes. Naturally, this story constraint is overused in too many scripts, and it is the good writer who can justify this tension-making plot device and make it believable.

The structure of a mainstream film story is linear. For a feature film it is generally (but not always) a classic three-act structure (see chapter 6). For a one-hour television drama it is more often a two-act structure with breaks into four parts for the commercials (assuming it will be shown on commercial television). Although this concept is certainly *form*, it should not be regarded as a *formula*.

Drama Is Heightened Reality with a Driving Pace

It means compressing the ordinary life of your protagonist into a created truth. Writers are reflectors of life, but not the real day-to-day, hour-by-hour life of a human being with all its minutiae of detail. You must create an internally consistent reality in the microcosm of your story. You are a god and the world you create must be real for at least 90 minutes.

In Michael Crichton's novel *Jurassic Park* the mathematician explains the chaos theory thus: 'Life is actually a series of encounters in which one event may change those that follow in a wholly unpredictable – even devastating way.' Crighton could not have explained better the essence of film writing. Use the technical skills you are about to learn to shape your imagination – and to stretch it.

CHAPTER 3 | THE WRITER'S CREATED WORLD

Your story must be created in visual terms. You will start with no more than an idea – perhaps a character that interests you or some plot twist, probably not even a whole plot. From these seeds you build a plot line and develop character sketches. You write a stepline of the points of the story. You break it into acts, then scenes, all still in outline.

Next comes the treatment and finally, after all the really hard slog is done, you can write the screenplay. How good it is depends more than you think on how thorough your preparation was. It's a good idea to write what you would like to see on the screen. Make the readers – producer(s), director, actors, backers, or distributors – see it leap off the page and make them want to bring your vision to life. It's important to remember that a screenplay is not intended for presentation to the public as a finished product in its own right – it is not a novel. If you're lucky, your script will be made into a movie. And of course, the film will be as strong as its weakest link. Don't let that be your script.

What qualities must a writer have? You must be a constant observer of life and have an open mind about what you see. To some extent you must be non-judgemental but have a strong sense of values. You might have to get inside the head of a murderer in order to create his character – which doesn't mean you have to go out and murder someone to see what it's like. It means you must have insight and perception into what motivates people to do what they do.

Reading a few books on psychology and studying your fellow humans (walking down the street or on a bus, at a party or in a restaurant) is good training for writers as well as actors. In the 1950s and 1960s the chic thing was for actors and writers to be psychoanalyzed, the idea being that if you understood yourself, you would better be able to analyse your characters. Certainly you must have a sharpened conception of life and a vivid imagination. You must have an ear for the way people speak: the 'sound' of dialogue – with its lack of complete sentences, its repetitions, and what it leaves unsaid.

Honing Your Dialogue

Nothing should be trivial in a screenplay. If it is, cut it or move it somewhere else. The structure or design of your story is its backbone, and it defines the relationship between the parts and the whole. It must have a thematic unity.

Dramatic dialogue is never real speech but it has to *sound like* real speech. It is compressed and heightened reality. In life, a conversation or a 'scene' doesn't necessarily reach a conclusion, but in a screenplay your scenes must have drive and come to a conclusion.

Try this. The next time you have a group of friends over, hide a tape recorder, and later, when they're not around, play it back. Notice how the conversation twists and turns, and never reaches a conclusion? That's real. If you were to write that scene, you'd probably find only a few lines you could use – and you'd have to make up the rest.

Discipline

You must learn the tools and techniques of this craft that you have chosen, have the tenacity to sit down at your desk and write for a certain number of hours a day and be something of a perfectionist – you should never quit the day saying 'that's good enough'. But even all that is not enough. If you don't have a certain amount of knowledge about the ways of the world (at least the world you want to write about) and an above-average wit and talent, this may not be the profession for you. Most of all, to be a good screenwriter you must have something to say, some insight that you want to impart. You could be a teenager who wants to write about people his age. That's great – all it takes is insight. You wouldn't be reading this book if you didn't believe you could become a professional scriptwriter – so let's get on with it and find out how it's done.

The Main Plot

The story-line is the plot and it begins with the *initial turning point* – the kick-off event that changes the pattern of the protagonist's life and sets him on his difficult journey. The 'event' that happens should throw the protagonist's world out of balance, causing a major reversal in his life, forcing him to make a choice and to take action. This event must be seen in the movie and must not be 'back story' (something that happened before the movie started).

What dilemmas your characters are facing will differ with the time, place and particulars of your story. Is your story set in the past, present, or future? Are the conflicts of the story due to religion, race, a love affair, a death, a contest, politics, extra-terrestrials, wars, school, parental control, the characters' social positions or their cultural and financial positions? The possibilities are endless.

But in order to destroy it, you must first establish the protagonist's world. That shouldn't take more than 15 minutes and hopefully less. From that point the protagonist progresses through a series of challenges. The audience want to know how he will react to each crisis. What decisions, what choices will he make? An 'event' does not have to be a large incident. It can be as small as a gesture, a look, a piece of information or a word from another character that lets the audience see something about the protagonist's inner life, about the way he perceives the world.

In a screenplay, the story reveals the 'education' of the protagonist through action. This differs from a novel, where this process can be described or suggested. To create your screenplay you must blend levels of emotion, imagery and dialogue with the protagonist's actions in opposing the negative forces.

Subplot

This is a second (or maybe even third or more) story-line, but it should not be unconnected thematically or structurally from the main plot – again unlike a novel where you can deal with multiple plots and the inner life of a protagonist. Subplots can be a counterbalance revealing other aspects, other points of view of your story or the main characters. They can be a contradiction of the main plot – a

contrast to create an asperity that enriches, echoes, or resonates with the main plot. They also work in minimalism – or in a soap, as we shall see. A subplot can radically upset the balance of forces in the protagonist's life. It must complicate the action of the main plot – or at least interact with it in some way. It is there to give dimension to the main plot and add to the audience's perception of the protagonist or his world.

The Kiss of the Spider Woman (1985, screenplay by Leonard Schrader from the novel by Manuel Puig) is about a flamboyant gay man and a revolutionary political prisoner sharing a cell in a South American jail. The film begins with the alienation of the two men because of their opposing beliefs and attitudes. The gay man (William Hurt, who won an Oscar for his performance), recounts to his cellmate (Raul Julia) the plot of his favourite film, which gradually draws them closer together. The main plot is shot in muted colours; the sequences depicting Hurt's fantasy life are in bright colours and give depth to the portrayal of his inner life. It is an excellent interweaving of plot and subplot.

The psychological drama *Belle de Jour* (1967, directed by Luis Buñuel, who also co-wrote the screenplay with Jean-Claude Carrière from the novel by Joseph Kessel) is a mini-masterpiece concentrating on an emotionally repressed housewife (Catherine Deneuve), bored by the social and sexual pressures of her society, who seeks escape in prostitution. Fantasy and reality intertwine in plot and subplot.

Multi-Plots

Soaps and serials have a great many story-lines threaded through them, which they are able to sustain because they are developed over a much longer timespan than a film. While one plot may be more important than the others they can all have stronger substance than a subplot. *Gosford Park* (2002) is an example of a multi-plot film. These are discussed in more detail in Chapter 4.

Is Your Story Character- or Plot-Driven?

Is the story predominantly about an interesting character (real or make-believe), and his life and times? You must decide this early on. Perhaps it's biographical (with dramatic licence): *Chaplin, Ali, A Beautiful Mind, Riding in Cars With Boys, Angela's Ashes, Iris, Frida* – all have been recent dramatized biographical stories that have made important films. *Moulin Rouge* was character-driven but fictional, as were *AI, Amélie, Bridget Jones's Diary, The Contender*, and the *Harry Potter* films.

Or is your story about an incident, a happening, a war or series of events, true or created? *Black Hawk Down* and *Lord of the Rings* were Oscar winners in 2002, and both were plot-driven stories.

There must be authenticity in structure, and internal consistency and believability in your tale, no matter how fanciful the material. *Jurassic Park* (all three instalments in the franchise), *Alien* (all four) and *Minority Report* are examples of films successfully dealing with subject matter out of our real world.

Question your Subject

Okay, so you have decided on the story that you want to tell. Even if it's a biographical tale, you have to choose the other characters who can work with your protagonist to tell it, and which ones (even real people) can be eliminated – or perhaps two or more characters can be combined into one.

For the audience to understand the story, what they see can reveal so much about the people, the place, and the conventions that dialogue is unnecessary.

To return to our six questions:
– *Who* are the characters that this story is about? (This is important even in a plot-driven story because the characters make the plot happen and the plot forces the characters to take action.)
– *What* is happening to them?
– *When* is it happening? Is it the present, the future, or the past?
– *Where* is the location? In what country? A city? The countryside? A war zone? A spaceship?
– *Why* is it happening to these particular people, and especially the protagonist?
– *How* does it happen? (That's the story-line.) For the moment, we will concentrate on *Who* and *What*.

Who are the Characters?
The Protagonist

This person can be a hero or an anti-hero – whatever you like. The word 'archetype' is bandied about these days but it does not mean your protagonist has to fit a standard set of rules. The important thing is that the audience believes in the protagonist when the lights go down, and so is able to experience the story through him. For the period of watching the film they want what the protagonist wants. His aspirations (even Hannibal Lecter's!) become the audience's, and it is his struggle to achieve his goals that keeps them glued to their seats. The audience lives through the rituals, crises, conflicts and decisions of the protagonist's life. It is an emotional experience that the analyst Jung called the 'participation mystique'. Freud called it 'projective identification'. Screenwriters call it *empathizing* with the protagonist.

If the protagonist achieved his goal in the first 15 minutes of a 90-minute story, you would have no film. Your story must develop and round out the various aspects and dimensions of your characters – what they think and feel.

A character's reactions cause a turning of the plot and that in turn causes changes in the protagonist's attitudes and way of thinking and therefore draws him into a further incident and another reaction, and so on.

Characterization

Find out where the inner conflicts lie in your protagonist (and the other characters), his desires, his point of view towards his life and those with whom he comes into contact.

Your characters will each have different distinctive idiosyncrasies, style of hair and dress, habits, and gestures, but don't confuse superficials with true character traits. Choose these carefully to emphasize the protagonist's personality and those of the other characters. It is a person's motivations – his reasons – that cause him to do what he does.

The actor can add to this dimension. You can inform him what type of character he is playing and his attitude – but only when the line itself would give no indication or would, on its own, suggest an opposite interpretation.

FRED: (*hiding anger*) Hi, there, Mary. Don't you look nice today?

Never over-explain – actors hate it. Sometimes the protagonist is an anti-hero, a strong-willed human being who wants something outside the law or common decency. He is a flawed hero who has not conquered his inner demons. We watch with fear, dread, terror, curiosity and, yes, empathy either secretly hoping he will succeed or anticipating how and when he will be caught. Whichever, the audience must have an attitude towards the protagonist or else they will not be interested in the story.

Who do we root for in *Silence of the Lambs* (1991)? From Hannibal's point of view, the cops and the psychiatrist are buffoons. Is it the FBI agent, Clarice Starling (Jodie Foster) we are rooting for? Obviously yes, but we also have undeniable empathy with Hannibal (Anthony Hopkins), or we wouldn't laugh when he makes his final phone call to Clarice to tell her he's 'having an old friend for dinner'. We would be furious that he got away – but we're not.

The audience needs somebody to root for and they must want the protagonist to achieve his goal. Even if he is a foul murderer like Hannibal, we must have some shred of empathy, a fascination with him – though this is not necessarily the same as sympathy. And if the major role in your story is really the antagonist, the question becomes how will the protagonist catch him? (*Columbo* uses this formula.) Everyone sees himself as 'good' in relationship to the world around him. For example, the husband in *The Piano* (1993) sees himself as being in the right when he chops off his wife's finger, but this challenges our sympathy for him. Actually, we may have no empathy for him either, considering him cruel.

Revealing your Characters

Your characters must reveal themselves within the framework of your story. The audience get hints from time to time of what happened before the opening credits (the back story), but our focus is on what's happening now. Our understanding of the characters must grow as each new scene unfolds. No matter how large the canvas of your story – for example, it

might be set in World War II, a macrocosm of history – your created world must be contained in a microcosm focused on a few major characters, your protagonist, and the things that happen to him. Through his eyes we must understand the wider world.

Spielberg said of *Schindler's List* (1993): 'With historical material you must combine various characters or you'd have 100 story-lines'. Keep a tight focus and involve your protagonist in every possible scene (particularly if you want to interest a star).

Research into your characters' world – where he comes from, how he got where he is at the beginning of your story. It can be an imaginary world (*Harry Potter*) or a real (fictional) world (*Bridget Jones's Diary*). Examine your protagonist's inner life – the drives behind his choices. Know your protagonist thoroughly, and decide as you plan your stepline at what points you will reveal the facts of his life. Only when you have a solid feeling for your characters will you be able to create choices for them.

Do not allow your protagonist to become too involved or reactive with your subplot(s) or that story-line will be in danger of becoming the main plot by default.

Text and Subtext of a Character

If a character works on more than one level you will have a much more interesting, more fully rounded, believable person. We all work on many levels: with our parents, our employers, our teachers, our partners. The root of your protagonist's nature is expressed in his conscious desires – in his pursuit of that which will return his life to normal after the *initial turning point* that altered his life. What he says reveals the text of the character.

The *subtext* is not what he has revealed in words. It is what he actually does or *thinks*, which can be quite different. The protagonist's *unconscious* desires become the *subtext* of his actions. For 'real life' drama, the protagonist works on these two levels.

In *Thelma and Louise* (1991), for instance, Thelma's boyfriend comes to visit her in Oklahoma and brings her the money she asked for. She doesn't tell him she's killed a guy. She talks about when they'll see each other again (text). She (and the audience) knows she won't see him (subtext). In *Carnal Knowledge* (1971), Jack Nicholson's 'conscious desire' is to pursue women. His 'unconscious desire' is to destroy women.

But there are protagonists who work on only one level and have *no* unconscious desires. Action heroes such as James Bond, Superman, Batman, Indiana Jones, or Spiderman are examples of such one-dimensional characters. These are the type of protagonists you meet in action adventures, comedy, fantasy and in minimalism, so these stories must move along swiftly and carry us with them because what you see is what you get. A protagonist can only be as many-layered as the circumstances allow.

What gives Bond and other action heroes the missing 'other dimension'? It is the pace of the action and we want to be swept along with it. Audiences don't want to anticipate Bond; they only have time to absorb one-dimensional characters in these types of stories. When Timothy Dalton, a fine actor, played Bond, he tried to infuse him with a subtext to round him out as a 'real' person. It didn't work. He was no longer the impervious icon that makes Bond what he is and has to be. With these types of protagonists we want his character not to change but to be just what we expect. Character subtext becomes a no-no in such situations.

Your protagonist must be a strong-willed person. Audiences won't relate to a wimp as a hero except in comedy (such as a Woody Allen, Gene Wilder, or Jim Carrey character).

When can you have a group of protagonists? When all are struggling against the same odds for mutual suffering or benefit (as in a strike: *On the Waterfront*; a shipwreck: *Titanic*; or a battle: *Band of Brothers*). But the main story plot must still focus through one or several central protagonists who carry the story for the others.

What Is Happening?

It is the protagonist's struggle that makes the steps of your story. Why can't he achieve his goal immediately? Because he is blocked by opposition. And what does opposition cause? At the core of all powerful story-telling is (you guessed it!) conflict – which stems from the behaviour of humans who each want different things. Where do you find this conflict? There are several possible sources.

A) Personal relationships: Who is the protagonist close to? Who does he love, hate, empathize with, sympathize with? In a single- or double-strand story-line (a plot and a sub-plot) the writer has time to develop scenes that explore more deeply the various characters' feelings and interrelationships. Not so in a soap opera with multi-strand stories, where the characters remain fairly one-dimensional.

B) Personal traumas: The traumas that a character suffers must be expressed in visual terms as much as possible. While it is the work of the actor to reveal the inner conflicts and machinations of his mind in a close-up, he cannot do this if the writer has not set down the character's emotional attitudes.

The writer must create the situations the character finds himself in and suggest his motivations. Star actors can hold the screen without dialogue and reveal their innermost thoughts through their eyes and expression alone. Actors like Tom Hanks, Daniel Day-Lewis, Anthony Hopkins, and many others have the power to convey their feelings through their eyes without words.

But deep inner contemplation is more easily dealt with in a novel. A character's thoughts (stream of consciousness) and inner life could take an entire chapter, while the physical action in the scene might be no more than tying a necktie, looking in the mirror, or applying lipstick. That action would take about ten seconds on the screen. Sometimes in films, particularly in French films, narration reveals the character's inner thoughts (see the section on voiceover narration in chapter 4).

C) Environmental frictions: The restrictions, rules, laws, mores, or conventions that govern the character's way of life are moulded by the circumstances in which you place him. The forces of nature – flood, hurricane, shipwreck, earthquake, and so on – can cause conflict. So can physical disabilities of the protagonist or someone close to him who is blind, amnesiac, crippled, or mentally ill, as in *Frida* (2002) where she is bedridden and spends months in a full body cast. Conflict can also be with wider society or the environment: a prisoner, an alcoholic, a drug addict, a victim, etc.

Whenever possible, you must concentrate on setting your protagonist in conflict in all three of these areas. Some examples in recent films that illustrate this concept are:

A Beautiful Mind (2001):
A) Difficult relationship with his wife.
B) Discovering that his best friend and his employer are both creatures of his imagination. Accepting that he is a paranoid schizophrenic.
C) Having to go through shock treatments. Trying to find a place at the university and a life he can fit into.

The Piano (1993):
A) The heroine's forced marriage to a stranger in a strange land.
B) Falling in love with the handyman.
C) Her piano in an alien world. Living with her unwillingness or inability to speak (it is ambiguous).

As you develop your stepline decide what is the central idea to be expressed – in other words, the controlling idea of your story. The theme that won all the Oscars in the 80s and 90s was the hero's dedicated pursuit of popular values and its consequences. For example, *Terms of Endearment* (1983), a story lifted from the realm of soap/sitcom to Oscar status by brilliant performances. In contrast, it was the biographical drama *Amadeus*, based on the stage play by Peter Shaffer, that took the awards in 1984. Besides telling the story of Mozart, it explored the envy and pride of the lesser composer, Salieri, which gave it the necessary conflict. Then in 1999 the black comedy *American Beauty* gave us an acutely observed look at a man in mid-life crisis and his sexually frustrated wife. All explored the usual drives for money, love/sex, power and their consequences.

Motivation and Justification

Screen stories require bold strokes. A film has little time for intellectual or internal subtleties – those are the province of the novel or the essay. But don't write only to shock. Go to

any film school end-of-term screenings or 'short film' festivals of new filmmakers and you will find at least one of the films will feature a guy sitting on a toilet or peeing against a wall or there will be blood and gore all over the screen – but all with *no motivation*. Anything can be justified if it is motivated. Without that, it's just there for shock value and is senselessly amateur.

The situations facing the protagonist must become constantly more challenging but in a logical way. They must put him at risk mentally or physically. Although he has the capacity to pursue his goal, the escalating obstacles prevent him from achieving it for at least 90 minutes of screen time. If he never achieves it, he should gain something else.

Empathy and Sympathy

The audience must be able to enter into the protagonist's personality and imaginatively experience what he is going through. They may not always share his point of view or agree with his choices, but they must feel in tune with (empathize with) the protagonist or they would lose interest in the story. Actors know this and when they portray a character it is uppermost in their minds. The actor Sam Waterston (*The Killing Fields*) has said that 'people want the experience of empathy with the hero'.

This point cannot be stressed too strongly. In *The Killing Fields* (1984) the producers departed from the original script – changed protagonists half-way through and introduced a Western hero instead of the Cambodian leading character in order to ensure the American/British audience would empathize with the central protagonist.

Decide what characters you must create to tell your story and why and where (in what scenes) you particularly need them. What purpose do they serve in revealing various aspects of the protagonist's life, background, and attitudes? The characters are there to help you tell your story and unfold your plot. Unless they serve that purpose, you don't need them. Never clutter your story with unnecessary characters or vignette scenes that are out of context with the plot's main drive. If you want a *scene as a counterpoint* (for humour, let's say) then find a way to make it gel with your plot or protagonist. Choose people and incidents that will counterpoint the protagonist's journey to his goal. You may discover that you have written three characters that actually could be combined into one, but make sure you don't develop a strong character in Act I who then fades from view in Act II.

One of the keys to knowing what a character or your protagonist will do in a given situation is to put yourself into his shoes. What would *you* do under those circumstances? Would that character, with the set of attitudes and idiosyncrasies that you have given him, act the same way you would? If not, why not? If you were to have his given mind-set, then what would you do? You'd be surprised how few new screenwriters ask themselves these questions.

If it is necessary that a character acts in a certain way at a certain point in the story, then you must justify that moment by giving him the proper attributes and abilities. Create for him specific character traits so that what you eventually want him to do is believable. He wouldn't swim a river if you made him afraid of water – but he might if forced to. What elements in his nature would prevent him from doing a certain thing? What would he do instead? Look for the alternatives.

To repeat: other characters are only there to bring out all sides of your protagonist's character and to move the plot. The protagonist must have many layers as do other main characters, but the minor characters can often be one-dimensional and have one specific trait by which we identify them and with which they will serve their function in the story.

Focus On Your Protagonist

Having decided on your protagonist and his quest, don't let a minor character take over the action and take away the spotlight. Don't give him all the good lines in a scene. You'll lose your protagonist – and possibly the star you want to play him. In *Blade Runner* (1982) the audience found themselves in empathy with the villain, a 'replicant' played by Rutger Hauer, instead of the protagonist, played by Harrison Ford, whose job it was to hunt down the replicants. After its initial opening, the picture was failing at the box office so the producer Michael Deeley and the director,

Ridley Scott decided to add a voiceover narrative to pull the audience back to Harrison Ford. It worked, though some fans preferred the original version, which, as the 'director's cut', has become established in its own right.

In *A Few Good Men* (1992, written by Aaron Sorkin from his own play) Jack Nicholson's scene-stealing cameo performance was due partly to his dynamic acting. But his three scenes were there on paper and allowed him to become the most interesting character in a mainstream Hollywood story.

In *Unforgiven*, Clint Eastwood's 1992 Oscar-winning Western (screenwriter David Webb Peoples) the theme asserts that what passed for law and order often had little to do with justice. Gene Hackman's performance as the sheriff won the Oscar for Best Supporting Actor, but didn't detract from the star.

The Hero Under Pressure

From the protagonist's point of view, in a moment of crisis he must believe that his decision – right or wrong, hazardous or death-defying – will make his situation better. Since the audience have seen a lot of movies before, they will anticipate – maybe even outguess what he might do. It is your job to keep them guessing. Both choices must look equally uncertain in their outcome. If it were easy, anyone could do it – but your hero must be a cut above average. Choosing the better of two unsavoury paths, the protagonist would logically go for the solution that seems to have the greatest potential for success even if it seems to the audience to be the worse choice. If he chooses one path because it looks easy but turns out to place him in a worse dilemma, that's even better. His choice should head your protagonist into one more moment of misadventure – at which point he must make yet another decision.

The momentum should escalate each time he reaches another crisis (another turning point in the story). Solutions become more difficult, putting the protagonist under more pressure. That is why so often in action drama, you will find the hero is under the pressure of *time*. He has only so many days, hours, or minutes to complete his mission. The more pressures (of every kind) you can put on your hero, the more involved the audience will be in watching him solve his problems.

Chapter 4 | ELEMENTS OF THE SCREENPLAY

Below is a checklist of some basic terms with which to familiarize yourself:

Plot: the structure or design of the story. It is not like life; it is an acceleration of life. It has a beginning, a middle, and an end.

Scene: one incident of 'action' taking place in one location. Your scenes must either expand or develop what we know about the characters or must move the plot. If you find that at the end of a scene, these values have not undergone any change or the plot has not moved forward, cut it. Be economical – or the producer, director, or editor will.

Back Story: information about what has happened to the characters before the film began. But avoid creating scenes solely to give this information – they must have more going on in them than that. Enhance the scene by developing your character(s) in some way, or making a plot point.

Plot Point: an incident or event that adds information and spins the action into another direction anywhere in the script. Something that forces the protagonist to make a decision – or 'go with the flow' and be swept along with the tide of events.

Story Structure: the story has a spine and is made up of character revelations and events. Like a fish that undulates in the water it must be flexible without breaking.

Theme: the central controlling idea of your story.

Imagery: the visual expressions of the theme. You will work them into your description of action.

Moment of Crisis: something has changed the status quo and now the protagonist must make a decision about what to do.

Twist: an unexpected development in the plot. This is just what the audience wants. What now?

New Direction of Plot: the protagonist's choices that lead the story in another direction.

Types Of Story Structure

What is story-telling? A situation isn't a story. A concept isn't a film. James Herbert, the celebrated horror novelist, told me the other day that people always come up to him and say, 'I'll give you a terrific idea for a story'. They follow this with something like, 'A man sees a brutal murder in the street'. James waits. But the would-be story-teller has finished. 'What happens next?' James asks. The story-teller shrugs. 'You write it. You're the novelist.'

A film script requires structure, texture, vivid but brief descriptions of the action and sparse, point-making dialogue. Mike Leigh (utilizing a repertory company of actors) and a few other director/writers get away with improvisation based on a firmly structured story-line. But their films are too often sometimes weak in story flow and dialogue. In *Secrets and Lies* (1995) although Leigh rehearses his actors to build their dialogue over a period of weeks, in my opinion, you can feel Brenda Blethyn struggling for words as an actress (not as the character) and repeating herself in the restaurant scene when she meets her long-lost daughter. Striving for spontaneity Leigh had kept the two actresses apart until they shot the scene. Blethyn didn't know the actress playing her daughter was black. This does nothing for the art of screenwriting that I prefer. Her repetitive ad-libs lacked any finesse. When Stoppard or Pinter repeat a line or word, it has structure and style because every word and stammer and pause is carefully orchestrated on paper. They allow their actors to be actors not scriptwriters. Improvisation is not commercially possible on higher budget projects.

We will be looking at the three main structures used in writing a screenplay. These also have permutations. Everything is there to alter if you've got something better to add. But it's good to begin with the basics.

Mainstream Structure

This is the classic form of story-telling and utilizes the traditional construction of a beginning, middle, and end told in the normal order. As mentioned before, a short film or a one-hour teleplay requires a two-act structure, while a feature film in linear story plotting requires a three-act structure. The story develops along a twisting and turning through-line. At the end of each act and also in several other places, the action will reach a climax. The climax leads to a turning point.

Like all good story-telling, the world of the mainstream story works by compressing and pointing the reality of life. It is the writer's created world as opposed to everyday life as we live it. Naturally, it requires conflict and interaction between the characters to hold audience interest. The *genre* of story is not the issue here.

By the end of act three, all the problems should have been solved in one way or another, but in any event, there is conclusion. The main device or driving force of the story is pitting the protagonist against the external/internal conflicts that beset him. The time line flows logically whether or not there are flashbacks and time jumps. Even if the story is total fantasy, there is a consistent reality within the parameters the writer has established. In the story, as in life, one event will trigger the next. There is cause and effect, action and reaction. This is the format most generally used in American and European films. But it is not the only one. As George Clooney pointed out, 'Good films raise questions and don't answer them all. They don't spell it out. You don't have to have it all handed to you on a plate. Leave the audience something to think about on the way home.'[1]

The following three films can all be classified as mainstream. If in doubt about the structure of any film, get it out of the video shop and list the steps of the story-line (that is, the stepline). In chapter 10 I have broken down the structure of two mainstream films in more detail.

Moulin Rouge (2001, original screenplay by Baz Luhrmann and Craig Pearce) is essentially a mainstream three-act structure. The genre is musical/fantasy/drama. A beautiful courtesan whose health is failing is engaged to marry an unsavoury nobleman. She falls in love with a poor but handsome writer. On this framework the director created a panoply of light and sound with driving pace and bold, courageous use of music and colour. This is really a film that relies on the vision of the director, Baz Luhrmann.

In *Good Will Hunting* (1997, original screenplay by Matt Damon and Ben Affleck), Will, a janitor at MIT (Matt Damon) is a closet genius but, because of his personal hang-ups, he prefers hanging around with his booze buddies rather than capitalizing on his mathematical prowess. A professor arranges psychological counselling for Will with Robin Williams, who helps him find his way – in the course of which the two men mutually exorcise their inner demons.

Saving Private Ryan (1998, screenplay by Robert Rodat) begins with a horrific recreation of the D-Day landings in World War II, during which Private Ryan (Matt Damon) is lost behind enemy lines. His three soldier brothers were all killed in one day so the U.S. government instructs a squad led by Captain Miller (Tom Hanks) to bring home the one remaining son, Private Ryan. Their journey leads through a classic three-act structure to find the missing Private.

The majority of Hollywood films are mainstream structures. Other examples show the diversity of subject matter and genre. Choose one of these to break down for yourselves and see why they fit this category: *Apollo 13, Fargo, The Piano, Gladiator, Kramer vs Kramer, Jurassic Park, Secrets and Lies, Casablanca, Sleepless in Seattle, The Truman Show, The Governess*. A film such as *Titanic* (1997) could be described as 'epic mainstream'. It's big and sprawling with lots of visual sweep, but is still an ordinary mainstream structure.

Midstream Structure

This format is not so clear-cut. The structure no longer has three acts (see chapter 6) but it still has an overall beginning, middle, and end. There are not three major climaxes, as you would have in a three-act structure. The order of events can be reversed to some extent or it can be composed of a series of separate episodes or incidents based on a central premise or theme with separate endings to each segment (which are related) and build to create a total understanding of the whole by the end.

In *Four Weddings and a Funeral* (1994, screenplay by Richard Curtis) we have a midstream structure with one main protagonist. The series of thematically related episodes are focused through the minimalist hero who drifts fairly untouched through the action or sequences and does not grow as a character. He remains resolutely as he was at the beginning: self-serving and immature – until the very end when he is forced to make a decision about his life. He doesn't get the girl so much as the girl gets him.

Pulp Fiction (1994, directed by Quentin Tarantino, who also co-wrote the screenplay with Roger Avary from their own original stories) is a masterpiece of structure. It utilizes its completely separate stories and characters, each one riveting within itself, to interweave and overlap with each other. Some characters travel through all the stories as the episodes move forwards and backwards in time. There is no central protagonist, more a series of protagonists. It is actually a structure in five acts. (See script breakdown in chapter 14.)

The Big Lebowski (1997, directed by Joel Coen, who co-wrote the screenplay with his brother Ethan). The 'Dude', Lebowski (Jeff Bridges), lets it all hang out in a parody of life in Los Angeles. An ageing hippie, Lebowski is mistaken for a millionaire of the same name. He survives a series of surreal adventures and plot twists that show us the mini-universe of the bowling alley and the drug and porn underworld peopled by eccentric characters. The structure is loosely woven through comedy and fantasy sequences leading to its resolution.

Midstream can also embrace a more broken-up, episodic structure. In one scenario, for instance, a man needs a coat, so he goes into a second-hand shop and buys one. Is that a story? No, but *Tales of Manhattan* (1942) was a collection of playlets about the coat's adventures with a different star for each episode. Definitely not a three-act structure, but very workable and under a midstream umbrella – or in this case, overcoat – each playlet has a beginning, middle, and end leading to the next story.

California Suite (1978) is a series of oddball vignettes written by Neil Simon, based on his own stage play, with a star-studded cast to keep all the separate stories rolling towards a final conclusion.

Best in Show (2000), co-written with Eugene Levy, directed by and starring Christopher Guest, is an outrageous and hysterical satire on dog shows and the owners and pets who inhabit them. It is a typical midstream format since it is composed of a series of set pieces based on the central theme: dog shows and their pets are the pits.

Short Cuts (1993) – Robert Altman wrote the screenplay with Frank Barhydt from Frank Carver's short stories. It is a brilliant piece of filmmaking and weaves the separate tales into a fine midstream tapestry, drawing together the threads of the different stories only at the end.

Multi-Plots

Like soaps or midstream structures, there can be six or seven separate stories woven together into a film that do not qualify as subplots because most or all of them are of equal value to the main plot. Audiences rarely see the inner conflicts lurking in every character in a large cast such as *Gosford Park* (2002). The focus can be only on a few central characters. The important thing if you are working with multi-plots is not to confuse your audience about who's doing what to whom. Sometimes it can be a case of the writer rubbing his belly and patting his head at the same time.

The audience might expect logical answers to the questions raised in the plot but they are not necessarily always provided. There can be an inconsistency about why things happen with no explanation. Sometimes the audience must work out what they think did or will happen. These films are not likely to be mainstream.

Minimalism

You could call this least-structured form an anti-structure. It is a static portraiture with no acts, as such. The story unfolds through a series of happenings that do not necessarily reach termination. There are no climaxes, although there may be a through-line of events with little or no pressures on the protagonist and the other characters. They are not changed emotionally or intellectually by what happens although events may have altered their way of life temporarily or even permanently. There are variations in mood and theme but not much conflict, giving the conclusion a feeling of inevitability. Charlie Chaplin's tramp character could be regarded as an archetype of the minimalist hero because he becomes the catalyst for changes around him but never changes himself.

Then what keeps the audience's interest? It is peeling back the layers to reveal the protagonist and his interrelationships with the other characters. The protagonist's role is not so much one of action as a passive reaction to events, loosely held together by the circumstances of time and place. By the end of the story the audience will have grown in understanding of the characters and will be left to decide what has really happened – or what may happen after the lights come up.

The French are not averse to this structure: Cyril Collard's (director/co-writer/star) *Savage Nights* (1992) was no more than a study of a man as he wandered through the last days of his life dying of Aids (which the filmmaker did, shortly afterwards). Claude Sautet's (director/co-writer) *Nelly and Monsieur Arnaud* (1995) and Louis Malle's (director/co-writer) delightful film *Milou en Mai* (May Fools, 1989) were minimalist. (Incidentally, Louis Malle once said, 'A confident director loves to have the writer on the set.' Most directors are not that confident.) Eric Rohmer favoured minimalist stories. His characters talk a great deal but not much happens. The New Wave low-budget filmmakers favoured it in the 1990s, as in *Orlando* (1992, directed by Sally Potter and adapted by her from the novel by Virginia Woolf) and *Clerks* (1994, written and directed by Kevin Smith).

The minimalist film *Memento* (2000, directed by Christopher Nolan) has already reached cult status. The director's own screenplay was based on a short story by his brother Jonathan Nolan. The central protagonist (played by Guy Pearce) has lost his short-term memory because of an attack on him and his wife that left her dead. At any one time he can only remember the previous ten minutes. Pearce's character never changes. There is a nice black touch when he finds himself running and can't remember if he is being chased, or is chasing the killer. If that sounds straightforward, it is not. Each segment of the story lasts only for the ten minutes of the protagonist's memory, and it jumps around in terms of chronology from one segment to the next. The fact that you never know quite where you are in the time frame keeps the viewer on his toes. Nolan noted that although he didn't make *Memento*

with the DVD format in mind, now that it has been released on DVD it enables the viewer to rewind, review, and even view the film with each scene in its chronological order. Does this mean that DVD will affect film structure in the future? You'd better believe it.

From the point of view of character, though not plot, the perfect minimalist hero was portrayed by Peter Sellers in his last film, *Being There* (1979, Jerzy Kosinski's script from his novel, directed by Hal Ashby). Sellers played Chancy, a gardener whose learning difficulties insulate him from all outside influences. He never changes, has no desires and never wants anything. A series of happenings change the world around Chancy without changing him, but he is the catalyst for the changes – which is what the story is all about.

There can be a film with no story at all - particularly if it lasts no more than ten minutes. A few years back, a Korean student of mine made a 10-minute film of a Koi fish swimming in a pond. Round and round it went. Fade out. It was quite artistic photography and the fish looked like he was enjoying it, but could you call it story-telling?

The following term a filmmaker made a film about a pistol being fired. The camera focused on the gun in a man's hand as it fired. The one bullet travelled many times to reach its victim – in this case, the same man. That, in a sense was story-telling because at least it gave us a hint of the man's inner chaos.

With the aid of Francis Ford Coppola, one innovative and experimental filmmaker, Godfrey Reggio, made a film (part of a trilogy) called *Koyaanisatsi* (1983) over a period of years between 1975 and 1982, which, while having no story or plot, would seem to make a comment on the world we live in versus nature. The title is a Hopi Indian word meaning 'life out of balance'. Reggio says, '*Koyaanisqatsi* is not so much about something, nor does it have a specific meaning or value. *Koyaanisqatsi* is, after all, an animated object, an object in moving time, the meaning of which is up to the viewer.'

The Art Of Story-Telling

As in physics, so it is in stories: all actions have reactions. When the protagonist's expectations are frustrated by the course of events the 'action' erupts into peak moments through the unexpected reactions of the protagonist or other characters. The protagonist's choices at such peak moments catapult the story into a new direction. His decisions also give us an insight into his mind. It is through his choices that we know and understand him.

But it is also good to leave a certain ambivalence about how a character acts, reacts, and what he says. Every word he utters does not have to be engraved in gold. You can leave a certain unexplained area for the audience to interpret. This allows them to think along with him.

This is very much the art of the story-teller because you, the writer, must know that what you have left unsaid and unspoken is still possible, believable and there to be discovered.

The Classic Story-Line with a Closed Ending

A 'closed ending' means that by the end all questions for the protagonist and in the audience's mind are resolved. The emphasis is on the external conflicts confronting the protagonist as he actively pursues his goal. We learn some, if not all, of the inner conflicts that face him because of the changes in his circumstances. The action may have flashbacks or even flash-forwards but the movement through time is logical and consistent and each step the protagonist takes will trigger the next step. This type of story gives an image of life as the audience understands it.

Having set the parameters of your story the reality of those parameters must always remain consistent. Your created world will have its restrictions and you must adhere to them.

The Classic Story-Line with an Open Ending

The audience is left to decide what the protagonist will do when the lights go up. Will he go back to the girl? Will he take the job? Will he pull the trigger? Not all the story points are resolved in an 'open-end' plot but one thing is certain: you never want the audience to outguess the writer. Following are some examples of open-ended story-lines.

The Italian Job (1969, written by Troy Kennedy-Martin, directed by Peter Collinson) was a first-class 'caper' film that leaves the audience with the perfect open end. The robbers, having pulled off a phenomenal heist, are in the getaway bus with their gold bars. After a crazy drive through the Alps the bus comes to rest on the edge of a cliff – about to go over. Michael Caine says, 'Hang on a minute, lads – I've got a great idea.' The last diminishing shot is of the teetering bus on the cliff's edge. Will it go over? Or has Caine thought of something that will save them? Audiences are still waiting for the sequel.

The Usual Suspects (1995, Christopher McQuarrie's elegant, tortuous, convoluted, Oscar-winning best original screenplay, directed by Bryan Singer). In this must-see film Kevin Spacey, the bland face of evil, relates his version of happenings told in flashback. The story is slick and the pace never lets up. It is intricately plotted and densely layered – a shell game of violence and betrayal. The resolution of Keyser Soze's identity undermines the entire narrative because everything you've been led to believe is turned upside down. You think it is a closed-end story but the plot delivers an open end as Spacey walks away free as a bird and not a suspect. So now we know who Keyser Soze is – but what will he do next? (We didn't get a sequel.)

Star Wars II: Attack of the Clones (2002) – the fifth film to be made in the Star Wars cycle, though the second in terms of its chronological sequence in the plot – is open-ended because it is only part of a larger whole. Unusually, it leaves the audience already knowing what eventually happens in the galactic battle to come, because those films have already been made.

When you have multiple protagonists and several separate but interrelated stories, some, if not all, the characters' separate futures will be open-ended. *Nashville* (1975, screenplay by Joan Tewkesbury, directed by Robert Altman, and considered one of his major films) was a minimalist structure encompassing some two dozen characters whose stories blend and cross over, but are not finalized. We are seeing only what the title informs us, a vista of life and music in Nashville.

One of the most open endings of all is *Unfaithful* (2002, written by Alvin Sargent and William Broyles Jr, directed by Adrian Lyne), adapted from the 1968 French film by Claude Chabrol called *La Femme Infidèle* (the first in a series of thrillers from Chabrol in which his leads are always called Charles and Hèléne). Now called Connie (Diane Lane) and Edward (Richard Gere), a well-off couple's marriage is disturbed by her affair. Edward kills her lover. The film's end sees Connie, Edward, and their child in a car. They kiss. Should they flee the country? Camera pulls back to reveal the car has stopped at a light – right in front of a police station. Was that an accident? Will they give themselves up – or drive on? We don't know.

The Writer's Working Method

There are two main types of story construction to lead the audience into your story. In the first, neither the audience nor the protagonist knows something until it happens. The audience discovers 'that which is unknown' only when the protagonist discovers it. In other words, they experience the action as it happens, through the protagonist's eyes.

Jacob's Ladder (1990, written by Bruce Joel Rubin, directed by Adrian Lyne) created a visually unique horror film based on Rubin's surreal story about a Vietnam veteran (Tim Robbins) who had been used by the army in drug experiments and as a consequence is now haunted by visions of monsters, winged demons, and memories of a dead son and of having been nearly bayoneted. The audience does not discover the truth, that he is already dead, until the end when he discovers it. This hugely underrated psychological thriller was a box-office failure, and the American critics hated it. It was at least ten years too early for its audience, but now it is a cult film.

The opposite situation in *Sunset Boulevard* (1950), when we know from the beginning that the protagonist is dead, because the protagonist himself announces it in voiceover, is really another example of the same approach, in that the protagonist and the audience know the same information at the same time.

The other main approach is when the audience knows something the protagonist does not, and they watch to see how he will react when he discovers it. This offers the audience the chance to be way ahead of the protagonist. In any case, obviously, you don't want the audience to never know what's going on – because they'll hate you.

In *Sleeping with the Enemy* (1991, screenplay by Ronald Bass from the novel by Nancy Price, directed by Joseph Ruben) Julia Roberts has run away from her psychotic, pathologically tidy husband. The audience knows he is on her trail, but she doesn't know. When she goes into her kitchen and finds her shelves all neatly arranged, it delivers a message no words could convey. The killer not only knows where she has gone, he has actually been in the house. This visual is a perfect example of the cinematic principle 'show, don't tell'. When I saw the film in the cinema, the audience actually screamed just seeing the carefully stacked cans. No bloody corpse, no ghoulish monster – just tin cans – a symbol of the obsessive husband's sadism and his threat of danger.

Ask yourself the following questions about the world of your story to ensure you maintain internal consistency:

What time period does your story cover? Is it 24 hours (like the TV series *24*) or a week, a year, or twenty or more years?

Location in time: Is it happening now, in the future, or in the past?

Geographical location: What are the specifics about this time and place that set it apart and makes it essential to your story? What country, city, house, planet, or space ship is the setting for your story? Where specifically is it happening? What locations would be necessary to tell the story? A ski resort? A business office? A country village? An ocean liner? List all the possibilities for a variety of visuals – keeping a thought for budget. How does that (or other factors) affect your story? Can you choose the most visual locations to open it up? This can be especially important in adapting a stage play.

Level of society: What are the human elements? What is the social context of these people? Aristocracy? Middle class? Working class? Jailbirds? You are going to invent a background for each of your characters so you must know about them – at least what the audience and the actors need to know. These factors create the boundaries to the world of your story. It puts limits on the possibilities of what your characters can reasonably do. These restrictions will actually be of great help to you. Keep your parameters wide enough to allow for all the elements of your story, but once set, do not exceed them. Your characters must be designed to have the necessary qualities that will enable them to carry out their choices under pressure within the framework of their world.

Even in such stories as *Aliens I, II,* and *III, Gladiator, Band of Brothers,* or *Enemy at the Gate,* we relate to a few characters – not the entire war or the whole of a city under siege. The world of your story must be small enough so that you can control all of it. The sharper your focus, the more choices you should have on a human level. Know the lives of the characters on every level: personal, social, the inner lives, the physical environment.

Is your story driven by *character* or *plot*? Decide early on. *Four Weddings and a Funeral* and *When Harry Met Sally* (1989) are midstream character-driven stories with not much plot. They are built around the characters who go through a series of happenings or 'little episodes' based on the central premise or theme.

Turning Points: Every time the protagonist meets a new crisis it turns the story from a positive to a negative, or the reverse, and keeps the audience off balance. What will happen next? Hopefully, something unexpected.

Counterpoint: Other characters are there to counterpoint the protagonist's actions and attitudes. Certain relationships escalate, and these can lead the story in another direction. There is a 'text versus subtext' to what characters will do. There are dualities and single-mindedness. What you are looking for is a good mix.

The Spine of the Story: This is called the through-line, and is the primary force driving the protagonist on his quest; the causal line that flows from the initial turning point to your final climax.

The Conflicts: These are the all-important forces of antagonism, the pressures put upon your protagonist, the cause of his struggle. We empathize with the protagonist as an underdog, under pressure. The cop fighting the deadline whose boss won't let him have enough time. *The Fugitive* (1993) in which the prisoner is trying to escape and prove his innocence. Even love stories have conflict, from *Romeo and Juliet* onwards. The conflicts in all stories lie between the protagonists' desires and their ability to reach their goals. Even protagonists with superhuman powers must face conflict. How could Superman become an underdog? You would have to create an adversary who is equal to or greater than he is – and yet, because he is Superman, he must, with some justification, still win.

Mood: This is heavily influenced by the genre of your story (see chapter 15). To a great extent, creating mood onscreen is the province of the director, but you should have indicated it in your script without being too literary. The visual elements – the colour, lighting, camera style, and acting style – are all parts of creating the mood of the piece. For example, Luchino Visconti's *Death in Venice* (1971) visually created a genteel, languorous turn-of-the-century ambience. It must be clear in the script what the mood of the piece is. It must have a through-line in the sense of overall style and emotional values and the spirit or atmosphere of your scenes. In other words, you wouldn't normally have high comedy scenes and then go into deep and serious drama, though of course there are exceptions because of plot, such as Martin Scorsese's *King of Comedy* (1983, screenplay by Paul D. Zimmerman). But in this case we are watching De Niro's performances as a comic, which is not part of his 'real' day-to-day life but rather, his hoped-for career as a performer. Roberto Benigni's *Life is Beautiful* (1997, discussed below under 'Comic Relief') goes from comedy to tragedy using fantasy as the grease on his axle. You should not keep the mood on one level throughout. There must be highs and lows, changes of pace.

Pace: The audience must not have too much time to ponder whether or not the story point you have just revealed to them is watertight (not that it won't be, of course!). They should be catapulted through your story, entangled in the action, leading them inexorably to the act climaxes and the *dénouement.*

This is not true in minimalism, since there plots are structured as permutations on a theme leading the audience to a keener insight into the characters, who in themselves don't change a lot. We just get to know and understand them better. Let the audience see the broad strokes of the protagonist's actions and then let them discover the details.

Tempo: The rhythm, measure, throb, or pulse of the 'action' in a scene is its tempo. This is not necessarily physical. It can be a psychological battle between two very quiet people having a discussion in a restaurant. It's a matter of pace, and *who's got the power* within the scene to control what is going on. A scene is highly charged when the power changes or the events alter the protagonist's point of view and actions.

Shorter scenes can build and can become part of a climactic longer sequence. Tempo should increase towards the act climaxes when your audience's interest may be flagging.

Story Design: There must be a compelling force to the narrative and a text and sub-text to what we see and hear. We must discover bit by bit where the story is leading. If it were all obvious from the beginning, we would not care to watch. The twists and turns should affect the protagonist's life or at least his point of view towards himself and/or others.

The story should arc up and down more than once, almost like a bungee jump. If you kept your audience on a series of high moments without relief, they would be exhausted, in the same way that they would lose interest and soon become bored if nothing much were happening. Like eating too much of your favourite ice cream, enough is good, but too much is cloying. Balance is essential.

Your plot must remain consistent with your central theme and be believable. The audience may 'suspend disbelief', but don't try their patience. If they get ahead of you, it's heads down and popcorn time for them, and curtains for you!

Thematic Elements: As you begin laying out your steps scene by scene, where is the conflict? What are the protagonist's goals? Do they change as the story progresses because of changing circumstances? What are the opposing forces and values at stake? Have you established your positives and negatives early on?

Chance versus Believability: Chance happenings in a story must be used wisely and sparingly. The initial turning point can arise by chance, but never use chance to justify the ending of your story. If you need to use coincidence (as in a random, unmotivated collision of incidents and/or people) to tell

your story then underline it, to close the gap in believability. 'Nobody could believe this could have happened again but ...'

In *O Brother, Where Art Thou?* (2000) Ethan and Joel Coen's delightful episodic comedy (in which an escaped convict tries to win back his wife) their picaresque adventures and meeting with other characters (especially the 'mermaidens'), too unreal for social drama, is perfectly acceptable in a fantasy/comedy based on mythic characters.

Building to your Climax: Movies are about the last act. There should be short, swift action leading to your climax. If you want the third act to have an up ending then your second act must be down – and the opposite can also work. Ironic endings require a positive then negative point of view, though one will usually seem the stronger choice. Tricking your audience with 'cheap surprise' may be a convention in certain types of comedy, but is only cheap in drama.

The Final Climax: François Truffaut said 'save spectacle and truth for the end'. After three or more acts, the plot reaches a major reversal in the protagonist's life. This is the moment of maximum tension. The 'great event', building from the crisis end of your second act, requires all the willpower and cleverness the protagonist can muster to achieve his goal. The situations become tougher every moment and puts him more at risk – whatever the disaster may be (mental or physical). The old line, 'cut to the chase', applies here. You want to make your third act no longer than 20 minutes in a 90-minute structure. And remember that that's what the audience have come to see.

The protagonist is not a weak-willed person and has the capacity to pursue his aims – but he may not get what he wants. He must risk losing in order to gain. He must struggle through a moment of truth, where the test is one of *decision*, not of *action*. The protagonist thus reveals the essential nature of his character through the choices he makes and what he does – not by the happenings he is confronted with.

The plot doesn't make the character. The character's decisions must, finally, control the plot. But it's the writer who tosses a coin in the air, flipping it to allow the audience to glimpse the other side. Try to add one more twist so that the end isn't what the audience expects. A good twist can cause the audience to see the whole film in a new way.

Try to suggest a final visual image that sums up the meaning of the film and leaves the audience with emotional insight into the human condition. Give your audience what they want – but not the way they expect it.

Sometimes a film's ending is changed because preview audiences don't like it. In *Fatal Attraction* (1987, written by James Dearden and Nicholas Meyer, directed by Adrian Lyne), the original ending had Michael Douglas in jail for Glenn Close's murder. But it was too *noir* for American audiences so it was changed to a typical slasher ending: he thinks he's drowned her – she revives – and then his wife shoots her.

Melodrama: Life is melodrama – just look at the front page of your daily paper. Murders, kidnappings, teenagers dying of drug overdoses, battles, wars, and plane crashes. But presenting all that dramatically is another matter. This is the art of the writer. The finest authors (from Jane Austen to William Boyd) all recount tales of melodrama. If you can distil your story into heightened reality and make it believable, you are on the way to being a good writer.

Momentum: Single scenes (for film) should average no more that two to three-and-a-half minutes, though in certain circumstances it's possible to get away with a lot more, particularly in movies adapted from stage plays, as in the eight-minute takes of Hitchcock's 1948 thriller, *Rope*. The length of a scene decreases to roughly one-and-a-half minutes for a TV drama. In a half-hour series or soap, scenes can be much shorter.

When you have a longer sequence in continuous time, although the location of the scene and characters do not change, the action can be kept vigorous by changing the focus on a particular character or introducing a new action. The entrance of a new character or the exit of one can alter who has the power or force in the scene and can keep the momentum going.

Although the camera is the director's domain, the shots – where they affect the story – should be imagined by a writer who is thinking visually, and briefly indicated in the script. You can indicate where you want the camera without 'calling' the shot. For instance, the note '*a closer look at her face*

reveals that she is about to cry, although she is still smiling' tells the director that you don't want a long shot at that moment, without specifying a 'close-up', which a director would resent as crossing the line into a decision that should be his to make.

You are focusing on the action of the character's inner conflict. During filming, the director may decide on another point of view and not follow your concept, so don't be too disappointed.

The 'Snake under the Bed' Theory: Cecil B DeMille had some advice for his chief writer, Jesse Lasky Jr, who was trying to put some tension in a scene. 'The audience will sit through a character lying in bed reading the phone directory if they know that there is a snake under the bed about to pounce.' Audiences love to anticipate trouble ahead for the protagonist because then they can worry about how he will overcome it.

Changing the Audience's Point Of View: In *Basic Instinct* (1992, written by Joe Eszterhas, directed by Paul Verhoeven) the audience (and the police) think Sharon Stone is guilty. Then the audience are led to believe the killer is the police psychologist. In the final scene, the possibilities are switched again. It looks like Stone is reaching for the ice pick – then no, she's not! But in the last frame you see it – under the bed (right next to DeMille's snake). This qualifies as a open ending, leaving the audience to decide whether she is the killer or not.

Expectations and Results: What the protagonist expects when his world is ripped apart and what actually happens; how the protagonist achieves his goal despite his challenges – or doesn't – these are what the audience pay to see. The results of the protagonist's decisions must hold the element of surprise. The audience want their expectations to be confounded. Keep them guessing as long as you can. They must speculate on the all important questions: what's going to happen next? How will this turn out?

Story Logic: A network of causes leads to one final result. In a sense, it a chain reaction. Your audience must believe the ending no matter what your plot line or genre. They have been having a psychological reaction to the inner thoughts of the characters for at least 90 minutes and they want to go home satisfied. Remember, you're not making this film with backers' money just for yourself.

More Questions To Ask Yourself:

1) What is your film about in terms of opposing values?

2) What is at stake for the protagonist if he loses?

3) What are the forces against him?

4) What does he gain if he wins? Seek the limits of his experience and powers to give dimension to the protagonist.

5) What are the 'politics' of this created world, this family, this relationship?

6) Who has the power in the relationship? Does this change?

7) What are the rituals of this world and its minutiae? How your protagonist eats, lives, travels, his quirks, habits, and so on.

8) What are the morals and ethics of this world?

9) What are the laws and restrictions of the period and place, household, or community?

Subject Matter And Symbols

Sex: Hitchcock (described by columnist Bernard Levin as 'the master of intangible menace') said, 'Sex should be suspenseful. If it's too blatant, there's no suspense.' Hitchcock preferred the paradox – the inner fire and cool surface of a Grace Kelly, ladies who become whores in the bedroom – as opposed to the 'let it all hang out' approach of a starry-eyed Marilyn Monroe or a blatantly overt Pamela Anderson. But elegance is not the image of the Millennium. Today's female stars expose as much skin as possible off screen and many movie makers explore the borders of soft porn in a cry for attention. If it's justified in the story, great. But if you put it there, make sure it is not just gratuitous. And Hitchcock had a point; suspense with a little sex is a big audience turn-on.

Symbolism: Objects can become supercharged with meaning. In *To Catch a Thief* (1955) Hitchcock used the image of fireworks in the sky seen through the window behind Cary Grant and Grace Kelly to symbolize their internal explosion. It's a cliché now (because so many other directors have copied it since) but in those more censored days, the visual symbolism got the idea across. Whether this was Hitchcock's invention or his writer's, I have no idea. But it illustrates the

sort of 'action' a writer might put into his scene description. How would you write this? Perhaps something like: *'Through the window behind them fireworks explode, echoing their suppressed desires'.*

Actions as Character Traits: In *Thelma and Louise* (1991, Oscar-winning script by Callie Khourie, directed by Ridley Scott) the way the two women pack their clothes for the trip tells us about the type of women they are without dialogue: Thelma packs everything sloppily; Louise packs carefully, neatly.

Symbolism as Character Traits: In *American Beauty* (1999, the black-comedy screenplay by Alan Ball, directed by Sam Mendes) Kevin Spacey fantasizes about teenage Mena Suvari and imagines her laid out waiting for him on a bed of roses, symbolizing his mid-life crisis with its sexual longings and frustrations. This is a fantasy image he creates in his mind, which differs from a symbolic image which the audience or a character actually sees. But the image was so strong it was used in advertizing the film.

In *Erin Brockovich* (2000, screenplay by Susannah Grant, directed by Steven Soderbergh) the image created by Julia Roberts' overtly sexy style of dress conveys a message to the other characters. It presents an icon that is in sharp contrast to her deeper character (text and subtext). It represents an overt defiance of convention, and a cry for attention.

In *Les Diaboliques*, the 1954 French classic (directed by Henri-Georges Clouzot and scripted by him with three others from a novel by Pierre Boileau and Thomas Narcejac) the imagery of water is used throughout as a symbol of dread and evil. In this must-see suspense-thriller classic, the wife and mistress of a sadistic husband, the headmaster of a school, decide to kill him.

Under the titles, a mud puddle holds our attention. The two women get the husband drunk and drown him in the bathtub. They dump him into the swimming pool. The car keys are dropped in the pool. There is constant rain. The pool is drained but the body has mysteriously disappeared. The husband is fleetingly glimpsed alive. We hear the sound of a dripping faucet. The wife finds the husband back in the bathtub under the water. When he bursts up out of the water the wife, who has a bad heart, dies of shock. The mistress has planned with the husband an untraceable way to kill his wife. (The 1996 remake is inferior – see the original.)

Points of View: Novice writers often allow more than one character to speak in the same 'voice' using the same phrases or expressions or way of speaking. In real life each person has an idiosyncratic style of speaking. Giving your characters separate ways of expressing themselves is vital. In stories of social significance, only one character (usually your protagonist, but not necessarily) can express the writer's point of view and perception. Obviously, some characters will be positive and some negative.

Back Story: Also called 'exposition', this term refers to what happened before your story began. Whatever your story, you will probably need to deal with a certain amount of back story, though be careful to limit yourself to information that the audience 'need to know' in order to understand the present situation and characters.

You should never have a character simply state a plain fact about himself. Instead, you can use a character's present attitudes and concerns – his reticence to take a certain action because of something in his past, for instance. For example, one character can accuse another of acting a certain way because of something in his past, which causes an argument. Arguments are good for revealing back story. Or, let one character discover a clue about something in another character's past – perhaps from a photograph, letter, or newspaper cutting. Just don't dump it all into one scene.

Remember, your characters know their own world, so make sure you don't have them tell each other things they would already know. Don't give the audience more than they need at that point in the story. Decide in which scene you will reveal *what* – and *how*, by planning it into your stepline (see next chapter).

In Ingmar Bergman's *Through A Glass Darkly* (1961, Oscar for Best Foreign Film), the film opens with the husband and the father going out in a fishing boat from a remote Baltic island. Against this interesting visual background and action, Bergman knew his audience would sit still to hear the two men discuss the wife having been in a mental home and her possible descent into madness.

We not only understand the whole back story but also get an understanding of the two men from their opposing points of view and attitudes: the husband's deep concern and the father's self-obsessed lack of concern and refusal to see the truth. The entire premise of the story and the characters has been spelled out in a few minutes at the beginning of the film through their attitudes.

'Show, don't tell' – but avoid visual clichés. How many times have you seen a film in which the camera pans across a group of photos on the mantelpiece to establish who's in the family? It's any easy cliché for a director to fall into, so don't make it easier for him by writing it into the script. Give him another way to establish the family connections.

Character Names: How many times do you forget what a character is called because the other characters rarely use his name unless referring to him when he's not in the scene – and then you're not sure who they're talking about. Be sure your audience is familiar with the names of your characters by having them referred to by name by other characters when they're talking to them, as well as *about* them.

The MacGuffin: A term invented by one of Hitchcock's writers, Angus MacPhail, and adopted by Hitchcock. The MacGuffin (real or symbolic) is the object which will give the person who gets it what he most desires (power, money, love, etc.) and to a great extent drives the plot, although in the end it may be of no significance. It is actually a 'red herring'. The name of this deliberately mysterious object was derived from an anecdote: Two men are travelling to Scotland on a train from London. In the luggage rack is an oddly wrapped parcel. 1) 'What have you got there?' 2) 'That's a MacGuffin.' 1) 'What's a MacGuffin?' 2) 'A device for trapping lions in the Scottish Highlands.' 1) 'There aren't any lions in the Scottish Highlands.' 2) 'Well then, I guess that's no MacGuffin.' [2]

A MacGuffin is neither relevant, important, nor, finally, anyone's business. It simply gets the story going. Hitchcock used it not as an entity but as a question in *North by Northwest* (1959) with the puzzling suspicion in Cary Grant's mind of what the spies were after. They're after the MacGuffin.

In *The Maltese Falcon* (1941, scripted and directed by John Huston from Dashiell

Hammett's book) all the characters are willing to kill to get the falcon statue but in the end it turns out to be nothing but a dud.

In *The Treasure of the Sierra Madre* (1948, written and directed by John Huston from the novel by B Traven) gold is the MacGuffin. In this great classic, the three men go together to prospect for gold. They get it, it destroys their lives, and in the end the gold dust blows away in the wind.

Comic Relief: It is important that even in the heaviest drama a light touch here and there and a gently humorous moment can counterpoint the drama and break the tension so that it can rebuild.

But sometimes mixing high comedy and heavy drama can be an uneasy blend. In *Life is Beautiful* (1997, directed by and starring Roberto Benigni, who also co-wrote the screenplay with Vincenzo Cerami) what begins as a light-hearted comedy suddenly turns to the tragic horrors of the Holocaust. The juxtaposition did not suit all the critics. As excellent as it was, it gave some the feeling of watching two separate films, regarding it as only a qualified success. With all its wonderful moments, I left the cinema not knowing what kind of film I was watching and unsure if I really enjoyed it or was just stunned by it. I watched it with an actress friend who had been a child in one of the camps. She was shaken by it and could not get it out of her mind. At first she hated it, and weeks later said that she had been moved by it. It certainly made people think.

Rhythm Editing: Rhythm is a word that often springs from the lips of directors. Rhythm in a single scene and in the entire movie, is under his guidance. The editor is the first audience that will see what the director has shot. His job is to be both critical and constructive to add finesse to the separate shots and scenes. The pace of cuts and intercuts can strengthen a sequence, add tension, give it meaning.

But it is to a great extent the domain of the writer to think visually and create the ambience for that flow of provocative images and moments to emerge. In fact, the writer should visualize the script as though he were editing it. The rhythm of story-telling is the writer's basic concern. The rhythm of life has two opposing moods: active and passive. And so too, there must be passive moments in a film giving the audience a chance to catch its breath and be ready for the next leap into action (not car chases – but story movement).

Goals: The goal of your protagonist need not be large. He does not need to be climbing Mount Everest against the worst blizzard in fifty years. The goal could be as small as a person trying to prepare tuna empanadillas for guests or studying for a degree in Maths. The element that turns it into a story is that something goes wrong and the protagonist is confronted with obstacles. Things are not as they should be or even possibly, as they seem. The tension in the story is created by what blocks the hero and how he finally achieves his goal (or doesn't). This can be called The Plot.

Imagery: As stated before, this is primarily the director's territory, but not always. The writer should imagine it and often can suggest it.

It is in the nature of images to engender emotion. They do not support intellectual analysis. If you see the American president speaking on television he often stands at his dais or sits in the Oval office with an American flag behind him. In August 2002 George W. Bush went so far as to speak on TV from Mount Rushmore, with the mighty images of former presidents looming down at him, as though in support. It placed him squarely in the viewer's consciousness among the greats where the image-makers wanted him. If he speaks to foreign heads of government (we now see Blair, Putin, and Bush together quite often) they are not just sitting at a desk, but are standing in front of their countries' flags. Whatever the message being conveyed, the image is one of strength, patriotism, and unity – making a direct appeal to the emotions.

Great films always include image systems. A film is composed of thousands of images. Don't go for the obvious, like a flag or a crucifix to represent patriotism or religious fervour. Leave that to the politicians, and look for the subtle visual message. We have seen that an image can tell the story without words. *Remember, the image is the message and the message is the film.*

Even a small visual image can imprint itself on the audience's subconscious. In *Blade Runner,* when Deckard (Harrison Ford) sees an origami twist of paper in his apartment towards the end of the film, he and the audience get the message that the police chief has been there.

K-PAX (2002, written by Charles Leavitt from Gene Brewer's novel, directed by Iain Softley) is the story of a man who claims to be from the planet K-PAX and the psychiatrist who treats him. The question the movie asks is at what point you believe the seemingly unbelievable. In the reflection on a window pane we see the merging of Kevin Spacey's and Jeff Bridges' faces – which mirrors the two minds drawing together to reach one point of view. You could write that moment in your script, and if the director is smart, he'll use it.

In *The Piano*, the piano's feet are in the sea when it is left on the shore. The sea represents freedom but the legs are bound. Holly Hunter pries open the packing case and plays. The image is a metaphor for her life and the piano – the symbol of her soul.

A Contradiction Of Images: If you set up something the audience understands in one way and then let them see it in a different way it's a bit of a cheat (but a good cheat) that hooks the viewer into watching more closely.

In *Witness (*1985, screenplay by Earl W. Wallace and William Kelley from Kelley's novel) the opening scene shows us a farmer riding up a hill in a horse-drawn wagon. It looks like we are in the 19th century. But then the title comes up on the screen: '*1984 Lancaster County*'. Then we see trucks and cars and we discover that this farmer is a member of the closed and anti-technological Amish community. It makes the point without a word that these people don't accept other people's definition of what it means to be in the 20th century.

Images Used to Underscore the Theme: In *The Seventh Seal*, Ingmar Bergman's 1957 masterpiece of world cinema, his allegorical theme poses the question: is there a God? A knight and his servant are returning from the crusade when the knight encounters the figure of Death. He refuses to accompany Death and gambles for his life in a game of chess – to discover if there is a God in a world stricken by evil, plagues, and corruption. Bergman uses overt images of flagellants, thieves, and people burning at the stake to underscore the evils of the uncertain world in which the

knight lives. The image of the chess boardchessboard reflects man as a pawn in the hands of Death and gives a deeper, more subtle meaning to the simple, provocative tale.

Alien (1979, script by Dan O'Bannon from a story by Ronald Shusett and O'Bannon, directed by Ridley Scott; its sequels have been *Aliens*, 1986; *Alien III*, 1992; and *Alien: Resurrection*, 1997) used sexual symbolism as a future-gothic technological turn-on. The images of the spacecraft as a womb and the penile symbolism in the design of the alien creatures plays on male–female sexual fears of birth and penetration, such as when an alien monster chews its way out of a man's stomach.

Dances With Wolves (1990, screenplay by Michael Blake from his novel, directed by Kevin Costner) was the first Western in 60 years to win a Best Picture Oscar. The image of the destruction of the bison symbolized the end of an era and destruction of a way of life for the Native Americans and the white man.

Flashbacks: There was a period in the 1970s and 1980s when the use of flashbacks was considered old-fashioned. Like all cycles this one has been back in fashion since the 1990s. In mainstream story construction it should be used judiciously at a motivated moment and not merely to reveal back story.

In the biographical film *Pollock* (2000, screenplay by Barbara Turner and Susan Emshwiller, directed by Ed Harris), the story opens with a high moment in Jackson Pollock's career when *Life* magazine features a spread on his work. From there it flashes back to his early days as a struggling young artist. It is here that the story actually begins. The plot moves forward again, past the episode of the opening scene, and follows the subsequent success of his career and marriage and the downward spiral of his life until his death in a car crash. The initial scene lets the audience (who may never have heard of Pollock) know up front that this is going to be a story about a famous painter. The structure makes for a compelling understanding of the artist.

In *Silence Of The Lambs* (1991, screenplay by Ted Tally from the novel by Thomas Harris, directed by Jonathan Demme), Tally used the agreed 'deal' of an exchange of information between Anthony Hopkins (as Lecter) and Jodie Foster (as Clarice) to make her tell him about the screaming of the lambs and the slaughter of young animals that she recalls from childhood. There is a brief flashback of Foster at ten years old with her father (Clarice's back story). She recalls how she saved a lamb. Lecter compares her attempt to save the lambs with her feeble attempts to fight the dark side of human nature. We get the back story through plot development.

Harold Pinter said, 'I can only write what comes out. I don't think too much about it. The act of writing is one when you push aside the kind of daily thoughts with which we live, and allow something else to happen.' Pinter is a man with an inner voice who tunes out the world and tunes in to his muse. Most writers do not start with that; they have to find it if they can. You must learn to open the creative channel. No one can do that for you. But practice teaches you to discover it, if it's there. Learning techniques helps make the path easier.

As the story builds in your mind and grows in outline on paper, let the characters take over instead of forcing them. Pinter also said he went crazy when a character came into the room in his script. He didn't know who 'the goddamn character was' and it took him three weeks to get the guy out of scene.[3] It's a great way to write if you're Pinter. He and Neil Simon each say they often write without an outline and no end in sight. When they're into the story and begin to know their characters, then they assess where and who the characters are and what they will do next. Possibly each writer outlines the story in his head, but Simon's plays and screenplays are carefully structured, and so are Pinter's although they may seem much more enigmatic. Their stories are 'character-led' so my guess is they begin with the character and then plan out the structure as they decide what the character will do in each situation.

But unless you are sure you're a genius, put your ideas on paper where you can look at them, analyze them, and build on them. Most of all, look for a story that you can tell better than anyone else. Bring something to it that is original and has your personal stamp on it, and that will be genius enough. Don't start writing your screenplay until the characters tell you what they are doing and why. They will begin to do this if your stepline has been sufficiently developed with the card system and your treatment is flowing.

Transitions of Time And Place

You can indicate the passing of time in different ways:

Changing Images: Dissolve through an object to a similar or related one. *The Shawshank Redemption* (1994, written and directed by Frank Darabont, based on Stephen King's story) covers 19 years. In his jail cell, Tim Robbins hangs a series of large movie star posters on his wall. The passing of years are indicated by the changing movie queens. But the posters served a dual purpose, which is good plotting. They make a valid story point about his eventual escape because we later discover they are hiding the tunnel he has dug.

Sound to Sound: Find key sounds that embody the tension of a transition: ocean to shower; car motor to train wheels, shell fire to fireworks; a scream to a train whistle – as in Hitchcock's 1935 classic, *The 39 Steps*. Sound transitions can be overdone, so use them sparingly.

Movement to Movement: Link two scenes by using a similar movement in both at the point of transition. For instance, one character might tip a glass over. Cut directly to next scene, where another (or the same) character picks up a glass. Or cut from the eyes of one character to the eyes of another – or to the same character in another place. Director Sammy Fuller said, 'exchanging a look with another character is a powerful character developer for a scene change'. Again, this is considered the director's area but put it in your script, if you see a place for it. At least the director will know you think visually.

Voiceover Narration: Narration can serve as a way of bridging a gap between scenes, particularly if much time has passed between the scenes. A narrator is generally necessary for documentaries, but for drama (or comedy), unless the situation requires it and when nothing else will work, it's good to avoid voiceovers, since the necessary information can usually be given in other ways, through the words you give your characters to say.

Having said that, some brilliant films (mainly French) have used it to give not only style, but an insight to the visual image. *Amélie* (2002) used voiceover with huge success. In *Tous les Matins du Monde* (1991) with Gérard Depardieu as an 18th century court musician, it got a little boring in my opinion. *Madame Bovary* (1991, Claude Chabrol's mediocre adaptation of Flaubert's classic novel, with Isabelle Huppert) filled the audience with *ennui* and dampened the sense of dramatic pace.

English-language cinema generally avoids the approach (in Hollywood it is felt to make a film too slow-paced) although Woody Allen frequently uses voiceovers to good comic effect.

In *About a Boy* (2002, written and directed by Chris and Paul Weitz, based on Nick Hornby's novel), the little boy, Marcus, provides voiceover narration to counterpoint the story of his relationship with a wealthy London bachelor (Hugh Grant). Grant envies his married friends but would rather not be one. Grant pretends to be a single father until he runs into his nemesis, 12-year-old Marcus. The voiceover narration adds humour and manages to preserve some of the tone of the novel.

Writing The Action

For the directions and descriptions in your script – everything that is not dialogue – use crisp, tight, visually evocative words – and bear in mind that some of the people who read the script with a view to financing it won't be artistically inclined. Keep it simple but colourful, so that you put the movie into the reader's head visually. Be brief, but specific, for instance: *'He ambles (pads, shuffles) to the door'*. It gives a precise idea of what you want. Remember, the action is always written in the present tense.

Avoid saying that something happens 'suddenly'. Almost everything in a film happens suddenly. There will be a few places you will need to specify it, but not many.

Use the camera as your focus – it is treated like a person in a script. Instead of saying 'we see' you can say: *'CAMERA focuses on MARY picking up the cup.'* This tells the director where you want a particular focus. But don't put it in if it is not making a specific plot point (for instance, if there is poison in the cup). You could also simply say: *'MARY picks up the cup.'* What would be the difference? The action in the latter case is not relevant to our understanding of the situation, but in the first instance we are really asking the director for a close-up, which visually emphasizes information that the audience knows but Mary doesn't.

Don't try to be too clever in your non-dialogue descriptions of action. You could say, *'the door slams like a gun shot'*, because that gives a specific reference to how it should sound, but don't use such similes just for literary effect.

Chapter 5 | THE STEPLINE, THE CHARACTERS, THE SCENES

What is a stepline? It is not a selling document. To be absolutely clear, it is nothing more than an event structure that you develop for your eyes only. You will continue to change points in your growing stepline.

In chapter 10 I have outlined two films in steplines. Because they are created from existing films they are probably more complete than the originals. They also identify plot and subplot. If you study them, you will see how the stepline works.

Preparation is the most important part of your work. Naturally, you start with an idea and develop it. Put your ideas down in a few sentences, broken roughly into paragraphs. Your first thought may be great, but at every point along the way, give yourself choices. In broad strokes suggest the steps from start to finish. But don't settle on the first concept that comes into your head. Think of a few alternative ways you might develop this or another idea. List all your alternatives separately and keep them.

Assuming this is the most sensational story idea you've ever thought of, you will develop it by starting with two ingredients: your stepline and your separate list of characters necessary to tell this particular story. The first thing you must do is break down the bones of your story into the points of your plot.

Plot means structure and structure means event choices. There will be at least 45 events (sequences) in a film. So your first step is a sequential breakdown giving each event a number. You are simply making a list of the things that happen. You may only have 15 or 20 to begin with, but you will be adding material and filling out areas as you go along. This isn't a breakdown of shots or even scenes, it's just an event structure based on your story idea.

The length and style depends on the type of story, but since we're beginning with a three-act plan, start with a page (or as many as it takes) for each act. This is a more complete breakdown of your beginning outline, and may be 15 to 20 or more pages.

See where the points of your story break into crisis moments, and begin to think about climaxes, turning points, and act breaks. Try to see how your story extends into the world around your protagonist. How does he affect the lives of those around him?

If you decide on changes in the structure, subplots, characters, and so on, it's easy to make them now. Story points will continue to change as your story grows. You will add and you will throw away, but if you begin with a solid stepline you will not end up with writer's block because you'll know what lies ahead (even though you may continue to change it). If your story falls apart during this stage of development and you cannot rescue it, at least you have saved yourself a lot of work and you still have your list of alternatives.

You'll want to put your protagonist under tension to make your story more urgent so make a separate list of 'pressure points' – factors that could put stress on him. List as many as you can think of. You may not use them all, but you may find you need more! Look for things that fall into the following categories: Personal relationships, Personal traumas, and Environmental frictions.

When you have put down all the steps of your story, look to see anything crucial is missing, or alternatively if anything can be eliminated. Is it logical? Justified? Motivated? Look for the friction points in your story. Compress the action as much as possible to keep up the pressure. Remember, for every cause there is an effect, and actions cause reactions. The protagonist is on a journey to put his world back in place. The audience will anticipate what they think will happen next. Don't let them outguess you.

If you can make your audience observe the action one way and then realize things are not quite what they seem, you've got a dramatic moment. The truth is out there – but not what the audience expected. By act three your audience should have a deep understanding of the protagonist and his world.

The spine of the story (the main plot) must run continuously from beginning to end, but if you have one or more subplots, they may run from the first act to the second act and end there – or from the second act to the third, or continue alongside the main plot throughout.

The main plot incorporates the moments of crisis requiring decisions from the protagonist. The act breaks (the ends of act one and act two) should leave the audience with a cliffhanger. The outcome of the protagonist's journey becomes the final climax. The protagonist may be flawed in some ways, he may be willing or unwilling at the start of the journey, but he must remain an active person so that at the moment of crisis, he is in control of his fate. It is the protagonist who takes the risks and sacrifices for the good of others or even for himself. There is often also be a 'resolution scene', to provide a winding down of tension after the final climax, and to prevent the ending appearing too abrupt.

Your narrative should be built around a simple, easily understood premise: three men plot escape from prison; girl wants to be a movie star; separated husband wants to get back with his wife; wife discovers her husband is gay, and so on. There could be 20 story-lines for each of these concepts. The more thoroughly you know your subject and your characters, the more original it will be because it is the small details and the insights into human behaviour that set one story apart from another.

Story-telling is not about reporting. Real-life reportage is filling our TV screens with Big Brothers or celebrities surviving in jungles. You've got to have a depth of understanding of your characters and interrelationships – something we do not get on live-action cop shows where we may never know the motivations behind the actions of the people we see.

Your plot is the ladder upon which your characters climb to success or failure, and your film is not about the plot but about the people making the climb. The stepline will create in broad strokes the blueprint for the screenplay.

When describing an event in your stepline, write down who does what to whom – not in dialogue and not even in complete sentences. Don't get carried away with vivid descriptions.

That comes later (in the treatment phase).

Your protagonist's life began before the movie started. The main action of your story begins at the initial turning point (ITP) in his life. So you will want to establish who he is as quickly as possible. The ITP catapults the audience right into your tale wondering, *what's he going to do about it? What will happen next?*

From whose point of view is the audience meant to be seeing this world? They must have a sympathetic, emotional response and empathize with the protagonist and at some point be wary of the antagonist. Your story should also offer the audience a new slant on their world or introduce them to a world they don't know. It should be built on layers of complexity, not just the complications of the protagonist's quest – but not so complex that the audience will lose their way. Weave your web slowly enough for them to absorb the steps.

Your story might present an idealistic vision of the world as we would wish it to be; one in which goodness triumphs. This viewpoint is not particularly popular today (except in fairy tales) because it leaves little scope for conflict and besides, a more pessimistic attitude towards our society prevails in the 21st century. Films today tend to show the worst of the world as it is, and sometimes a world in which evil triumphs or nearly triumphs, but it is also a more redemptive and palatable world in which the good guy wins. Good may squeak by, by the skin of its teeth. Think of *Silence of the Lambs, Unfaithful, Catch Me If You Can, The Good Thief, The Italian Job, The Talented Mr Ripley, In The Bedroom, Grosse Pointe Blank* and even *Chicago*. All have baddies as heroes. But there is a duality to life and both good and evil exist side by side. It is the balance that can make for an interesting group of characters and an exciting story, so avoid making your characters black and white in their attitudes.

Ethan and Joel Coen's *Fargo* (1995) spins a quirky tale set in the snow-crusted world of a Minnesota winter in which a heavily pregnant and fairly 'uncool' police chief (Frances McDormand) is pitted against the evil goings on. The story focuses on relationships, character and ethics. The lives of *good* ordinary people are caught up in an evil web. Imbued with the Coen brothers' traditional off-beat humour it offers a surreal approach to the traditional black comedy/crime/thriller genre and has been called 'a modern masterpiece'.

An ironic point of view can work for black comedy and drama alike. For example, when the protagonist achieves his goal he finds it's too late (for example, Scarlett in *Gone With the Wind*). Or it can seem that he is being led further from his goal – only to discover that he has reached it. Or he can unwittingly take actions that lead him away from it forever. He can be encumbered with someone or something he thinks will make him miserable, only to discover true happiness. Or he can turn away from a path or a person whom he later realizes was indispensable to his happiness. In *Pollock* the artist gets rid of his wife, who had kept his life in balance. Then he discovers that without her he's out of control.

The right subject for you is something you know about or have a special feeling for. Hopefully, it's a subject that is timely and will catch some producer's eye. A young filmmaker who doesn't know enough about life, or doesn't have enough respect for story, character, the nuances in a relationship or the complexities of the human condition will most likely write something superficial. If you write about a mass murderer, your research does not include going out and killing a few folk. You can read up on the psychology behind that kind of criminal and maybe consider visiting a few jails – from the outside of the bars! You could interview a few detectives or barristers. Truman Capote spent months with one of the killers (safely jailed) who was the subject of his book *In Cold Blood*.

Be willing to discard things that you have worked on. A writer's most essential tool is his wastebasket (or in the case of a computer, the delete key). But there is no harm in keeping a separate file of ideas that didn't quite work for you the first time yet might be useful somewhere else. It's not a bad thing to review half-baked ideas. Sometimes, looking over a list of rejects, you see another angle that would make one of the ideas work.

The Characters

A film character isn't a human being in the same way that your dialogue is not real speech: they should be a form of heightened reality. You will hope that your creations will be works of art. Choose characters that can help develop your plot, resonate and form a counterpoint to the story or some part of the protagonist's life. Preferably write about characters who have emotions and experiences you have felt or have seen or at least have understood in yourself or others. To get emotional response from the audience, you must dig into the life histories of each of your creations and give them dimensions, although not all of it will end up on the screen. You are not writing dialogue at this point – doing so prematurely could ruin your structure. We will look at dialogue in chapter 9.

On a separate document containing biographies of your characters, whether hero or anti-hero, list your protagonist's attitudes, his points of view when confronted by the type of problem he will face in the plot. To decide on the right choice your character will make in the situation, make a list of the possibilities open to him. His choices under pressure reveal his deeper temperament. To give him more dimension than James Bond or Superman, his inner nature can be in contrast to how he appears to others. His true character will be revealed by things he does as much as by what he says.

Make it Real

To try and develop your characters, imagine your protagonist as a real person – possibly someone you know – or even a person you have read about. It doesn't hurt to imagine an actor you could see playing the part. You may be lucky enough that the actor you have in mind will end up playing it! And even if it's played by somebody else, it could be a lucky break. For example, *Amélie* is about a Paris innocent who sets out to become involved in life rather than just observing it. It was written by Jean-Pierre Jeunet and Guillaume Laurant for the brilliant English actress Emily Watson. She turned it down. Did the world end? No. It was delightfully played by button-eyed Audrey Tautou who made the part her own. The film was a great hit and won many laurels.

Love your characters. Relish them, especially the baddies. Write apparent contradictions into your parts, such as the intellectual rationality of the maniacal killer Hannibal Lecter in *Silence of the Lambs*, or the big time fraudster (Charles Grodin) who appears caring about his fellow man but is cynically trying to undermine his captor's hold over him (Robert DeNiro) in *Midnight Run* (1988, written by George Gallo, directed by Martin Brest).

If you're a believer in astrology, try making an astrological charts for your characters. Choose what star sign you think your character fits, and then focus on the attributes of that sign. There are plenty of books on the subject to give you a lot of character traits to start with.

Character Subtext

When Harry Met Sally is a good example of the subtext of a character. In this midstream story-line each segment reaches a conclusion but does not resolve the two protagonists' relationship. In the text of their characters (what they say they want), they do not know their goals, but in the *subtext* (what they do about it) they are inevitably driven into each other's arms at the *dénouement*. In a twist on 'boy meets girl', they start as friends and we follow an episodic trail over a period of time until they realize they are in love. In this type of plot structure, select the events in your protagonist's life designed in an ever-escalating sequence.

Below is a copy of a note written by Cecil B DeMille to Jesse Lasky Jr about *Samson and Delilah* – 'Jesse – Samson has lost his

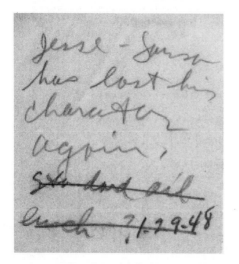

character again'. (On the bottom, crossed out, is a note about a lunch with some people from Standard Oil. These were their backers.)

The Three Main Dimensions of a Character

The Inner Self: How he thinks, the way his mind works, his control of his emotions, what he feels deeply, his level of ease with his own body and his mental state. What are his firm convictions? His fears? His vices? His likes and dislikes? A little thing like loving spinach made Popeye famous.

Personal Relationships: How does he deal with others? How deep are his friendships, family ties, loves, and hates? For whom would he risk his own life? Who would he gladly kill? What would prevent him? What do others think of him?

Society and the Physical Environment: How does he relate to the world around him? Does he fit in? Is he a leader or a follower? Is he happy in his environment, anxious, fearful, or strong? The phases of your protagonist's life – the aspects of his place in society, the effect of his background on his present attitudes and situation – all must be accounted for in a general way in your biography. This will help you (and the character) make decisions later. This does not require literary style. You are about to embark of a difficult journey, so give yourself the best possible choices with which to begin. Start with who the protagonist is. Why have you chosen him? What does he want? Who are the people in his life?

The Antagonist and Subsidiary Characters

This is the most important opposition to the protagonist, and can be a single person or a group of people (like a team of cops, or bandits, or an army) but the focus must be through one person. In *High Noon* the whole town stands back from Gary Cooper. He has to fight alone. The antagonist in this case is Frank Miller's entire gang but is focused through Miller himself, who must face up to Cooper in the end.

A good antagonist is the best way to create the contrary relationships and contradictory points of view that maximise opportunities for conflict between your protagonist and the surrounding characters. Use these characters to reveal all that the audience needs to know about the protagonist. Remember that things are not always what they seem, and what characters say may not be true (in the story). Other characters can reveal information about the protagonist that he keeps hidden himself.[1]

Each human being is unique. Find the eccentricities that mark out this uniqueness by making each person as different from the others as possible. What are their specific traits, ages, appearance, relationship with other characters, and so on? What intimate details of their imagined lives can you provide? Ask yourself which character doesn't seem to be adding anything to your story as it is developing, and see if there is a way you can do without that character. If not, how can you make him more interesting or important to the story? What kind of character do you need to bring out a certain aspect of your story, and what kind of scenes could that character fit into? Can you combine the attributes of two characters to make a single more exciting one? Look for traits that fall into the following categories: personal relationships, personal traumas, environmental frictions.

Don't let a minor character take over the action. Keep your focus on your main character. An example of this working in an unexpected way occurred in the original Inspector Clouseau film, *The Pink Panther* (1963). In Morris Richlin and Blake Edwards' script David Niven (playing Sir Charles) was meant to be the star. The accident-prone Inspector was supposed to have been a supporting role but his slapstick 'take' on the part was so hilarious that Edwards inserted new scenes for him and Peter Sellers became an international star in the many hilarious sequels that followed.

Remember, you're not writing a book in this stepline. This can all be written in brief notes, decipherable only by you.

The Scenes

In writing the screenplay, your story will be broken into scenes. A Scene consists of a group of shots that together compose one continuous action. Each scene will carry the story a step further. Every scene should be important for telling the story or developing characters, and there must be some level of conflict within it. A scene heading might read: **INT. BEDROOM – DAY.**
– which simply means that the scene is an interior (indoors) and takes place in the bedroom, in the daytime. Another could read: **EXT. HOUSE - NIGHT.**
The average length of a scene in the average final screenplay is between two-and-a-half and four pages (see the notes on layout in chapter 7 to understand how much script this represents). It can be longer if something is happening that changes the pace of the action. In your stepline, you should set out each scene in a few sentences. List the plot points or subplot points that the scene encompasses. Again, the most important question to ask yourself at that point is: does the scene move the plot or develop the character in some way? It must do one, but it would be infinitely more clever if it did both. What are the values of the scene? Has the event changed anything in the life situation of the characters so that it is not just exposition? What benefit and importance has this scene given to the rest of the story? Look for the protagonist's inner unconscious desires and his conscious desires. It is necessary to reveal both at some point. Some unconscious desires are displayed by a character's actions as opposed to his attitude. If the scene is only about the information contained in the dialogue, you're in trouble. It should have layers.

A shot is an unbroken view through one camera. In a final shooting script each shot may be listed by the director as CLOSE-UP, MEDIUM SHOT, LONG SHOT, MASTER SHOT, and so on. By that point it is no longer the writer's decision. Those shots are written into the final shooting script by the director. That's why a clever writer who knows he needs the camera focused on a specific action will write things like: 'CAMERA lingers on her smile as it slowly fades and tears fill her eyes.' If the director respects the writer's intent, he will keep his camera in a CLOSE-UP.

The curve and stretch, highs and lows within the scene are called the beats. A beat can be caused by a change in circumstances of the protagonist and/or one of the other characters. These can be changes in human behaviour, mood changes, new motivations, new points of view within a single scene. For instance, a description of the beats of a scene might be characterized as '*Anger* turns to *pain* – then to *love*', or written out as: 'A man and woman fight. He slaps her. She cries. Then he kisses her and they make love.'

Cutting a scene in the middle of a beat (editing) heightens the pace and the audience's reaction. The writer can indicate where his scene ends, although finally, that is the director's and editor's decision if they choose to change it. If the director gets something special from the actors, he may want to incorporate it into the scene. Of course, the reverse could happen and your scene could land on the cutting room floor. Your major concern is to make the scene so exciting on the page that the actors will give it their all, and the director will love it.

Scenes build into larger units. A *sequence* is made up of a series of scenes leading to a change or reversal in plot or in character development. When a series of sequences have created a major reversal in the life of the protagonist, you reach an act climax. Remember that 'decision leads to action'.

Something to be careful of as you lay out your scenes are *holes*. These are gaps in the logic of the plot or in human reactions that might cause your plot to lose credibility. Although it's true in life that people often appear to do things with seemingly little justification, in your distilled view of life, in which actions flow from character, try not to write unbelievable actions and reactions unless you can actually make a point of it. If a character does something that you need him to do in the story, but it is out of character, try to justify it. Either supply logic or else show the audience the hole.

An example of this kind of problem can be seen in *Monster's Ball* (2001, script by Milo Addica and Will Rokos, director Marc Forster) the story could have used deeper probing. The logline of the film was: 'A lifetime of change can happen in a single moment'. Was that the producer and director's excuse for serious holes in the logic that were treated superficially? The father (Billy Bob Thornton), a racist prison officer somewhere in the American South, tells his son he's a coward and he never loved him. The young man immediately shoots himself. The grandfather looks on – which we can excuse because he's senile. We have no idea of the deeper problem between father and son nor the absent wife/mother (Is she dead? Has she run away?). Thornton quits his job, which is clear enough – we don't have to see him re-examine his attitude towards the electric chair or spell out his guilt at his son's death. When he has sex with Halle Berry he revises his racist attitude towards African-Americans. To make way for Berry to move in with him, he dumps his father in an old people's home.

But what are *her motivations*? Did she move in with him only because she has no place to go? Do we know what she feels about Thornton? Why did Berry say nothing to him when she discovers he is the officer who pulled the switch at the electrocution of her husband? Instead, she has a screaming fit of passionate grief all by herself. When he returns the audience expects her to face him with the truth. Instead, she swallows her emotions and they sit together on the steps facing the tombstones of his son and family and eat ice cream. Fade out. It is not what the audience expects, so is it what they want? Presumably, a sparsely motivated but happy ending. While it got Halle Berry a well-earned Oscar for a fine performance, it would have been a much stronger film if the character motivations had been probed in the script.

Box office can tell a story – and figures add up. In its first 81 days *Monster's Ball* grossed $17 million in the States. *Gosford Park* grossed $35 million in the same time span. *A Beautiful Mind*, a deeply probing film, made $149 million in 87 days. We are not talking about science fiction or action films – these are all dramas, indeed social dramas on a mega-scale. What BO would the film have made if Halle Berry had not been nominated and received that Oscar? It gives one pause to think.

When Is A Scene More Than A Scene?

In *The Mummy Returns* (2001), the director/writer Stephen Sommers, who had previously made *The Jungle Book* in 1994 and also the first of *The Mummy* franchise in 1999, has made a film that makes Indiana Jones look plodding. For sheer bravura and fun this picture is tops. The theme or logline asks, 'Can the heroes stop the end of the world?' The story is set ten years after the first film. The couple (played by Brendan Fraser and Rachel Weisz) now have a little boy (whenever you can, stick a kid in your story – children are great for the BO and are always a good way of interesting producers in your project). Every scene in this film is an event. For the final action sequence Sommers used the device of intercutting three separate action scenes into one:

1) The two women's hand-to-hand fight.
2) The march of Imhotep's Jackal army against the good guys.
3) The hero's hand-to-hand fight with Imhotep (the mummy who returned) which is then topped by the Scorpion, who fights them both. This creates a long sequence of rip-roaring action – beyond which there is nowhere further to go unless the characters jump out of the screen and into your lap. For an action film, having three events happening at once is magic. If this is your genre, then this is the kind of action/fantasy film you want to write. *The Mummy Returns* is worth a careful study for construction, action, character interaction and relationships. The characters are all fairly one-dimensional and the plot is simplicity itself, which is the way it should be in this genre. There is no time for deep introspection. The film broke a non-holiday BO record, and made about $200 million in its first 38 days of release, coming fifth overall in that year's box office.

With Lucas's company, Industrial Light and Magic, and its many followers and competitors, incredible standards of computer generated imaging (CGI) have been achieved. Today, anything you can write can be portrayed on screen. Nobody goes to see this type of film to delve into the human condition. Social drama is something else, demanding a less spectacular approach that does not rely on special effects but focuses on character, relationships, and motivations.

Who Has the Power?

One character will always have more power than the other in a scene. If there is conflict, as there should be, one character will be in control. But that can change within the scene and when it does, it can make for great drama

or comedy. In the powerful thriller/comedy/road movie *Midnight Run* (1988), Robert De Niro's bounty hunter travels by plane, train, car and anything else that moves with his prisoner, Charles Grodin, a soft-spoken but bent accountant who has embezzled $15 million from the mob. The tough De Niro, with the gentle Grodin handcuffed most of the way, is the man in charge. But Grodin constantly undermines De Niro's thinking with mild, sympathetic questions until there is a reversal of power.

In one scene they are eating on the train. De Niro is taking no crap from Grodin, but by the end of the scene Grodin's niggling questions – *'Why are you eating that?... Don't you know it's bad for you?...Who loves you?'* and so on – have made De Niro so insecure that it has created a complete role reversal. De Niro rises from the table, his defences wiped out, vanquished. At the end of the film he is so turned around that he helps his charge to escape. This is an important film to study for *role reversal*.

Analyze the elements you have put into each scene: Where does the conflict lie? Who drives the scene? What does your protagonist want at this moment? What do the other characters want? What's keeping them from getting it? What ingredients are at risk in the scene? Are the positives and negatives working for you? Decide in which scenes you can reveal some of the back story. How can you reveal it without simply 'telling' it but making it emerge from the plot or character? Look for the emotional tension in the scene. Then, ask yourself what effect the continued action of the plot will have on the protagonist's character. You have established who he is from the moment we see him, but we want to see the changes in him that take place when he is confronted by obstacles.

Remember that the choices your protagonist makes are the plot movers. You will no doubt work on this stepline for several days, weeks, or more. Don't be too quickly satisfied. If you are working on a computer, it's easy to insert steps later where you see you need them, to eventually build up into writing your treatment.

Decisions lead to the resolution of the story. The action happens, climaxes are reached and changes are made because of your characters' decisions and choices. It is not simply the protagonist's quest to reach his goal that is the essence of your story, it is his developing understanding of self and the changes it brings to his life. That is what gives a story texture and richness.

Pulling it Together

Put the action in a logical order unless you have a specific reason for not doing so.
If you are working on a story told partly in flashbacks (or a totally reassembled story-line like *Memento*) first put down the action in a straight 'real time' order. You can break it up later and fit the pieces where you need them, but setting it out in a single forward continuum helps ensure there are no unwanted gaps in logic in your stepline. It's like working a jigsaw puzzle. Even if the action is not revealed in flashbacks, you need to be able to choose when you're going to tell a particular part of your story. This is where the card system (see chapter 7) is a big help.

Develop and work on this scene stepline until your story flows with proper turning points, sequences, and crises and reaches the climaxes you were aiming for. At this point, you will no doubt still have gaps in the story. Leave spaces where you don't know what should happen. Get down the broad strokes first.

Once it is complete, this stepline can be pitched (orally) to a story editor or a producer or director, but you should never give a stepline to anyone. It is not a selling document. Assume the producer has no imagination. Each sentence is bulging with meaning to you, but to someone else, it is just a sentence. What you *can* give them in paper form is a treatment, which is the next step, discussed in chapter 7.

Whodunits: Three Main Plot Structures

Detective and police stories inhabit a world of their own. For television it has been a busy world. There are three main structures to consider.

Closed Plot

A closed plot ties up all the loose ends of the story-lines by the final scene. The British TV series *Inspector Morse*, based on the books by Colin Dexter, unfolded suspenseful mystery tales of murder with a twist of dramatic irony featuring a grouchy, slightly alcoholic bachelor detective who can't stand the sight of blood. Somewhere along the way, the audience usually suspects who the killer is – but they could be wrong. For Morse, which were all closed-end episodes, the series could have gone on forever, and it only ended when the character of *Morse* died (as did the actor who played him, John Thaw, a little while after).

Australian crime writer William Marshall, had his hero paraphrase Sherlock Holmes's 'Once you have eliminated the impossible, whatever remains, *however improbable*, must be the truth'. Marshall's Detective Inspector Spencer said, 'When all the possible answers have been eliminated, whatever remains, however impossible, has to be the solution'. This served as justification for a gap in story logic.

The great Raymond Chandler added, 'If in doubt, have a man come through the door with a gun'. Chandler (whose *Blue Dahlia*, 1946, won a Best Original Screenplay nomination) was a notoriously forgetful writer. When I was writing the *Philip Marlowe* series for HBO, I was surprised to discover that in a three page short story, Chandler could change the colour of a girl's hair or eyes. His adapter and his readers forgave him.

Agatha Christie's tales generally function by offering a handful of suspects, any of whom might have had some plausible motive and opportunity. We don't know the killer and we keep trying to guess, along with the detective. We are being thrown a lot of 'red herrings' along the way leading us to the inevitable conclusion that 'the butler did it'. Agatha Christie's Miss Marple and Hercule Poirot, Raymond Chandler's Philip Marlowe, and Dashiell Hammett's Sam Spade have had a long shelf-life.

Open Plot

In this case, the audience sees the murder committed. It is seemingly the perfect crime. You know who the killer is already, so what keeps you hooked is why it was done and how will the detective catch him with some ingenious coup de grâce. There is always a flaw in the murderer's logic that will lead the detective to his suspect.

This is dramatically a much weaker structure than a closed plot and therefore everything depends on having a charismatic detective.

It is the detective who is the real protagonist. The killer is the antagonist, trying to bluff the detective at every turn. But the wily detective lays a trap for his opponent. When he finally confronts the killer, the power of his evidence is so compelling that the murderer has no choice but to reveal the truth and confess. Richard Levinson and William Link's *Columbo* (which began a spate of TV detectives) is a good example of the audience knowing more than the villain – who doesn't know that Columbo (and the audience) know he's guilty. The charm lies in how the detective goes about trapping the villain while the latter thinks he's getting away with it. That will hold the audience's attention for as long as it takes.

The Mixed Plot

The American TV series *CSI* and its spin-off, *CSI Miami*, are mostly mixed plots. Generally, there are two stories being told at the same time. Unfortunately, the two-story plotline has little time to develop characters. The victim is already dead and the villain is often suspected – so there is little mystery. They concentrate of the computer generated images of body parts, and the story emphasis is on police procedure.

Resolutions

In thrillers it is often necessary to enlighten the audience with a resolution scene in which all the loose ends are tied up. In the final scene of *Psycho*, for instance, everything about Norman Bates's behaviour and motivation is explained by the psychiatrist. The Agatha Christie 'dénouement' scene in which Poirot (or any other detective) explains to the other characters and suspects (and the audience) what really happened, creating a ritualistic confrontation with and confession from the killer, looks fairly creaky now. In modern detective stories we generally learn enough of the facts as the story progresses to avoid the necessity of this conclusion.

Remember when you sit down to write a detective story that if the audience knows more than your detective does, they may have sympathy for him, but little empathy. That could be generated in other ways, as it is in *Columbo* by the warmth of the detective's character, but alternatively you may be heading for comedy as with the inept Inspector Clouseau.

Hitchcock was a master of dramatic irony – making you think you know what's happening, but then discovering that the truth was something else entirely. A few contemporary films have come up with some clever ways to explain what needs explaining before the lights go up. The entertaining Argentinian film *Nine Queens* (2000) is about a couple of scam artists who out-scam each other until the very last frame of film when all is explained by what you see, not by what you are *told* – and it's not at all what you thought.

Wild Things (1998), a low-budget thriller, was written off by some critics as a 'sexed-up feature-length MTV film'. It had no big name stars but deserved attention for its inventive story-telling. Its excellent, convoluted plot by writer Stephen Peters keeps you guessing until the final credits – when you finally think you know what's actually happened. But you don't. Scenes intercut with the credits tell quite a different story about who killed whom. In commercial Hollywood films, too often today the producer adds a resolution scene to what they consider a 'heavy' or 'downbeat' story. It is a dramatic device, usually inserted as a result of feedback from a preview screening, that often makes a serious writer cringe. There is no doubt that the major studios see it as a necessity because they consider the larger mainstream American audience not 'ready' for dark or serious drama, or resolutions which depend on audiences drawing inferences rather than having things explained to them explicitly. From your point of view as a writer, you must make sure that any such scene penetrates your protagonist's new-found point of view, and is believable in terms of his character.

In *The Piano* (1993, Jane Campion's Oscar-winning screenplay mentioned earlier), the story is set in the 19th century. Holly Hunter is sent from Scotland to New Zealand with her daughter and her beloved piano to marry Sam

Neill, whom she has never seen. Although she can hear, she has chosen not to speak since childhood. Her husband discovers she is having an affair with Harvey Keitel and chops off her finger. She sets out for a new life with the piano, her daughter, and Keitel, but while being rowed out to a waiting ship the piano falls out of the boat and she goes down with it. Underwater, she unties the rope attaching her to the piano, symbolically choosing, life, the future, and Keitel, rather than death, the past, and the weight of the piano dragging her down; a highly dramatic scene. With a little imagination the audience can realize that she'll be all right with Keitel. She'll be fine. The picture is over. Let's go home.

But the producers felt the audience needed a feel-good ending to make the point, so a resolution scene was tacked on, showing Hunter learning to talk and wearing a replacement metal finger that Keitel has made for her.

Your audience has been having a psychological reaction to the inner thoughts of the characters. In the darkened cinema they have been 'living' in the world you have created. A slow 'curtain' – even a tracking shot – gives the audience time to regain its equilibrium, time to absorb the impact of that last exciting crisis, and maybe wipe away a few tears. The viewers must switch off and distance themselves, back to the real world. This last visual moment may be the choice of the director, but there's no harm in you, the writer, putting on paper how you see it.

On the Right Path

You have started quite simply, with an idea. It could be some incident or some character that excites you. Then you have created a stepline, building the story points across a three (or more) act structure. If your stepline has been thoroughly thought out and you have roughly broken it into acts and scenes and given yourself enough possibilities of action, character relationships, and development, you will know where your story is taking you.

It is better not to start writing your treatment until you have the acts blocked out in your stepline. You, as the writer, have a goal to reach. Like your characters, that goal may develop and change more than once in the writing. But at least you have a path to follow that will keep away the dreaded writer's block.

CHAPTER 6 | THE THREE-ACT BASIC FORMAT

The 90-minute, three-act format is is the most popular and conventional Hollywood format for a mainstream film. It is generally used for some very important box office film favourites and for TV Movies of the Week (made-for-television films). It contains the following elements (the times are approximate):

ACT ONE (30 minutes)
Main Plot
Initial Turning Point (10 to 15 minutes in)
Introduction of Subplot
Main Plot Crisis

ACT TWO (40 minutes)
Main Plot
Subplot
Mid Act Crisis
Cliffhanger

ACT THREE (20 minutes)
Main Plot
Subplot
The Major Crisis and Decision
Resolution Scene

Here is a chart of this structure, showing the peaks and troughs in the action – the high and low turning points.

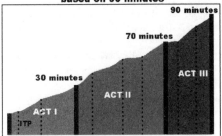

Mainstream Structure for a Feature Film based on 90 minutes

Key: (ITP = Initial Turning Point) 10/15 minutes.
- - - - - = Key moments of crisis within the Acts.

You can never anticipate what you will think of, once you actually begin writing your treatment (see chapter 7), and when you get into the screenplay, characters begin to

have a reality of their own. They actually can tell you what they should do at a given moment, if you know them well enough. This is the wonderful part of writing but don't let it lead you down another road into another story than the one you're trying to tell.

The length of acts given here is based on the 90-minute format mentioned above. Naturally, if your story is longer, then the length of each act is correspondingly increased – certainly acts one and two can become longer, but you want to keep the last act as tight as possible in relation to the whole. An alternative approach to lengthening the structure is to break it down into four or even five acts.

Act One
The Main Plot

The protagonist is following his normal life pattern in pursuit of success, sexual satisfaction, power, money, achievement, or whatever. The initial turning point changes his course of action and turns his life around. Through his forced journey and the series of crises that he overcomes he finds fulfilment and happiness – or the reality of a cruel world.

Act one includes the initial turning point, which poses the major plot enigma, establishes the theme, and prepares the audience for an emotional reaction to the protagonist's journey. It can deliver one or more major reversals to his life.

The Subplot

The secondary or subplot(s) can begin in act one and can finish in acts one or two, or go through to act three. The subplot should provide a frame for, or enhance or resonate with the world of the protagonist and develop the dramatic premise or situation he is facing and his interrelationships with other important characters. The subplot must counterpoint the main plot and help us, ultimately, to understand it. It might seem totally unrelated but somewhere along the line a connection must be made. It can begin before or after the initial turning point, or could be used to set the stage for the initial turning point. it can work on two levels by revealing to the audience what they need to know about the protagonist while developing a separate plot line. Subplot characters (the protagonist's friends and/or enemies) can interact. There can be hints at secrets. Clues can be dropped that will develop later.

When Harry Met Sally (1989, screenplay Nora Ephron, directed by Rob Reiner) is a midstream story with a strong subplot dealing with another couple's relationship, their marriage, their apartment, their furniture, their squabbles. The subplot develops out of their relationship with Harry and Sally and counterpoints perfectly the lives of the main characters. But it never dominates or slides into the main plot and it helps us to better understand Harry and Sally.

The Others (2001, written and directed by Alejandro Amenábar) has a mainstream structure with a strong subplot. The subplot in this case is interwoven from the start and is an alternate reality – or is it? Nicole Kidman does not know that her servants are ghosts who have their own reasons for being in the house. The audience learns this when she does. She also doesn't know that she and her children are also ghosts (so, in fact, her reality is equally 'alternate'). We only find that out when she does, and the subplot has crossed over into the main plot.

Climaxes

The mid-act climax deals another reversal – an obstacle to the protagonist's progress. Obviously, you don't kill off your hero in the middle of the first act. But if you do (in a flashback structure such as *Sunset Boulevard*, *Psycho*, or *Pulp Fiction*) something else must be working for you.

The first-act climax brings the act to a close, and so must occur no more than 30 minutes into the story. It can be either a positive or a negative situation. To create a dynamic rhythm in the story, let it swing back and forth from positives to negatives, highs and lows throughout.

To summarize, this is how you develop the basic format:

Points Of Main Plot And Subplot are introduced.
Main Plot: Briefly establishes the protagonist's world: aims, goals, relationships, loves, associates, children and so on.
Initial Turning Point: An event that happens in the first 10 to 15 minutes (earlier is better) which changes the course of the protagonist's life.
Subplot: New characters are introduced who resonate with the actions of the protagonist.
Main Plot: The protagonist cannot cope with his new situation. He must make a decision.
Subplot: Through other characters' attitudes and actions, aspects of the protagonist's character are revealed.
Main Plot: A crisis leads to an intense moment of decision for the protagonist.

Act Two

The second act should advance the story and the protagonist's relationships and problems from act one. In a 90-minute format it should run about 40 minutes, bringing you to about 70 minutes into the film. It sets up and pays off some of the obstacles and turning points. Your subplot lines (if any) can start or end in this act. There should be at least three peaks to the action that should reach a greater crisis at the end of the act.

This second-act climax is called a cliffhanger (based on the concept of leaving your character hanging on a cliff). The audience is waiting for the protagonist to 'fall' (if it's Sylvester Stallone, he doesn't) and it sets up the problems to be resolved in the exciting end of your story in the third act. The second act offers a false ending. It seems like the end of the story ... but it may not be. In *Shadowlands* (1993, the biographical story of C S Lewis adapted by William Nicholson from his own stageplay) just when you think Joy (Debra Winger) is dying and the picture is over (end of act two) she recovers. She does die at the end, but by then the audience is ready for it.

The false ending (see below, act three) is also an option at this point.

To summarize:
Main Plot: The protagonist makes the first attempts at choices about his destiny. Other characters help or hinder him. Relationships

are changing in the protagonist's world. He is faced with yet another crisis, another decision. Because of events, the protagonist is changing emotionally and beginning to see his old life in a different way.
Subplot: Will others adjust to the changes in the protagonist? How does he affect them? What affects him?
Other characters must make decisions, too. Some subplots may end in this act. Others may begin in this act.
Main Plot: The interaction of the protagonist with the other characters begins to alter. He loses some friends and gains some others. Two or three more serious crises escalate the pressure on the protagonist. Decisions must be made. Some secrets (if any) are revealed. Second-act climax: the cliffhanger.

Act Three

The third act should last about 20 minutes, completing the 90-minute format. Naturally, if you are working on a larger time frame, the last act should be proportionally longer. Too often one watches a film that seems to go on forever. Why? Because the distribution of climaxes isn't well thought out, and act three becomes too long. You don't want your audiences coming out of the theatre saying, 'I thought the picture was over 20 minutes before the end'.

Scenes must escalate in value – the excitement must build. The pace becomes faster, the action heightened (whether it is character- or plot-driven). The third act climax should be quite different from the act two climax. It is often said that the audience comes to see the last 20 minutes of a film. Give them what they want but not the way they expect it; the action must not be predictable. That is the secret of keeping your audience awake. But don't try to wrap it up with a quick surprise ending that lacks logic (see the discussion of *Monster's Ball* in chapter 5). They may give the star an Oscar but the story won't satisfy the audience.

In action and horror genres especially, there are often false endings – think of *Aliens* or *Nightmare On Elm Street*. In *Fatal Attraction*, just when we think Glenn Close

is dead in the bath she pops up again (an idea taken straight from *Les Diaboliques*, discussed in chapter 4). Though effective, it occurs so frequently that it's in danger of seeming hackneyed. As mentioned above, a false ending could even be placed at the end of act two, but, wherever it's placed, it is always the reverse of the final climax. You cannot reach another climax without escalation.

A resolution scene that winds up all the loose ends and doubts in the audience's mind would be placed after the final climax. It shows the protagonist on the road to a new understanding of life. An American producer will want it. Chances are a British producer will not.

In a happy ending, the protagonist finds a fresh sense of himself through his changed values. Abandoning the pursuit of success and self-indulgence, he achieves true success – which is real happiness. Fade Out.

I have talked about *open endings* in which the inner conflicts of the characters are unresolved, or their resolution is unclear. Will he go back to his wife? Will he go back to the desert? Will he be caught by the police? Of the questions raised in the story, some will be left for the audience to decide. With *closed endings*, all threads are tied in a neat bow.

'Formula' writing is only basic structure. When you know and understand why it works and have figured out the interaction of the main plot with the subplots, you can build on it and develop your own permutations. This is not constricting to the creative process; it can define it. I have included several other formats of equal versatility in this book.

To summarize the third-act structure:
Main Plot: The protagonist's world is disintegrating around him.
Subplot: crosses over with the main plot: the stories merge.
The Major Crisis and Decision: *Unexpected events lead the protagonist to the brink. The protagonist decides to do what he must do to achieve his goal – but it is not what the audience expects. Having achieved his goal, the protagonist makes a new start with adjustments to his loved ones and associates. Some, he breaks with – some he bonds with.*

Chapter 7 | THE CARD SYSTEM AND THE TREATMENT

Scene Cards

When you feel it is working fairly well, your stepline is ready to be transferred to the card system. Most professional screenwriters and many novelists will use scene cards for constructing their story. These use index cards with dimensions of about 7.5 x 12.5 cm (3 x 5 in), which you can buy in packets at the stationer's. There is a smaller size, but this is more workable. These will become the building blocks for the full treatment, on which you will base your screenplay. The story and cards will change and grow as you develop your ideas.

On your stepline you may already have 20 or 30 story points or key scenes indicated. Now on separate cards you are going to break down the elements of each scene. These scene cards can be push-pinned (thumbtacked) to a story board – which is nothing more than a large cork board, also purchased in a stationer's or home furnishers. Usually you need two of the largest boards for a feature film, since you will end up with 55–80 cards. With this system you will be able to study each sequence of events and each scene, eliminating those that aren't working and adding more scenes where needed. You can move them around to finesse the story structure and details. If you don't have a board you can always lay the cards out on the floor or a dining-room table.

Each card contains a wealth of information about the scene. It tells you the location, day or night, the characters, the 'through line' of the scene (does it move plot or develop character?), what the element of conflict is (physical or a difference in points of view?), and what each character wants. It also lists any important visuals.

It is better to still avoid dialogue at this stage because it can trap you into attitudes, which you need to keep flexible. That doesn't mean you shouldn't jot down a good line when it comes into your head. Put it on the back of a card, or code it to a scene (card) number on a separate document.

Using the Card System

```
                        Card No:
Scene Location - Time (if relevant)
Important Visuals:
Characters:
A Plot Scene or Character Scene?:
Conflict: Physical?  Different Points
of View?
Who wants What?

(use back of card for      29.
dialogue ideas)     Hospital - Day: (3 months later)
                    Henry, Black Male Nurse, Henry's
                    daughter, Wife.
                    Daughter afraid of Henry. Nurse
                    sends Her to talk with Henry.
                    Henry's POV: Doesn't want to
                    go home.
                    Daughter shows him how to
                    tie shoelaces.
                    Henry makes a decision to go home.
```

Film Example: 'Regarding Henry.'

The first card illustrated here tells you what the elements of your scene are and how to list them. The second card is from a scene in *Regarding Henry*. I have used it because you will find a complete stepline of that film in chapter 10.

Although you may be typing your cards or writing them in ink, always number them in pencil in the corner so you can renumber easily when you add more cards and change their position in the structure.

If you have the cards in a box you can put a coloured divider between the acts to see how they are shaping up as far as balance of length; if you're laying them out on a board you can use different coloured cards, or colour the edges to differentiate them. In a midstream construction, keeping a quick visual track on the relative lengths of your acts is extremely useful because you may be working with more than three acts, or have interlinking episodes, moving back and forth (as in *Pulp Fiction*). Or, if you are plotting a long story with multiple plots, you can use the different coloured cards to represent different subplot or story-lines.

Locations could also be colour coded, if it is important to your story and budget – a point a writer should never forget. It will make a good impression on a producer if, when pitching your idea, you shown awareness of the number of locations your story needs, and hence an awareness of cost.

You can also keep track of each character by underlining his name in a different-coloured pen so that you can see at a glance where he appears and – particularly if it's a minor or subplot character – whether the gaps between his appearances are too long. Where can you salt him into another scene to keep him alive for the audience? Where can you get rid of him?

Story themes such as action, exposition, comic relief, or love story could be coded with a highlighter pen to see a glance the interaction of the various story elements (note that these are themes within a story, not genres that define your story overall). You can then tell if two heavy action scenes are back-to-back, or if there is a dearth of comedy where it would help to lighten a sequence.

What do your characters have to discuss in a scene? Have two scenes of a similar value and with the same characters come too close together? Where can you move one of them?

Once you have the overview of the complete plot that your cards give you, it is time to ask yourself again the question that you should always keep repeating to yourself: *Does the scene move the plot or reveal something about a character?* If it doesn't, throw it away! If it contains something you really want to keep, add that element into another scene that *does* move plot or develop character.

This card system can also be used for writing a novel or a theatrical play. It is an advantageous building block in the construction of any major piece of writing. When you have completed your scene cards and are satisfied with your story-line, crisis points, and characters, you are ready to write your treatment.

The Full Treatment

You might compare a treatment to an abbreviated novella, told in as colourful a style as you can muster. It must create a visual picture of the action and convey the thoughts and feelings of your characters. This requires good, straightforward, non-elaborate writing ability. Remember, the treatment has no dialogue, except for an occasional line set out like speech in a novel!

This is a selling document, meant for somebody to read. When you pitch your story or idea to a producer, the next thing he may ask you for, if he likes your idea, is a treatment. He may pay you to write this, depending on your agent's ability to negotiate and your own clout. At this point he may prefer to see a treatment to a finished screenplay (if you have not already written it) because he can see where you are going in some detail and decide whether he feels the story is good enough to pay you to develop it into a script.

If the producer feels it's worth putting his money where his mouth is, he can suggest his ideas and changes before you write the dialogue of the actual screenplay. He might also steal the idea, so don't pitch the story or give anyone a copy of the treatment until you have mailed yourself a copy of whatever you have (which you keep unopened, to prove if need be that the contents were put in the envelope on or before the date of the postmark), or you have registered it with the

Writers' Guild of America, the Writers' Guild of Great Britain, or the equivalent organization in your country (see registration and copyright in chapter 17 and list of organizations in appendix 4).

Length

The treatment can run anywhere from 25 to 60 or more pages. It should lay out the complete story in an exciting but tightly dramatic way with all the details of what happens and who the characters are. (Obviously when you actually write the screenplay many of these things will be embellished, and some will be thrown out.) You can break your treatment into acts. If it is not a mainstream three-act structure, then break it into episodes (see the outline of *Pulp Fiction* in chapter 11).

The technical requirements are simple. The treatment is always written in the present tense, just like a script (he *goes* to the store; she *looks* at him etc.). Use a clear and unfussy font that is easy on the eye, such as Arial, Helvetica, or Times – avoid ones that are too heavy, have unusual spacing or attempt to mimic handwriting. I prefer to use Century Schoolbook (which was recommended to me by my novelist friend James Herbert as the perfect typeface.)

Layout

Use 1.5 line spacing with a 2.5 cm (1 in) margin on the right and a 3 cm (1.25 in) margin on the left (to allow a producer room to make notes). I prefer to align the pages in the 'justified' setting (if you're not using a computer, that means the margins are 'even' on the right-hand side). But this is a personal preference. Add punch-holes on the left side, as with a script, so the pages can be put in a binder. Write in paragraphs (each new paragraph beginning with an indent) within a scene, as you might in a novel. In the header you can put the title and your name, with the copyright symbol (©) and the year, e.g. *'This is the Title*, Pat Silver-Lasky © 2003'. Leave a two-point line spacing between the scenes, and number your pages in the upper right-hand corner, not at the bottom.

You will have a cover page which will have the title, 'Original Screenplay Treatment by [your name]', the © symbol and year, and in the bottom left-hand corner, your address, contact number, and email, or those of your agent.

To catch a producer's eye and interest, start by expressing the theme of the story – you could start by putting a logline at the top of the first page. Define the mood and the look of the film as you write it. You want to give the reader a vivid description of the people as they meet them and the action as it happens.

Writing the Characters' Attitudes

Indicate the characters' inner thoughts when and if it is something the audience should know at that point, and something an actor could reveal by his facial expression. You have no actor to express these emotions for you, and since there is no dialogue in a treatment, you can say things such as: *'He holds back his anger and tells her he's leaving'*, or *'She asks him where he's been all day, but he doesn't answer. Instead he walks out of the house, slamming the door'.*

This is telling the reader the character's attitude as well as his action. It is a good idea to read your treatment out loud to yourself or onto a tape recorder, or to a friend. See where they begin to lose interest. Feel if your writing has a flow. Watch for too much repetition.

The following section of a treatment is from a TV series of mine currently in development with British Destiny Films. The character description of Bierce is from an earlier part of the series treatment. The action is set in London in 1873.

Strikingly handsome, Ambrose Bierce wears his light blond hair cropped in a duck-tail, his moustache thick. Extremely soft-spoken, immensely prickly, women find him irresistible but men often choose to hate him. His acid cynicism and his reputation for verbal viciousness gains him the name of 'Bitter Bierce' and earns him enemies. He carries a pistol – and has been known to use it.

The following is the beginning of the treatment for one episode:

THE BOTTOMLESS GRAVE

A floating, dream-like image, the figure of AMBROSE BIERCE moves slowly forward through a smoky, gloomy mist. Bierce pauses to peer down, and then in slow motion, jumps – to vanish completely – as though he has hurled himself into the bowels of the earth. A woman's shrill scream breaks the silence.

Bright lights replace the gloom. The scream expires on the lips of a woman: young, beautiful, but pale and consumptive. A creature of her times. In a room of elegantly dressed men and women she is staring in shock. It is a reception for the American author Mark Twain and for the English poetess, EMMA BREN-WALTER. It is at Emma that everyone else is staring.

Ambrose Bierce comes towards her across the gas lit room, not dream-like now, but very real. 'Usually I frighten dogs and children,' he assures her, 'but the ladies have generally reacted kindly towards me.' Emma Bren-Walter explains that she has seen him before. Last night – in a dream. Coming towards her, and then hurling himself into the darkness of the earth in some inexplicable way. She is embarrassed. But surely he must be laughing at her.

Bierce is no man to laugh at the inexplicable. He turns his attention away from the literary lions of the moment to hear Emma whisper in her deep, throaty voice, her strange tale. Her father, an eccentric amateur inventor, died only a few days ago, causes unknown. She has only come out this evening at her uncle's insistence, because an award was being given her for a recent poem.

In accordance with Bren-Walter père's instructions, he was laid to rest in the family cemetery in a grave especially prepared by himself. But since her father's death, it is not only Bierce that Emma has seen. She is certain she has seen her father – and not in a dream. Her uncle, Dr Bren-Walter – a formidable man – comes over and takes her arm possessively. Intrigued by the idea of the ghost, Bierce invites himself to stay the weekend at Bren Hall, the residence of the Bren-Walters.

Emma is waiting to greet him with her uncle and his son Alfred – a sinister echo of his father. In the gloomy Jacobean hall, Bierce witnesses a shadow figure – a figure *he can see right through* – flit across the walls and vanish with a strange whirring sound. The visit is filled with incident. Locked doors fly open. Mysterious footsteps. The kitchen maid finds the pantry in disarray, food strewn on the floor. But no sign of an intruder – nor a secret panel. Only a few peep holes cut through the walls, large enough to pass a fist through.

In response to a soft knocking on his bedroom door, Bierce opens it to no one. But there is a gift of sorts. A silver salver lies on the carpet. On it, a tin of rat poison.

ACT BREAK

Even if no producer is involved and you've written the treatment only for yourself, when you have worked out all the kinks in your story you are ready to launch into the screenplay. If you are just starting out professionally, the treatment may be enough to get you an agent. But the agent will want to see at least one or two scenes of the screenplay written out with full dialogue – not necessarily the opening, but scenes that will show the characters in a high-tension moment.

CHAPTER 8 | ELEMENTS OF SCRIPT FORMAT

Don't start on your screenplay until you have a firm grasp on your story, having written a stepline and a treatment, and feel that you know your characters fairly well.

A professional-looking script will get read, so layout is important. You can buy scripts on the Internet and download the latest layout information because, if you open this book ten years from now, preferences may have changed.

A PROFESSIONAL PRESENTATION

Be sure you follow all the rules. Otherwise the reader won't get past page one, and will assume you're not a professional. The page count of a standard 90-minute film script is 110 to 120 pages on American Quarto paper (also known as letter size, 8.5 x 11 in), which is difficult to purchase in the UK, though a few screenplay stores supply it. Pinewood Studios has a store, or you can check out the Internet. It is perfectly acceptable to use A4 paper (210 x 297 mm) for submission in the UK. Script length is approximately 105 to 115 pages on A4. This length includes simple but visually detailed descriptions of action as well as dialogue. Major epic features can run to 190 or more pages. (Don't make that your first screenplay!). The font traditionally used for scripts is Courier, and it should be single-spaced.

As for timing, you should figure one minute per page for American Quarto paper and one and a quarter minutes per page for A4 paper when typed in 12-point Courier. This is approximate, depending on longer descriptive paragraphs of action that take only seconds on screen – for example animation or computer graphics action episodes.

Scripts are single-spaced but there are double spaces between dialogue and action. Number your pages in the upper right-hand corner (you can set your computer to do this automatically). All of this can be made easy and automatic for you with scriptwriting software. I use Final Draft. There are also a few other makes on the market that I am told are equally good. It is the best investment you can make if you're serious about becoming a scriptwriter in the 21st century.

If you are submitting a script to a Hollywood production company, there are certain conventions you should observe apart from the use of American Quarto paper. The script should have three holes punched on the left side and be fastened with brads (binders with a pair of bendable prongs attached to a circular washer) with the prongs at the back of the script and the washer at the front. American companies insist on the 12 point Courier font because they base the timing of the script on that form. British producers are not (yet) as strict but it is a good idea to get it 'right' from the start.

What Producers Want

The writer today is asked to write a 'Master Scene Screenplay', which means one in which the scenes are not numbered and the transitions from one scene to the next in terms of camera directions are not marked. It makes for easier reading. The writer is no longer required to write camera directions – in fact directors dislike it. Indicate few – and only ever *necessary* – shots to make your story clear to the reader, for instance, for a probable Point of View shot: 'HIS POV'.

Elements of the Screenplay Form

The layout for a single colunm layout for script is shown on the following pages. A script is composed of different types of information (called the elements) such as DIALOGUE, CHARACTER NAMES, TRANSITIONS, SLUG LINES, DESCRIPTION OF ACTION, PARENTHETICAL DIRECTIONS, CONT'D (used at the right-hand bottom of a page when a scene continues on the next page - quite often today omitted), V.O.(Voiceover), O.S. (Off Screen), and Cont'd (where the same character continues speaking after a break for action or description). Each has its own margins, its own justification settings, and, sometimes, its own type style.

THE SLUG LINE is the scene heading that tells us where the scene is located. There are specific rules governing the way each of these elements is written, e.g.:

```
INT. DARK OFFICE - NIGHT.
The office is dark. There is a man standing in the doorway. We cannot see
       his face in the shadow.
```

A PARENTHETICAL: A specific direction for the actor set in parentheses under the character's name. It can also come at the end of dialogue.

```
                          FRED
               (barely above a whisper)
               Help … Help me, somebody …!
               (falls to the floor)
```

If the direction is not just for one specific actor but will affect other characters in some way, it should not be used parenthetically, but should be put into the general ACTION description.

Character Names are always written in capital letters in action and dialogue headings – but never in the dialogue itself.

```
BILL gets up from his desk, coming over to the fallen FREDDIE.

                          BILL
          Freddie … are you okay? Wake up, Freddie!
```

In your ACTION description, always start a new paragraph where you know there should be another camera angle. It will tell the director where the focus should be without your telling him how to shoot it.

```
Across the road BRENDA sees MATTIE waiting for her. She starts out into
       the heavy traffic.

MATTIE peers through the traffic, not having spotted her friend.

BRENDA fights her way between the cars. They are honking at her.
One DRIVER waves a fist at her.

BRENDA finally reaches MATTIE, out of breath.

                          BRENDA
               Well, Mattie? Didn't think
               I'd come, did you?
```

The director can see that each paragraph is another shot. Don't write the track shots or be too technical. Instead of asking for a CLOSE-UP you could say something like:

```
His head looms close into camera showing the scar on his cheek.
```

Whenever referring to the camera, treat it like a character name, without 'the' and in caps.

```
CAMERA moves across a vista of desert.
```

The shooting script (which includes all the CUT TOs and camera directions) is prepared later by the producer and/or the director.

Examples of Dialogue and Scene Layout

To illustrate some of these points I am including a page of script from the episode 'The Work of the Devil', from the television series mentioned above, *Bitter Bierce*, currently in development with British Destiny Films.

```
                        SOSITRICE
                   (starts for door)
              Leave the tray. Mary will collect
              it later.


                          BIERCE
                   Thanks, Sossie.
```

She exits. He takes a last bite, leaving most of it on his plate, gives his hair a pat in the mirror, dons his coat and starts out.

(NB: The director may see this action as several separate shots – or all in one take. That is his decision, and since it is not vital to the plot, I do not offer a suggestion.)

INT.HALL. BOARDING HOUSE - DAY.

As BIERCE comes out of his room, the door to the next room opens and a young girl (DONNA) comes out. She is fragile, ethereal, and for December, too lightly gowned in a white silk dress. She carries a pale blue silk cape and a small draw-string purse. A broad-brimmed hat hangs from her shoulders decorated with flowers and wonderfully beribboned.

DONNA throws him a hasty sideways glance from beneath long lashes and moves to the staircase.

She glides gracefully down the stairs, pulling on her blue cape as she goes.

BIERCE watches her, wondering which sister she could be – entranced by her gentle beauty until she exits the front door.

INT. BRANDON'S CLUB BAR - DAY.

BIERCE's reflection floats for a moment on the surface of a silver bowl of claret punch. The ladle dips in, breaking the reflection.

BIERCE lifts his claret cup to his lips. He is standing with HOOD. The room is filled with GENTLEMEN having after-lunch brandies, claret, coffee, chat.

```
                          HOOD
              I've lined up a publisher who
              might print your Devil's Dictionary, Bitter.
```

IN B.G. JOHN BRANDON is in jovial conversation with the American writers BRETT HART and JOAQUIN MILLER whose hair flows to his shoulders and is colourfully dressed in 'Daniel Boone' style (no hat). MARK TWAIN is with them.

The above should give you the layout. Since this is an example of a Master Scene Screenplay the CUT TOs are not inserted.

Chapter 9 | WRITING YOUR SCREENPLAY

The Essence Of Story-Telling For The Screen

A screenplay is really a series of instructions to director and actors. You create the scenes and dialogue, suggest motivations, and then you must leave the rest in their capable hands. So what type of screenplay does a director want to film? Ask most, and they will tell you that the film they want to make is the screen story that comes alive in their head when they read it.

Melissa Mathison, writer of *E.T.* (1982, directed by Steven Spielberg) and *Kundun* (1997, directed by Martin Scorsese), said that 'great moments in films are created by emotional moments that require no words'. The screenwriter creates a specific reality and must find ways to express it.

The planning and preparation should have ironed out most of the smaller kinks in your stepline and treatment. Now it's time to see if they really work, and you won't know that for certain until you get into writing the actual screenplay. With the aid of your cards you can now start sketching out your scenes and begin to bring your characters to life. As you start working scene by scene, be open to new opportunities. Don't be glued to your stepline or treatment. Things change, and new thoughts come to you. The cards are there to shift around or throw away as required.

For example, perhaps you have indicated a scene between two characters on board a ship. Now you will have to be more specific and decide where exactly on the ship. Maybe it doesn't work and you decide to place the scene somewhere else – or add another character. Perhaps the story isn't progressing as you want. The characters have nothing relevant to say to each other. Although you will constantly be changing things, writing the script will be much easier when you know the broad strokes of where you're going. When you quit for the day, you won't be at a loss the next morning about where to go next.

A good day's work might be five pages. On a day when you're really flying, you might write ten pages. I always make it a rule to reread yesterday's work and tighten it up before getting on with the new. It gets me into the mental state for writing the next scene.

Once you have your story plotted out in your stepline and treatment, it is not even necessary to begin the writing process at the beginning of the script. You may have a strong sense about a particular high moment between two characters and what they might say to each other. Start with that scene and write it down as quickly as you can. Obviously it would be wrong to have a character spouting three pages of monologue, but at this stage, it doesn't matter. Get all your thoughts down on paper. Remember to create images – both visual and aural – that will tell some part of your story without dialogue.

Dialogue

You've been waiting for this – your chance to put words in their mouths. The dialogue should begin to flow spontaneously the more you delve into your characters and know what they're thinking.

William Goldman (scriptwriter of *Butch Cassidy and the Sundance Kid*, 1969, and *All the President's Men*, 1976) said: 'In your first draft, dialogue doesn't matter. You can work at that. The structure has to be right. There may not be a formula, but there's an organizational rhythm to a film; ruthless simplicity.'

The function of dialogue is to move the plot, reveal information about characters, and show their points of view. If you have wit and can make it clever dialogue, you are on your way. It's not like dialogue in a novel, nor is there any such thing in real life as a monologue (although I've had a few acquaintances who can hold court for far too long). In the theatre an actor can have a monologue that lasts several minutes, but in films, most single speeches don't extend beyond about 15 seconds. For a strong story point, it could be as long as 30 seconds. There must be action and reaction or you'd soon grow weary of listening.

Think of writing dialogue like adding Tabasco to a stew. Use it sparingly, economically. Try to hear each character's voice in your head. Use short, simply constructed sentences so that your audience will understand it instantly. Remember, unlike a novel, your audience cannot flip back a few pages to catch something they missed earlier.

Dialogue must *sound like* real conversation without *being* real conversation. It is the way people talk, which is not always in complete sentences. You're not writing a letter. People drop pronouns and phrases. Dialogue should be directed to a purpose because a scene must make a point. Dialogue can turn the scene in another direction.

Capture the 'sound' of your characters' voices in your head. Only then will they begin to tell you what they will say. A caution: dialogue can be deceptive on paper because it is there to be spoken by an actor and heard. When the actor says it, it may sound better than what you thought you wrote. Or it may sound so completely wrong that the actor has to ad-lib – with the director's approval.

Writing is Rewriting in Screenplay

I cannot emphasize that enough: writing is rewriting! Maybe this first scene has sparked a deeper understanding of your characters, and you can apply it when you develop other scenes. It may have made it possible for you to go back to the beginning with a slightly better knowledge of your characters.

You will eventually refine each scene, make it more visually interesting, cut it to proper length, and check the flow of the story's through-line. You might have written a great line for a certain character but it somehow doesn't add to this scene but you may find it could work in another scene. By getting your first thoughts down on paper, you may have captured the essence of what you are trying to say by allowing you to hear it in your head. Character relationships and story come first – but never forget the visual aspect.

Less is More – Don't Overwrite

Christopher Isherwood said, 'Lots of fine writers who come to Hollywood don't understand that the *image* is primary. They say, "The bastard's cut my dialogue!" They think you write movies in a vacuum and then send them to the [sound] stage to be photographed.'

David Pirie said, 'Beginners write too much dialogue. Make it pacey - keep it spare'. Learn to read your dialogue out loud. Use a tape recorder and play it back to yourself. Get a friend to record a scene with you. Listen to the rhythm of it.

DeMille (the Spielberg of his day), upon reading a scene heavy in dialogue, handed it back to his chief writer, then pulled a pistol from his desk drawer and passed it to him saying, 'If you want to destroy me, Jesse – use a gun. It's quicker.'

Don't be too explicit in your instructions – leave something to the actor's imagination. You can write brief parentheticals on movement or attitudes that will help the actors/director see and understand the action to interpret and fulfil it, but if you do, keep them short, punchy and descriptive. Don't ever tell him *how* to slam the door, tell him why he does it – but only if *it's not obvious*. Actors want to understand their motivations. *How* they illustrate them is their special expertise – they don't want to be given acting lessons.

A good trick to remember when you want to point something to the audience: put the reference in one character's speech that you want another character to pick up on, as close to the end of the first speech as possible. It makes a big difference in the rhythm of the scene. Here's an example from the same script excerpted in the previous chapter.

```
              HOOD
It's the man next to him - John
Brandon, theatre critic for the
London News. Brandon's offered to
introduce you around to the right
people.

BRANDON turns directly into CAMERA
as they approach. His manner is
mild and outwardly jovial — at
the moment.
```
(NB: this last direction is important for the actor, since his character later goes insane.)

HOOD (Cont'd)
Gentlemen, I'd like you to meet
Ambrose Bierce. John Brandon,
Esquire — and the famous Mr. Mark
Twain - a man whose every book is
a classic…

TWAIN
I hope not, Hood. A classic is
something everybody wants to have
read - and nobody wants to read.
I'd prefer to be popular like Mr.
Bierce here. Verbal viciousness -
with a touch of the blood sport
about it.

BRANDON
(pensive)
My trouble is - I'm not vicious
enough in print. (brightens) They
say you've had threats on your
life, Bierce. It all makes you
quite colourful - if true.

BIERCE lets his coat drop open
revealing the pistol at his hip.

BIERCE
I shall endeavour to live up
to my reputation, Mr. Brandon.

Twain picks up on the word 'classic' with a
twist of humour and Brandon picks up on
the word 'vicious' – which leads him into the
subject of threats. This scene also shows how
simple description of the action informs the
actor, and how, when the same character's
speech is interrupted by a direction, a '(cont'd)'
is placed after it to inform the actor that it's still
his speech. There is also a parenthetical
'(pensive)' because it's important to the story at
that moment for the actor to convey that
attitude and mood which the dialogue on the
page might not convey on its own.

Watch out for alliteration and double
meanings that could cause an unwanted
laugh. Reading it out loud may reveal such
words. Don't let your audience focus on words
– but on the undercurrent in the scene.

Never write dialogue when you can make
the point visually. For example, in *Witness*
(1985), Kelly McGillis serves Harrison Ford a
meal. Her boyfriend and grandfather watch
them as they eat. There is no dialogue. Their
attitudes are reflected in their observation of
Ford. It's written into the script but it's the
actor's task to give it to us visually.

A script is image and action versus words.
In European films there are an average of
1,000 to 1,200 lines of dialogue. In American
films it is closer to 500 lines.

Read my Lips

When hearing O.S. (Off Screen) or V.O. (Voice
Over) dialogue the audience is disconnected
from the speaker and can lose a lot of the
speech. Although the majority of us are not
conscious lip readers, we unconsciously
partially read them as we watch someone speak.
The proof of this is that when you see a film
that is badly dubbed, you know at once that the
actor's words do not fit his mouth movements.
Remember to keep these O.S. speeches simple
and if possible, avoid words that can have
another – or sound like another – meaning.

Writing Pauses

To an actor, pauses aren't just holes in the
dialogue. They are the beat where something
else is happening between the characters. It
might be the moment when someone first
understands something, or a transition from
one way of thinking to another. The writer is
signalling the actor that words are not
necessary to make this transition, but *a
change in attitude is*. A pause can transform
the action of a scene. This can be indicated in
a line of dialogue by a dash – or three dots…

BRANDON
(pensive)
My trouble is — I'm not vicious
enough in print. (brightens) They
say you've had threats on your
life, Bierce. It all makes you
quite colourful — if true.

Each character's voice should stand out with
it's own distinctive style and flavour from all
the other characters, because people express
their personalities in how they speak. In
theatre, sometimes an actor (even a good one)
will pick up the speech pattern or rhythm of
the other actor in a scene. The same can
happen to you when you write dialogue.
Guard against this to keep each voice unique.

The Inner Life of a Character

An actor who can hold a 30-second close-up without dialogue is said to have *star quality*. Dustin Hoffman, Gene Hackman, Jack Nicholson, Matt Damon, Meryl Streep, Anthony Hopkins, Juliette Binoche, Robert DeNiro, Marlon Brando, Maggie Smith, Judi Dench, Sean Connery, Bruce Willis, Julianne Moore and Michael Caine are just some of the current stars who can invite the camera into their thoughts and feelings and reveal the emotional levels of their unconscious mind to make a character into a real, many-faceted person – even in an action sequence. A good actor by a single look or movement of his hand can say more than words can tell.

Often actors know what they can express in very few, or no words. Johnny Depp frequently asks for his dialogue to be cut, preferring to show his feelings with his face. He follows a tradition set by Gary Cooper.

When Jesse Lasky Jr was writing *North West Mounted Police* (1940), DeMille kept him on the set for rewrites. Jesse had written two long speeches for Cooper, who came over to him, script in hand. The actor flipped through the pages to his first speech (practically a monologue) and said, 'You see this speech, Jess? It's really great. Wonderful!' He took a pencil and scratched an 'X' through it adding, 'But what I want to say here is, *Yup.*' Then he flipped over a few pages and came to another long speech. 'And this one's terrific. Sheer poetry.' Out came the pencil. Scratch it went, right across the speech. 'And what I want to say here is, *Nope.*'

He did, and it was all that was necessary. The moral of the story is don't overwrite. Leave something for the actor to do besides speaking your lines.

Isherwood said, 'You can be a great writer and be utterly unsuited to movie work. Being a movie writer is a very special kind of talent and it involves much else besides writing; you have to have a strong visual sense. The image is still far more important than the sound. And the sound can't exist in its own right, it has to be played off the image.'[1]

The Idea is the Key to a Good Story

Count on your audience to identify everything they see and hear, and to give it a meaning within the framework (and limitations) of their own understanding of the world. Keep a tight focus on the elements of your story as you write each scene.

D.H. Lawrence said: 'Never trust the artist – trust the tale.' In other words, don't expect the actor to give you what you haven't expressed either in dialogue of description of his attitude, *when not obvious*. It's got to be on the page for the actor to interpret it. He will add his charisma, but you are the creator – he, the interpreter. You won't get credit if your script turns out to be an accident, even a happy one. Check the rhythm and tempo of the action, check your character's points of view and attitudes for a balance of highs and lows – and be prepared to rewrite scenes when the director wants it.

Life is minimalism carried to the extreme, which is why dramatizing life as it is on a daily basis isn't drama. Fact and realism alone may be truth, but not artistic truth. Distil your 'slice of life'; compress it with high points and pace – which real life rarely offers. Most importantly, give the audience a point of view by which to see the story.

Sometimes you may find that your story looked fairly good in the stepline and the treatment, but when working on the screenplay, some of the scenes just don't want to be written. What do you do? Try rethinking the scene or sequence of scenes. It is not too late to ask yourself the great 'what if?' questions:
– What would be a catastrophe if it happened to the protagonist right now?
– What would be wonderful if it happened? What are some of the choices he could make and where would each lead?
– Who are the most powerful forces of opposition?
– Have you chosen characters who provide your story with the maximum conflict?

No one is going to stop you from changing things that are not working out. The earlier you do this, the easier it will be.

Straining the Believability Factor

For a character to be believable within the parameters you have set for him, his actions should be justified even in such unreal worlds as that created in *Star Wars II: Attack of the Clones* (2002). George Lucas may offer state-of-the-art technical wizardry, but does it excuse terrible dialogue and predictable plotting – not to mention the improbability of Jedi Master Yoda (who hobbles on a cane throughout the film) suddenly being able to fight like a kick boxer in a lightsabre battle? His opponent is the excellent villain Christopher Lee, who makes even the most improbable characters and dialogue believable.

In *Minority Report*, (2002, written by Scott Frank and Jon Cohen, based on a short story by cult writer Philip K. Dick, directed by Steven Spielberg), set in 2054, Tom Cruise manages to escape from squads of 'flying' cops and leaps from futuristic cars on a perpendicular freeway. He has his eyeballs replaced in 24 hours – and a few other incredible happenings. But it's great fun under Spielberg's guidance and if Cruise isn't too cerebral an actor, he's great at action. We accept it because the parameters of his world are set and retained, the dialogue is excellent, and there are plenty of highs and lows.

This film is a study in pace. It has got to be in the script, but it is up to the director to get it onto the screen. If you want to write this sort of film remember that much of the final experience depends on computerization and digital effects. As a writer, give them the characters, the story, the pace and they'll give you the impossible.

Know the limits of what your audience can absorb from the screen. In writing stage directions, don't ask your director to focus on a newspaper article or a letter and expect the audience to be able to read it. Unless it is as large as a headline the written word can't easily be read on the screen. Invent a reason for someone to read it out loud – or even, as a last resort, to himself. Or use a voiceover of the person who wrote the letter. Or have the character read the news article to somebody else. Or get another character to come in and tell them the news – 'Have you seen the paper?' – or have them see it on TV.

Writing Stage Directions

Keep all location descriptions to a minimum, pointing out only features that are important to your scene. The location you get may be nothing like what you wanted. But if certain values are essential, they should be there. Create your mood in as few expressive phrases

as you can. Give a brief description of a character as he enters for the first time – or if a change has taken place. Only tell the reader what is necessary to know. Most producers hate reading scripts anyway, so try to keep him awake!

Polishing

When you have written the final scene in your screenplay, you're not finished. If you're working on a computer, print out a copy. Put it aside for at least a week. When you come back to it, try to read it with a fresh eye. Lines of dialogue will glare at you. You may find too many repetitions. Tighten speeches generally, and cross out any words in a speech that add nothing. Ask yourself: does he need to say this line? Will the other sentences in the speech tell enough? Eliminating words is one of the best things you can do in writing dialogue.

Do all the scenes work? Do some add nothing at all but words? You may find you have lost an important character in one scene or perhaps one of your characters has actually added nothing to the script. Should you eliminate him?

How is the overall length? Does it need tightening? Or is it too short? Are all the climaxes working? It should take you a week or more to give the script a good polish – but it won't be the last one. Put it away for another week, then read it again. This time fine-tune the polishing.

If there is nothing more you can add for the moment, send a copy to yourself by registered post to keep in case of plagiarism (remember not to open the envelope when you get it back, just put it away in a safe place). When this is done, it is time to call in a friend whose judgement you trust. Get some feedback. If you have an agent, give him a copy, and get his feedback too. Listen to all suggestions and weigh them. If several people point out the same problem, you'd better give it some thought. If you reread it after a few months, you may realize there are many changes you can see that would make it better. Discuss it with someone before making the changes. Writers have been known to rewrite the wrong things.

When all loose ends are sorted out, you are ready to submit. A professional writer should be able to write a first draft 90-minute screenplay from a very good treatment in six weeks. You may take much longer – the important thing is to do it right, not fast. Don't submit before you're sure of it yourself. Remember, this is still a first draft.

Accents

When is an accent enough and when is it too much? In writing a film where the characters are actually speaking in a foreign language but you want them to speak in English, there is a bizarre convention about speaking with an accent. One is seen in, for instance, *K-19: The Widowmaker* (2002, written by Christopher Kyle from Louis Nowra's story, directed by Kathryn Bigelow). Since all the characters are Russian, the decision was made for the actors to speak English with a hint of Russian accent, with the idea that the audience accepts they are really speaking Russian. This was very acceptable.

The other approach – which can be seen in, for instance, *Amadeus* (1984, written by Peter Shaffer from his own play, directed by Milos Forman), in which most of the characters are German-speaking Austrians – is for everyone to use a standardized English-language accent (in this case, an American accent – including the small number of British actors in the film), which is taken to stand for the native language of the characters, in this case German; non-German-speaking characters have degrees of accent depending on their familiarity with German: the fluent Salieri a very slight one, the less fluent Kappellmeister Bonno a more pronounced one. Since this is more logical than presenting people as speaking their own native tongue with a 'foreign' accent, this second approach is becoming steadily more widely used.

A separate issue is that of the range of regional accents that are acceptable within an entirely English-language context. Ken Loach and his writer, Paul Laverty, advocate the opposing point of view. Their films (they've made four together) all tend to be set 'up North' with downbeat endings. *Sweet Sixteen* (2002, partly financed by the National Lottery through Scottish Screen) is a slice of life in Greenock outside Glasgow. Laverty chose Greenock for the 'majestic vistas and the characters'[2]. He spent research time listening

to 'dozens and dozens of kids talking. Don't underestimate standing on street corners.' His writing is 'an organic process, keeping at it until it's right', asking himself 'is this realistic? Does it make sense?'

Laverty said he wanted their speech to resonate in the dialogue and tell a story that was not predictable. While some critics liked the film, it has been called 'sour and old hat' and the atmosphere 'relentlessly miserable ... A tedious compendium of housing estate clichés that never rises above the level of agit-prop.'

Laverty established a family network of characters. Liam, the sixteen-year-old lead was a hangover from their previous film, *My Name is Joe.* Played by a local boy, Martin Comston, and other first-time actors, it was impossible to understand anything except the 'f-word', which was used three or four times in every sentence. Comston commented, 'It's just another word. It's the way we talk to our friends.' Loach was annoyed that because of the strong language and violence the Censor Board gave it an 18 rating although it has no sex scenes.

But the decision to use the strong local accent of Greenock, and dialogue authentically laden with swear words, meant that it had to be shown with subtitles even in other English-speaking countries, and received a more restricted certificate because of the swearing. Although it won high praise in the United States as it did in Europe, these would certainly both have been factors in limiting its box-office appeal there. After the screening I asked Loach if he had any trouble getting distribution, since this was not a documentary and he had made no concession to dramatic license in the interests of intelligibility. He replied that he had 67 prints in distribution in the UK and 120 prints scheduled for the Continent (a limited distribution). Although he was 'open-minded and comfortable with subtitles' he had held 'exhaustive' tests in the Midlands, where several hundred people saw it. Loach claims 75 per cent of the audience understood it and overwhelmingly reported that it made no difference. However, in my opinion, if you want to make a film using authentic dialects, you must make some allowance for the other 25 per cent of your audience. Loach disagrees: 'You have to be true to the way people are. In the end I think I did the right thing.' He added, 'Subtitles are a distraction, but of course we will add subtitles for the US and other foreign countries.'

There is a difference between documentary and drama. By telling his story with non-actors who did not modulate their speech for clarity, the film was forced to play mainly arthouses, even in the UK. The film's distribution was very small – though it won a few festival awards. The debate continues ...

Dialogue Versus Action

The following figures are given generally for Hollywood mainstream films; naturally they vary for straight action films, European drama, etc.

Film: a typical Hollywood commercial film is 80 per cent action and non-verbal communication and 20 per cent dialogue. Audiences engulfed in big-screen movies want to see, not just hear.

Play: is the reverse – 80 per cent dialogue and 20 per cent action. We can listen to poetry on the stage and accept it as reality. Words can lift the level of human expression in the work of great playwrights from Shakespeare to Pinter. But actors in the theatre cannot express the sub-text of the characters' inner lives using their faces alone, with the same subtlety that can be achieved in film with the closeup, which can de-verbalize the emotion with a look.

TV Drama: Because the viewer is sitting close to the box and it's right there in the house, the audience wants to see and hear. So for the most part the dialogue and action are about half and half in a 60- or 90-minute drama.

A half-hour segment on TV (generally sitcom) is, in effect, a short film. It has a beginning, middle, and end, all in under 30 minutes. This is a highly disciplined form, all the more so bearing in mind that in the UK on all but the BBC, commercials must be accounted for (and in North America they take up an even greater portion of air time – as much as a third). Your story introduces characters, situations and the initial turning point in the first five minutes. It follows the normal mainstream format except that it will generally encompass a two-act structure for a one-hour segment (broken into four quarters for commercials).

You may find yourself writing a segment for a running series, or creating a series of your own. Every quarter of your script needs a cliffhanger even more than in an ordinary film. The advertizers don't want the audience flipping to another channel.

TV Soap: A soap is slightly different because it is generally built on a half-hour format with many strands of story-line. The dialogue averages 75 per cent against 25 per cent action – budgets are too tight to take the episode far afield from its standard sets. Scenes almost never last longer than a minute and could be much shorter. Although the characters are generally one-dimensional, the action is built on peak emotional conflict and current, highly charged social issues: abortion, rape, adultery, cross-cultural relationships, criminal pursuits, homosexuality, and so on. The stories are open-ended, keeping the viewer tuning in week after week to find out what's going to happen next.

Below is a diagram representing the breakdown of dialogue versus action outlined above.

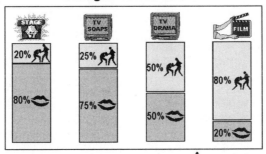

Dialogue versus Action

Key: Dialogue 👄 Action 🏃

CHAPTER 10 | MAINSTREAM FILMS FORMATTED

Breakdown Of A Mainstream Film Structure

The following two films (both of the social drama genre) identically follow the mainstream formula given in chapter 6. *The Doctor* (1991, screenplay by Robert Caswell, directed by Randa Haines), which starred William Hurt, had critical acclaim if not large box office. *Regarding Henry* (1991, starring Harrison Ford) was a slightly bigger financial success ($38m and $43m respectively). I have outlined the formats for comparison because they illustrate perfectly how two completely different stories can be built on exactly the same schematic frame. The theme for both films proposed that if the protagonist could see how his life had been degraded by his ruthless desires, he could change himself for the better. By abandoning his current lifestyle, he can find his way back to genuine values. Check them out of the video shop and compare them to the outline.

I have set these out in the style of an initial stepline that you would make for your own story. This is not broken into scenes, only steps of the story. When you get to the card system, you would break this down into the scenes before writing your treatment, and eventually your screenplay.

Regarding Henry (1991)

Screenplay: Jeffrey Abrams

Genre: Social drama – happy ending.

Theme: The unrelenting quest of success and self-indulgence.

Logline: Ruthless high-flying lawyer fights back from a brain injury – using his brains to find new meaning to life and real happiness.

ACT ONE

1) **Plot:** Sets up tough 'success-oriented' character of the lawyer protagonist. His relationships and attitudes:
To his wife: too busy for her; orders her about; in charge of her life.

With his daughter: doesn't bond with her; no interrelationship.
With his co-workers: they think he's a dynamo.

2) **1st Subplot Clue:** Protagonist wins a case against older couple versus hospital by clever (ruthless) manipulation of evidence.

3) **2nd Subplot Point:** Wife makes intimate phone call.

Hook: Is she having an affair?

4) **3rd Subplot Point:** Secretary is somehow too intimate with Protagonist.

Hook: Is he having an affair?

5) **Main Plot:** Initial Turning Point (about 12 minutes in). A chance occurrence. Protagonist goes to corner shop to buy cigarettes. Gunman shoots him.

6) **Main Plot:** In hospital, Protagonist can't walk or speak.

Crisis: Will he or won't he pull through?

7) **Main Plot:** Protagonist is a vegetable, hospitalized. It has changed the course of his of life. Wife by his bedside, doing her duty. Husband has no memory, can't function.

8) **Subplot:** Friendly black male nurse introduced (the Mythic Mentor figure, see Chapter 13).

9) **Main Plot:** Protagonist's partners (the Threshold Guardians) take wife to dinner. Her life has changed. Can she survive without his earning power? She reveals nothing.

Cliffhanger: What will she do? Is their marriage over?

ACT TWO

10) **Main Plot:** Black male nurse and a physiotherapist retrain Protagonist to walk, speak, etc.

11) **Plot Point:** His daughter is afraid of him. There are higher stakes.

12) **Crisis:** Hospital tells him to go home, but he doesn't want to. Protagonist must make a decision.

13) **Plot Point:** Black nurse (who understands the psychology of the Protagonist) sends daughter in to talk to him. She helps him tie his shoelaces.

14) **Main Plot:** Change in relationship: a complete reversal between daughter and father. He needs her. She warms to him.

15) **Moment of decision:** He chooses to go home.

16) **Plot Point:** Protagonist cannot adjust to his old life at home.

17) **Plot Point:** Goes to office. Will he fit in at work?

18) **Plot Point:** Discovers he won his last case because he hid evidence. Confronts partner (the Mythic Shapeshifter). Now Protagonist wants to help the old couple.

19) **Plot Point:** Protagonist is not his old self. Partners begin to worry what he will do next.

20) **Crisis:** He is disoriented in his old life. But how can he live with the new?

21) **Plot Point:** Protagonist's illness has destroyed wife's world. Will she stay with him? Does she love him enough?

22) **Plot Point:** Wife's crisis: with his new life, she can't survive financially in her former lifestyle. Her decision: cut down lifestyle. Stay with husband, move house.

23) **Main Plot:** Wife decides to send daughter away to boarding school.

24) **Character Reversal:** Protagonist is totally dependent on wife's decisions.

25) **Main Plot:** He makes friends with his daughter. Their relationship grows. They bond.

26) **Main Plot:** Wife brings black male nurse to visit husband – and help him to adjust.

27) **Crisis:** Protagonist discovers love letters to wife from his partner. (Audience learns when he does.)

28) **Crisis:** He confronts her! She says that's all in the past. She loves him now. He rushes out. He must make a decision.

29) **Subplot crossover:** At office, he discovers his own infidelity with secretary. Realises he has been just as bad as his wife!

Cliffhanger: What now?

ACT THREE

30) **Main Plot:** Protagonist's life is in shreds. His office won't give him his case files because they are afraid of what he might do.
Crisis: Protagonist must make a decision.

31) **Moment of Truth:** He quits the law firm. Says fond farewell to secretary.

32) **Plot Point:** Goes to old couple he was cheating; gives them the hidden evidence.

33) **Plot Point:** Goes home to wife (to live happily ever after?).

34) **Obligatory Scene (Happy ending):** Accompanied by wife, Protagonist gets daughter out of boarding school. Moves family to small house with dog (kitsch touch) to play 'happy families'. The protagonist will start a new life – a lawyer with a different set of values.
Fade Out

Those 34 steps could break into 75 or 80 scenes. Compare the following stepline breakdown to the one above. *The Doctor* had a stronger screenplay on many levels, and was graced by a many-textured performance from William Hurt.

The Doctor (1991)

Screenplay: Robert Caswell, from *A Taste of My Own Medicine*, the memoirs of Ed Rosenbaum.

Genre: Social drama – happy ending.
Theme: The unrelenting quest of contemporary values. By abandoning the pursuit of success and self-indulgence, the doctor achieves understanding and real happiness.
Recurring sub-theme: Bad advice from the medical profession.
Logline: An egotistical heart surgeon who shows no feelings or emotions (no heart), finds it and becomes a better person.
Imagery: The image of heart works on several levels.

ACT ONE

1) **Main Plot:** Protagonist, a brilliant but arrogant (heartless) heart surgeon sings and jokes in operating room while his patient lies on the table.

2) **Subplot introduced:** Doctor teases black nurse who won't sing.

3) **Plot Point:** Good relationship with surgeon-partner in his practice.

4) **Main Plot:** Takes interns on his rounds, advises them not to become emotionally involved with patients.

5) **Main Plot:** Relationship with wife: jokey, but impersonal. He keeps her at arm's length.

6) **Plot Point:** Bad relationship with son. He has no time, doesn't relate.

7) **Plot hook:** His throat troubles him. Goes to see his G.P. who tells him: don't worry about it. (Gets bad advice from medical profession.)

8) **1st Subplot:** A new kitchen being installed.

Wife frets that he is never there to help with decisions.

9) **2nd Subplot:** Partner's patient is suing them both for malpractice. Partner wants him to testify for him. He makes no decision.

10) **Plot Point:** His Mexican patient is waiting for a donor heart.

11) **Main Plot:** Protagonist goes to woman throat specialist. A series of tests. He is angry at his casual treatment as a patient. Finds it inhuman (heartless).

12) **Main Plot:** Initial Turning Point (about 12 to 15 minutes in). Throat specialist discovers growth on vocal chords.
Hook: Is it cancer?

13) **Main Plot Crisis:** Protagonist discovers Yes! it is cancer. Must decide on treatment.

14) **Plot Point:** Protagonist wants them to operate to remove it. His doctor advises radiation with 80 per cent cure rate, versus possibly losing his voice.

15) **Decision:** He takes her advice. (2nd piece of bad advice from medical profession.)

16) **Main Plot:** As a doctor, he expects priority treatment. Angry at being treated just like everyone else. Takes anger out on staff.

17) **Plot Point:** His fears of death draw him into himself: Shuts out his wife.
Hook: What will become of him?

ACT TWO

18) **3rd Subplot:** Meets young woman, June, also undergoing radiation. He finds he can talk to her about how he feels. She understands (the Mythic Mentor.)

19) **Main Plot:** Protagonist ignores partner's advice to give up his practice even though he's too ill to operate.

20) **Subplot:** June knows she is dying of brain tumour. She faces it calmly.

21) **Main Plot:** Through knowing June, he begins to have humility and see other people as humans (begins to 'have a heart').

22) **Subplot:** Mexican patient's wife tells Protagonist he must find him a kind, loving donor heart. (Attributing emotion to the replacement heart.)

23) **Main Plot:** Wife and Protagonist growing further apart. He cannot share his emotions towards his possible death.

24) **Subplot:** To partner's disgust, Protagonist talks to patient who is suing and in trouble. Will he help the partner (the Mythic Shapeshifter) or the patient?

25) **Decision:** Protagonist helps patient to get car keys.

26) **Main Plot:** Too ill to finish an operation he walks out of operating room, leaving shocked partner to take over.

27) **Subplot/Main Plot Crossover:** Takes June to desert to fulfil her dying wish. They never get where they were going – and end up dancing in desert sunset.
Decision: He realizes he needs help; cannot fight it alone. Phones wife (in a convenient phone box); feeling lost.

28) **Sub-plot:** Discovers partner lied about patient's lawsuit for malpractice. Partner is guilty. Knowing this, should he defend him?

29) **Decision:** Must break with partner.

30) **Main Plot:** Learns his cancer has grown bigger despite doctor's advice. He must have operation – and now it will be more dangerous! (3rd piece of bad advice from medical profession).

31) **Main Plot:** In an emotional turmoil in the middle of the night, goes to see June but can't bring himself to go in.

32) **Subplot:** June dies. He is devastated.
Crisis: He feels no-one else understands his fear of facing death. What will he do?

ACT THREE

33) **Main Plot Decision:** Protagonist changes surgeons. Goes to man he personally dislikes but respects and trusts his good advice. (There is an anti-Semitic suggestion here, but since the memoir's author is Jewish, one assumes this was meant to point out the irony that people respect Jewish doctors – though they may feel socially negative towards them.)

34) **Subplot:** Protagonist breaks with partner over lies and misconduct.

35) **Emotional Crisis:** Goes into operating room as a patient:
Hook: Will they get all the cancer out?

36) **1st Subplot payoff:** In the operating room, black nurse (who wouldn't before) now sings. Shows she 'has a heart'.

37) **Main Plot:** Recuperating at home, sees wife yelling at builders. She is taking her anger at him out on them.
Decision: Makes a new start on marital relationship.

38) **Plot Point:** Realizes son is alienated. Starts to win him back (this area not as developed as the daughter in *Regarding Henry*).

39) **Time jump:** Fast forward to when he's well.

40) **Main Plot:** Having survived his ordeal – back at work (not with old partner) takes new interns on rounds. Forces them to spend 24 hours as patients (with their pants off) to learn to treat patients as human beings (teaches them to 'have a heart').

41) **Subplot/Crossover:** Refuses to testify for ex-partner, even though he, too, will be sued. He now treats his patients like human beings – and cares.

42) **Subplot/Crossover:** He performs heart operation on the Mexican patient but no jokey music. Has doctor changed? After operation he peels off gloves and pats unconscious man lovingly on head.

End of film? Hardly. There's a ...

43) **Resolution Scene:** Doctor receives June's letter – her last words to him. Reads it (her voiceover) on a visually sentimental sunset-lit roof. He is at peace with himself. He has found a heart.

Fade Out

There is a definite unresolved lapse in logic: this letter must have been written a long time earlier, so why read it out loud now? Because it winds up the feel-good factor of the film. With a little imagination, a reason for the delay could easily be found: for instance, if his wife had just found the letter and given it to him. Except for this 'schmaltzy' ending, this was a better, more subtly characterized film than *Regarding Henry*.

CHAPTER 11 | MIDSTREAM FILMS FORMATTED

A Midstream Film Structure

As Truffaut said, 'All films should have a beginning, middle, and end, but not necessarily in that order'. The following example is not in that order.

I have chosen *Pulp Fiction* because the structure of this dazzlingly designed film of the 'low-life' American society is composed of many characters and cross-plots. The several stories are skilfully woven together with disregard for the time factor, partly so that the chief protagonist of one story-line that threads through the others (played by John Travolta), is not seen to be killed at the end of the film. We have actually seen Travolta killed in an earlier scene – and although we realize he is already dead as he walks out of the cafe at the end (as far as time-frame is concerned), we do not leave the cinema weepie-eyed. The construction has 'happy-ended' the film in an otherwise cold-blooded, brilliant, black-humour piece of work.

This is certainly one of the best films of the 1990s with a construction as intricate as a jigsaw puzzle. The dialogue counterpoints what the people are doing, so the dialogue is not about what the scenes are about. The talk is consistently about trivial matters often unrelated to the actual action, and the contradiction helps to make it funny. You will benefit from studying the video with the outline to better understand how Tarantino broke the format down.

Pulp Fiction (1994)

Screenplay: Quentin Tarantino and Roger Avary
Genre: Crime/drama/comedy
Before Titles:
1) **Cafe Scene (really a flash-forward):** A modern Bonnie and Clyde discuss what type of venue they want to stick up. They kiss. Each takes a gun. She stands up, shouts:
Move and I'll kill every mother-fucking last one of you! CUT!

Loud Rock Music and Titles

Part One: The Two Hitmen

2) **Car Sequence:** Vince (Travolta) and Jules (Samuel Jackson), two spaced-out hoods smoking pot as they drive. They don't discuss their mission – instead:
Vince: What do they call a quarter-pound hamburger with cheese in Amsterdam? A Royale.
They stop car. From boot they casually take out handguns.
We should have fucking shotguns!
3) **Int. Lift:** Going up, we know not where. They discuss a guy who gave Marcellus's wife Mia a foot massage and was thrown out of a window. Vince has a 'babysitter' date with Marcellus's wife that night. They argue if foot massage is as intimate as eating pussy.
4) **At Door:** Jules, an eloquent sociopath, says, Let's get in character.
5) **Int. Men's Flat:** Three guys eating breakfast. Jules announces they are from Marcellus, their business partner. Quotes Ezekiel and shoots one guy. Vince fires. Mad gunfire! CUT!

Part Two: Vincent And Marcellus's Wife

6) **Night Club:** Marcellus (Ving Rhames) giving fighter Butch (Bruce Willis) a big bribe to throw his fight in the 5th round.
7) Vince and Jules drift in, discuss his pending date with Marcellus's wife. Her claim to fame is making a pilot for TV that never got shown.
8) Vince insults Butch, who then watches Marcellus hug him.
9) **BLACKOUT. V.O.** Jody (Rosanna Arquette) and girlfriend discuss body piercing – a sex thing – turns every part of your body into the tip of a penis.
10) **Pusher's House:** Vince arrives. Angry because somebody hit his car. Buys heroin (says coke is dead).
CLOSEUP: Ritual shooting up with hypodermic, spoon, flame etc. (was this necessary? we got the message without it).
11) **Intercut Car Scene:** Vince driving alone.
12) **Marcellus's House:** Vince arrives, stoned. Finds note from Mia (Uma Thurman) to come in. Note is read by Mia in V.O. (audience

cannot be expected to read the written word on screen). Vince lost in elegant modern room. Mia watching him through TV intercom. She snorts coke. CAMERA does not reveal her face.

13) **Int. Car.** Mia's face finally seen. She says, 'Don't be a square'. Draws it in the air. (Computer Graphics used to make a square. This is the only time C.G. is used. Using an unrealistic visual technique only once disrupts the 'style' of the piece. It is usually best to use it more than once or not at all.)

14) **Restaurant:** Waiters dressed like movie stars, diners eat in fake cars. Mia tells him about her pilot film. Won't tell him her joke. Orders a $5 milk shake. Discuss its merits. She denies the guy ever massaged her feet, and forces Vince into a dance contest (taking advantage of Travolta's talents).

15) **Marcellus's House:** Vince goes to bathroom, has an argument with his reflection: he is attracted to Mia – *it's a moral test of one's self.* Decides to go home instead.

16) Alone Mia snorts Vince's heroin, thinking it's cocaine.

17) He returns to sitting room to find her passed out. Tries to revive her.

18) **In Car:** Mia unconscious. A crazy drive to pusher's house, on mobile to pusher to get help.

19) **Pusher's House:** Shouting and arguing about a book on first aid. Marks position of her heart with a pen. Who will give her the life-saving shot? Vince is forced to do it. She revives. **Arquette murmurs:** That was fuckin' trippy!

20) **Marcellus's House:** Vince walks her to door. She finally tells him her joke about three tomatoes. Daddy tomato squishes baby lagging behind – and shouts, Ketchup. Vince blows her a kiss.

Second Story Sequence

21) **Flashback (not immediately obvious that it is the boxer's back story):** Little kid watching cartoon on TV. Mother brings in Captain Koons (Christopher Walken) in uniform, to talk to little boy. Serious. Koons holds up boy's great grandfather's watch. His birthright. Hidden up his father's arse for five years during Vietnam war and two more years up Walken's. Boy grabs watch. Quick Cut To:

22) **Int. Taxi:** Sexy Lady Taxi Driver, waiting. We don't know for whom.

23) **Boxer's Changing Room:** Butch wakes up before fight.

Hook: Will he throw it? If he doesn't, he's in trouble.

24) **The Fight:** Willis makes a Decision: Wins fight. Accidentally kills opponent. He's in BIG TROUBLE!

25) Willis escapes through window. Leaps into Woman's Taxi and they drive off.

26) Backstage Arena – later: Vince and Jules saunter in – ordered to get Butch. Can't find him (this really takes place *much* later than what follows).

27) **In Taxi:** Driver wants to know what it feels like to kill a man. Drops Butch at a motel.

28) **Motel Room:** Butch joins ditsy French girlfriend who has packed their bags to escape. Her conversation is all about pot-bellies and tummies.

She asks: If they find us will they kill us? Will you give me oral pleasure?

29) **Morning:** He looks for his grandfather's watch (we now get the connection). Goes berserk because his girlfriend left his watch at their apartment. He must go back for it.

30) **Butch in Car:** Alone, vents anger at losing watch, returns to apartment.

31) **Ext. Apartment:** Butch cuts through field, sneaks into his apartment.

32) **Int. Apartment:** All quiet. Finds watch, stops to make himself toast.

33) **Int. Toilet:** Vince on the toilet.

34) **Int. Kitchen:** Butch discovers a shotgun; picks it up. Realizes someone is in the toilet.

35) Vince comes out. Sound shock: **Toaster pops up** and gun goes off together! Vince thrown back onto toilet, dead! Willis wipes prints from gun, leaves. (The film has just lost its main protagonist and we're only half way through. So how does Tarantino get out of this one?)

36) **Ext. Apartment Bldg:** Butch gets in car, drives around front of building – is spotted by Marcellus in street with groceries. Butch tries to run him down, crashes.

37) **In the Street:** Butch gets out of car. Marcellus shoots, chases him into ...

38) **Gun Shop:** Butch and Marcellus fight. Marcellus knocked flat. Owner knocks Butch out, and then makes a mysterious phone call: A spotter just killed a couple of flies.

39) **Owner's Cellar Room:** Marcellus and Butch are bound and gagged by owner and a deviant friend. They bring a guy out of a cellar chamber in black leather torturer gear and tell him to guard Butch. They take Marcellus into inner room. Butch breaks loose. Starts to escape. Hears sounds of torture. Decides to return to save Marcellus.

40) Looking for a weapon he picks up hammer – exchanges it for a chain saw – discards that for a Samurai sword. (Escalation of weaponry has a visual comic effect.)

41) **Inner Torture Room:** One baddie is buggering Marcellus across a barrel. Butch breaks in and kills him. Knocks the other out.

Butch: Are you okay?

Marcellus: No man, I'm pretty fucking far from okay. (To owner) I'm going to get my evil on your ass.
Butch: What about you and me?
Marcellus: There is no me and you. Not no more. (Logic flaw in episode: nobody in street called police at car crash. Here Logic must bow to Action. You could have had cops drive up just after they leave, but who cares?)

42) **Ext. Street:** Butch takes torturer's chopper (motorbike) – goes back for French girl.

43) **At Motel:** She doesn't want to leave – talks about not getting blueberry pancakes. Finally she agrees to climb on chopper.

Part Three: The Bonnie Situation

Flashback To: (continuation of initial scene)

44) **Int. Men's Flat:** At shooting (when Vince was still alive). This time, a third man is revealed hiding in toilet.
Repeat action of shooting (as in first scene). The guy bursts out of toilet. Shoots at them – misses. They shoot him.
Jules, the religious psychopath, says they were saved by the hand of God. They collect briefcase for Marcellus and take the one friendly black guy with them.

45) **Int. Car:** Jules talks about a miracle of divine intervention. Black man in the back seat. Jules says he's going to retire.
Crisis: Vince accidentally shoots black guy in face.
Jules: We gotta get this car off the road. They drive to ...

46) **Jimmie's House (played by Tarantino**

himself): They leave the body in the car in the garage.
Jimmie: Did you notice a sign in front of my house that said Dead Nigger Storage?
Allows them to wash the blood off themselves. Afraid Bonnie (his wife) will see blood on towel. Worried about Bonnie divorcing him. Gives them coffee. Jules phones a friend for help who says he is sending 'The Wolf.'

47) **The Wolf's House:** The Wolf (Harvey Keitel) takes call during a party. He writes: 'One body – no head.'

48) **Screen Caption: '9 Minutes 37 Seconds Later.'**

49) **Jimmie's House:** Keitel at door says: I'm Winston Wolf. I solve problems.
He tells them they will follow orders. Looks at corpse, orders coffee, cream, and sugar.

50) Wolf's orders: Stick body in garage. Scoop up all the little pieces of skull and brain and give car a good once-over. Pools of blood are thicker and darker. Must camouflage the seat. Tells Jimmie his 'Uncle' Marcellus is rich. Gives him money to do the clean-up.

51) **In Garage:** Vince and Jules argue about who should clean what. They finish, pleased. Wolf makes them strip and puts a hose on them. They put on shorts and shirts and look like a couple of dorks (by this time we have forgotten that we have seen Vince dead).

52) **In Cars:** Vince and Jules drive two cars to ...

53) **Monster Joe's Car Lot:** Joe demolishes the car in a compressor – with the body in it.
Wolf tells them: Because you are a character, doesn't mean you have character.
They head for something to eat.

54) **The Cafe (a continuation of the before-titles scene – which was a flash-forward in the first place):**
At a table sit Vince and Jules, who has Marcellus's briefcase. They discuss eating pork: If a pig had a better personality, he'd cease to be a filthy animal. Jules repeats he's quitting the business.

55) **At Another Table:** The Boy and Girl from opening scene are now seen at a point earlier, before they got up (a flashback in a flash forward scene),

56) Vince heads for the toilet. (Tarantino has given him this as an idiosyncrasy.)

57) **A repeat and continuation of action of boy/girl stick-up from opening.** Girl waving gun gets everybody's head down.
Manager tells customers to be calm.
58) **Int. toilet:** Vince reading.
59) **Back To Restaurant:** Boy/Girl put money into a garbage bag. Boy goes to Jules, who keeps his cool. Boy looks in his briefcase. (Audience doesn't ever see inside – only that it seems to glow. The content is a **MacGuffin**.) Jules has the power in the scene, efficiently takes money from boy.
Girl stands on counter with gun, confused.
60) Vince comes out of toilet, covers girl.
61) Jules gives the boy back the money the boy stole. Holding him at gunpoint, he discusses the meaning of the passage from Ezekiel. Then he sends them out.
62) Jules and Vince pick up the briefcase, stuff guns in their waistbands, and walk out in their dorky shorts. We have an 'up' ending.
Fade Out.

Since the last time we see Travolta he's alive we can temporarily forget that we earlier saw him killed in a scene that takes place later.

The film has one major dialogue fault, which is that Tarantino does not differentiate the 'voices' of his characters sufficiently. All of them speak with the same mixture of eloquence and kookiness. You should not let your characters all speak with the same voice.
Nevertheless this is a masterful piece of work.

The Horror Genre

I have chosen *Nightmare On Elm Street* to illustrate the Horror genre. Writer/director Wes Craven created an intelligent and chilling Oedipal conflict in which the line between nightmare and reality is blurred. This is ingenious and original. The image of Freddie Kruger may be schlock horror but it is not mindless rubbish. This landmark film follows every rule of scripting suspense in creating the nightmare world of terror. Craven's chilling concept made this a pioneering classic in the genre and led to six sequels and a TV series.
Sounds and imagery are key elements of horror. See how often these come into play in this film. This has been broken into scenes, which is fuller than a stepline and could be the basis of a card system.

Nightmare On Elm Street (1984)

Screenplay: Wes Craven
Theme: What is seen is not always what is real. Do you believe in the bogeyman?
Logline: Four teenagers experience identical nightmares. Only Nancy can save them from the horror of the bogeyman, Freddie, by staying awake.
Character Elements for Nancy, the Protagonist (reflected and echoed in the other characters): *Inner conflict*: Nancy's fear of Freddie. Personal relationships: with boyfriend Lane it arcs from plus to minus. Is he a murderer? With her mother: Is she a drunk? With her father: Can she depend on him? *Environmental Conflict:* The alien world of dreams and fear of the unknown.

TEASER (an attention grabbing sequence before the story begins).

1) **Night:** Dirty hands shape metal claws.
Sounds: Heavy breathing. Claws ripping fabric.
2) **Shiny Hall – Night:** CLOSE-UP Nancy running away in sheer nightdress (back-lit to show sexy body outline). A sheep runs out (a metaphor for counting sheep). **Sounds:** Maniacal laughter.
3) **Boiler Room:** Nancy runs. Sounds: water dripping, whispers, laughter, steam. The claw ripping a curtain.
4) Freddie, seen from rear. Nancy runs away. Nancy backs towards fiery furnace.
5) **Horror crisis:** Freddie pops up behind her.
6) **Nancy's Bedroom:** Nancy wakes up. Mother enters and calms her.
7) **Day: The Street:** Little girls (images of Freddie's former victims) skipping rope, singing 'one two ... '. Transition to:

ACT ONE
8) **Rick's Car:** Nancy and friends coming to school. Overt sex talk:
Lane to Tina: I had a hard-on and it had your name written all over it.
First mention of theme: They all admit to recent nightmares.
9) **Tina's House – Night:** Her mother away for night. All four friends are staying over. Slight humour: Rick plays trick on his parents with phoney tape to sound like he's somewhere else. Second mention of theme: both girls

have had same dream. Hear strange sounds outside.

10) **Scary moment:** Boys hiding in bushes, jump at Rick and Lane.

11) **Teenagers having sex O.S.:** Lane takes Tina up to her mother's bedroom. Sex noises. Third mention of theme: Lane admits to nightmares, too. All go to sleep.

12) **Scary incident:** Large cross falls off wall into Nancy's bed.

13) **Horror crisis:** Tina hears noise – somebody throwing things at window.

Tina (challenging, yet fearful): Who do you think you are – whoever you are?

14) **Horror crisis:** Nancy sleeping alone. Wall behind her becomes rubber. She wakes, holds cross. She knocks on wall, but it's now solid. Tina goes outside alone! (The requisite 'foolish thing' pretty girls do with little clothes on in horror movies.) **Sounds:** Voice calls her name. Water dripping – rubbish bin lid rolls out.

16) **Horror crisis:** Freddie's shadow appears at end of alley with arms six feet long.

Tina: Please God …!

Freddie: This is God! (Holds up fingers) Tina, watch this! Freddie chops off his own finger. Green bile gushes out.

17) Freddie attacks Tina. She fights him and his face peels off to a bloody skull. (So far, the villain and intended victims have been established.)

18) **Initial Turning Point** (the other incidents were building up to this): Lane wakes to find Tina under the covers. Her stomach is ripped open and she flies to the ceiling, knocking him back. She drops on the bed in a bloody mess.

Crossover: dream has become reality! What next?

Nancy and Rick enter to find Tina's body – blood everywhere. What to do?

Moment of decision: Lane runs away.

19) Police arrive with Chief of Police (Nancy's estranged father). Window is open. Weapon: a razor-like device.

Back Story points revealed: Tina's mother away with boyfriend. Tina has no father.

20) Nancy explains why she didn't want to sleep alone: her nightmare premonition.

21) **Nancy's House** – Day (first change of pace): Nancy watches TV news. Lane is the subject of a manhunt.

Back Story Revealed: We learn Nancy's father and mother are separated. Mother an alcoholic and not supportive.

Nancy leaves for school against mother's wishes.

22) **Bogus Scare:** Figure follows Nancy to school. She is dragged into bushes. But *it's not Freddie, it's Lane,* who wants to tell her he's innocent.

23) **Plot Point:** Nancy's father and police capture Lane. A troubled Nancy goes to school.

24) **First Theme statement:** From Classroom Teacher: What is seen is not always what is real. Quotes Shakespeare. A canker operating in nature.

25) **Horror crisis:** In the school corridor Nancy sees Tina's body in a plastic bag calling her. Blood floods a trail. She follows it! (This is an irrational decision. In Horror flicks protagonists always walk right into danger – ignoring fear and most of all, common sense!) Body bag drifts down hall. Nancy follows. Bumps into another girl, who chides her.

Shock: then turns into the claw!

Calling after Tina, Nancy follows the bloody trail down the stairs! (One of the unwritten rules of the Horror genre: protagonists always go down – not up. *Up* is light, *down* is dark – unless of course it's creaking stairs to the attic.)

26) **The Boiler Room** (scary setting): Nancy returns. Sounds: Water drips. Frightening noises. **Shock:** Freddie appears.

Nancy: Who are you?

Freddie rips his flesh, oozing green, backs down halls, cackles – then attacks her. She screams.

27) **Plot point:** She burns her arm on boiler.

28) **The Classroom:** Nancy wakes. She fell asleep in class. Dilemma: Was It All A Dream? Teacher sends her home.

29) **Nancy's home:** Serious Crisis. Nancy finds burn on arm! It's *more* than just a dream. She has 'crossed-over' from reality to dream and back to reality.

Decision: She must stay awake!

30) Nancy goes to the jail to see Lane. (There is a subtle point being made here about logistics. Distance between the locations

would only be logical in a dream.) Lane tells her he dreamed of Freddie the night before.

31) **Home:** Nancy in bathtub. Sexual image – her knees apart. She forces herself awake but as she closes her eyes – **Horror crisis!** Claw pops up – in the water between her legs! Mother comes in, wakes her in time. But does Nancy get out of the tub? No, she falls back to sleep.

High Down Angle into Tub: Nancy is pulled under the water! (These are the kind of shots that you can, if you want, indicate in your script.)

Deep Underwater shot: She is struggling to break free.

32) Mother enters and wakes her.

33) **Nancy's Bedroom:** Crisis decision – she must stay awake. Nancy takes 'no doze' pills and watches TV.

34) Rick climbs in window. He hasn't had dreams.

Theme stressed: Nancy: Do you believe in the bogeyman?

Crisis Decision: To fight back, Nancy asks Rick to guard her. She falls asleep.

35) **Horror Sequence:** Nancy goes outside alone in the mist. **Sounds:** Thumping heart-beat music. Rick hiding behind tree (to protect her?).

She walks down dark, spooky streets and sheds. Looks in jail window (dream-like, no logical progression of place is necessary). Nancy sees Freddie in alley, yells for Rick. He is gone!

36) She sees Tina's body standing in shroud. **SFX:** Huge centipede comes out of Tina's mouth. Slimy worms at her feet.

Nancy: Are you there?
Freddie: I'm here!

37) **Horror Chase.** Nancy makes it back to her house.

38) **Nancy's House:** She locks door. Starts up stairs. **Horror Crisis!** Stairs are liquid. **SFX:** She sinks though them, ankle deep. Freddie breaks window of front door. Claw arm reaches in.

39) Nancy makes it to her bedroom. Rick is still asleep.

Character progression: Protagonist (Nancy) losing grip on reality: She looks in mirror.
Nancy: This is a dream. It isn't real.

40) **Horror Crisis:** Freddie bursts through mirror – throws her onto bed. She fights him off. He slashes pillow. Feathers everywhere.
Story Structure Point: Death is always near – but never final (or else your story is over). Remember, you don't kill off your hero in the middle.

41) **Sound:** Alarm clock wakes Nancy. She scolds Rick. Mother knocks on door. Rick hides on roof. Closes window. Mother comes in. Everything seems okay. Mother leaves. Nancy sees window is open and Rick is gone!
Mood: Premonition of Evil.

42) Nancy finds Rick, rushes to jail with him to see Lane. They won't let her in. Begs her father to see that Lane is okay.

43) **Intercut Horror sequence: SFX** – Lane being choked by the sheet winding around him. He is swept up to the ceiling. When they arrive to cut him down, he is dead!

44) **Day – Lane's funeral** (mood is gloomy): Nancy tells her father the man is still loose. Describes him. Weird hat, dirty sweater, etc. Father's response: orders ex-wife to keep Nancy home.

45) **Mother's Crisis Decision:** Going to get her daughter some help.
Cliffhanger: What *kind* of help - and will it help?

ACT TWO

46) Mother takes Nancy to Institute of Sleep Disorders. They wire her up.
Theme: what is seen is not always what is real. Repeated by **Doctor to Mother:** Dreams are mysteries. We don't know where they come from.

47) Nancy beginning to dream.
Horror sounds: Slushing water. Her brain waves go crazy on the machine. They wake her up. Her arm has been cut in the dream and she has captured Freddie's hat!
Escalation of Nancy's decision:
Nancy: I brought something out of my dream. I grabbed it off his head. (Crossover of dream to reality)

48) **Ext. Nancy's house – Day** (establishing shot): We need this to tell us where we are, because it's all been so hectic.

49) **Int. Nancy's House:** Nancy hears mother on phone to father. Tells him she doesn't believe Nancy's story.

Character Conflict Scene: Between Mother and Nancy.

Nancy's POV: Lane didn't kill Tina — and he didn't hang himself! It's this guy. He's after us in our dreams. The hat has a name in it: Freddie Kruger.

Nancy: Do you know who he is? Tell me! He's after me now. Accuses Mother of being a drunk. Mother slaps her.

Mother: Freddie Kruger can't come after you now. He's dead. Believe me.

Nancy: You knew about him all this time and you've been acting like it was something I made up?

Mother: You'll feel better when you sleep. (Audience has got to think this is a stupid line. But they won't have time to think.)

Nancy: Screw sleep! She breaks Mother's vodka bottle.

Mother: It's just a nightmare.

Nancy: That's enough! She leaves the house.

50) **Pretty Bridge Scene** (A light, contrasting setting to relieve the dark horror and audience's tension and get them ready for the BIG HORROR). Nancy and Rick. He tells her he isn't sleeping either.

Strong Plot Point: Rick tells her about Balinese dream skills. Where they get their poetry. **Rick:** If you turn your back on monsters, you take their power.

Plot Point: Nancy is reading a book on booby traps (establishes action for later).

Crisis Decision:

Nancy: I'm into survival.

Rick promises to come to her house and sneak in. Nancy goes home.

51) **Int. Nancy's house:** All the windows now have bars. How can Rick sneak in?

Nancy: Oh, gross!

Following sequence reveals Back Story told in active not passive style:

52) Nancy's cellar: Mother drunk, takes Nancy to boiler room. Tells her Freddie Kruger was a filthy child murderer – who killed twenty neighbourhood kids. The police let him go, so she and the neighbours caught and burned him in this very boiler room.

Mother: He can't get out now, he's dead, honey — because Mommy killed

him. (Shows Nancy the claw, hidden in incinerator). I even took his knives.

53) **Int. Rick's House.** telephone rings. **Sound: ring is extra sharp.** Nancy tells Rick she hasn't slept in 7 days. **Decision:** She plans to bring Freddie out of her dream.

Nancy: Meet me on the porch at midnight — and whatever, don't fall asleep.

54) Midnight approaches. Nancy taking stay-awake pills.

55) Rick's Mother wakes him – he has fallen asleep.

56) Nancy's Mother tucks her in. But Nancy drinks coffee and gets dressed. Her arm is bleeding. Phones Rick again.

57) **Putting pressure On Situation:** Rick's father upset at his relationship with Nancy. He hangs up on her call and takes phone off hook. Now she can't reach Rick!

58) **Horror Crisis:** Nancy's phone rings! It's Freddie. She pulls it out of wall, but it still rings. She answers.

Freddie: I'm your boyfriend now.

Escalating Horror with SFX (great visual): phone becomes lips and tongue. She stomps on it. Runs.

59) Nancy tries to get out front door (locks on inside), but Mother has key, is drunk, and won't give it.

60) **Rick's Bedroom: Horror Crisis:** He is pulled inside a gaping hole in the bed by Freddie's arm that comes up right through the sheets. He is yanked down hole with the TV set after him. Blood shoots up like a geyser, covering the ceiling. His mother enters, screams.

61) **Ext. Nancy's House and house next door.** Ambulance. Nancy's father arrives. Waves at Nancy. She waves back, weakly.

Cop: I've never seen anything like it in my life. (Cliché)

62) **Rick's Living Room.** Blood dripping through ceiling.

63) **Int. Nancy's House:** Nancy's crisis decision. Phones Father. Makes a deal. Be at her house in exactly 20 minutes! Break down the door. Arrest Freddie when she 'brings him out'. (*Arrest* a bogeyman?)

64) **Protagonist Taking Positive Action:** Nancy rigs her booby traps, light bulb, hammer, wire, etc.

65) Nancy's father can't face the death room. It's too horrible even for a cop!

66) Nancy comforts Mother. She goes to bed and prays.

Nancy: Okay, Kruger, we play in your court.

Gigantic Cliffhanger: Will Father really come in time?

ACT THREE

67) Nancy's dream: Nancy starts downstairs to cellar (Always Down!). Freddie's claw glove is gone. More dark stairs – down. **Sound:** Echo of iron door swinging. Clank! Maniacal laughs. Whispers. Bogeyman chant: I'm gonna get you ...!

Down more 'Trip Stairs' to the spooky boiler room. Sounds: Steam, noises, dripping, dead baby coos.

Nancy: Kruger ...! (Echoes) I'm here!

68) Nancy in the dark, moving towards a light ahead. It's Kruger's living quarters. She finds her cross in his bed. POV towards his hand, his profile. **Sound:** Mysterious clicks.

69) She is in front of furnace now. Nancy picks up Rick's bloody earphones. Drops them. Nancy: Come out and show yourself, you bastard! Checks her watch. Suddenly Freddie is beside her.

70) She runs – down – down – jumps! Falls into – her garden! **(dream logic)** Kruger leaps out from bushes.

71) **Int. Nancy's Bedroom:** Nancy wakes in her bed. **Nancy:** I'm crazy, after all. Freddie pops up in her room, back-lit. (His silhouette is more frightening than full view. The less you see the more horrible you can imagine it.) Nancy throws hot coffeepot at him. Rushes into next room.

72) **Positive Action:** Nancy sets her booby traps. Runs down to front door, screaming for help. No father. Behind her Freddie calls: I'll split you in two! She taunts him into her trap.

73) Light bulb explodes. He falls. More calls for help. She runs *down* into the spooky basement (not outside where it's safe). Freddie follows.

74) **Escalating Horror:** Nancy covers Freddie in petrol. Sets fire to him – leaves him burning. Calls Father – who finally breaks down door.

75) **SFX:** An unseen Freddie's footprints are burning holes in carpet! Nancy and Father follow them up to Mother's bedroom.

76) **Mother's Bedroom:** Freddie on top of Mother as Father and Nancy rush in. Father throws blanket over burning bodies. They disappear. The bed is empty.

Nancy: Now do you believe me? (Audience is vindicated. They knew all the time.)

77) Nancy sends Father downstairs. Her door shuts. Freddie pops up through the bed sheet.

Freddie: You think you was gonna get away?

Nancy: You're not alive. This whole thing is just a dream.

78) **Big plot point:** She turns her back to him. CAMERA holds on her face. **Sound:** Freddie's heavy breathing.

79) **Major Crisis Decision:** Nancy turns to face him.

Nancy: I want my mother and friends again. I take back every bit of energy I gave you!

Freddie: Whhhat ...?

Nancy: You're nothing. You're shit. Turns her back on him again. He lunges at her – but dissolves and falls through floor. (Why? Because he has no energy if she is not afraid!) She opens her door.

80) **Reality:** Day. Everything looks back to normal. Nancy's arm is mysteriously okay. It is a foggy day.

Mother: Baby, I'm gonna stop drinkin'. Did I keep you awake last night?

Nancy: Do you believe this fog?

Justification of Theme: Mother: Oh, I believe anything is possible.

81) Nancy's friends arrive in car to collect her. She gets in.

Hook: Or is everything back to normal? The car is mysteriously locked and driven away with them in it.

82) The murdered children (as seen at opening) are singing, skipping in street.

83) **Dénouement**: Great SFX shot of Freddie's arm shooting through window of Nancy's front door and dragging Mother inside through the tiny, high window (all is not over).

Fade Out (ready for the next six sequels).

Try watching some of these films with the outlines to get a complete sense of the construction.

CHAPTER 12 | TV FORMATS

Television Drama

Every medium has its own demands and requirements. Television films have much shorter shooting schedules and the pace and energy levels are much faster. For television the *dialogue versus action* ratio is more or less half and half (see diagram of the breakdown for the three mediums at the end of chapter 9).

One Hour TV Format

This is based on 54 minutes of story (in the UK approximately 48 A4 pages including credits, titles, and so on). This is broken by four commercial breaks. In the US, they use American quarto paper (see the section on layout in chapter 8) and if the script is written in 12 point Courier font (which is mandatory there) the script will time to roughly one page a minute. In the US there are many more commercial breaks and producers want the film to time to about 48 minutes, roughly equal to about 48 pages of quarto paper. These times vary according to the particular production, and your producer will inform you of the specific show's requirements.

Movies of the Week

MOWs are 90-minute or 120-minute plays, mainly social drama, detective stories or mysteries. In the UK, there are generally five or six commercial breaks for the MOW and the story-line is divided into six segments with climaxes or reversals at the end of each segment. Subplot reversals can be used for hooks at commercial breaks. For example, on ITV's two-hour production of *Sparkling Cyanide* (October 2004) there was 95 minutes and 33 seconds of story, out of 120 minutes airtime. This consisted of six commercial breaks adding up to 24 minutes and 30 seconds.

Mini-Series

This can be a two-parter of one hour or an hour-and-a-half, or the script can be formatted in one- or two-hour segments. There will always be a hook at the end of each segment for a mini-series. The cliffhangers used for commercial breaks are mini-climaxes.

Today, multiple story-lines and subplots are essential for almost all TV drama. Straight dramas and detective and cop shows have picked up on the multi-strand plot formats of the 'soaps' because the networks believe that audiences can no longer concentrate on more than one and a half minutes of story-line and get easily bored if they can't follow two or three stories at once. It's all part of 'dumbing down' and there is little time for 'in-depth' characterization. As with features, multi-plot dramas will be more cohesive if one of the plots is major and carries the spine of the story. But in crimes shows, the tendency now is to have two stories of equal importance (such as in *CSI* and *CSI Miami*) with two teams solving the cases.

As in films, multi-plots on TV can contradict the main plot and illuminate it. But there should be a thematic unity with the main plot. In the cop sagas the audience is focused on getting to know the cops, not the victims.

Filming 'Murder'

The difference between filming for TV and for the big screen is one of budget and time, as can be seen by the example of the four-part BBC mini-series *Murder*, directed by Beeban Kidron and written by Abi Morgan (who began as a student at the Carlton TV writers' workshop), which aired in May 2002. The theme was the ricochet effect of a murder. When Angela's (Julie Walters) son is brutally murdered her world is shattered. The action is viewed through Angela's eyes. The effect of the tragedy spreads outwards to encompass the people who know her as friends and neighbours.

The production company Tiger Aspect's producer worked closely with Kidron and Morgan throughout the development stage. Kidron said that close collaboration and working as a team is the best way to achieve a successful film. She and her writer were in total harmony. Julie Walters' brilliant performance was a plus.

At a BAFTA interview in May 2002 Abi Morgan said that in creating a story like Murder 'research tends to get in the way'. But several stories came from people she met while investigating her plot. She worked on keeping the thriller element ticking over while trying to escalate the five or six stages of grief that Angela goes through. Morgan stressed that it is necessary on film to distil an image to a single line, to tighten and condense. She spoke about the rhythm of a scene and its flow. 'You have to take on board what the actors say about their scenes. Otherwise what ends up on the screen is not real.'

But during filming, whole scenes and parts of scenes had to be dropped because of the tightness of the shooting schedule. One scene that worked well on paper didn't gel in the editing room. Morgan rewrote it and Kidron (within the tight budget) was able to re-shoot the scene. The new version worked, although when a line was dropped by an actor it changed the entire rhythm of the scene. With no time or money to re-shoot again, it was edited to keep the camera on the other character's face while the correct line was dubbed in as a voiceover.

Kidron said, 'The discipline for TV is much tougher than for film. You are shooting, cutting and editing throughout with less resources, less time.' In the case of Murder she was shooting the four episodes all at once, 'out of context and trying to keep in my head all the elements without forgetting anything'.

Half-Hour Format

Half-hour mysteries such as The Twilight Zone and Night Gallery used to be made regularly, but these seem to have gone out of fashion. Today this time-frame is mainly used for soaps, comedy and sitcoms, with 26 to 28 minutes of script depending on the commercials.

Documentaries

Quite a few screenwriters get their foot in the door by writing documentaries. The latest 'viewer grabbers' in documentaries for television are in the fields of archaeology and history. Computerization has widened the horizons of this genre because now the filmmaker can offer a glimpse of what the ruins looked like when newly built. The written narration (and the narrator) is vital to holding the audience's attention.

According to Philip Day (producer/director/writer of the series Lost Worlds) documentaries that are financed by American money, or expected to be shown there, are subject to strict rules of format. The narrator's script must impose questions every four or five minutes, which it then attempts to answer. As with drama formats, there is a cliffhanger before every commercial break and a reprise at the beginning of each section. Philip Day says, 'The Americans' expectation of their audience is such that they treat them almost like imbeciles. They assume the audience knows nothing.' But, because the Americans control the major finance, he adds, 'we've got no choice but to accept it.'[1] The effect of this change can be clearly seen in series such as Horizon, where the intellectual level has noticeably diminished. Some series made primarily with a domestic audience in mind have escaped this tendency, such as the BBC's The Nazis: A Warning from History (1997).

With interactive TV, a documentary can add film clips to back up its linear construction of events. It can make the viewer a creator of the online dialogue by allowing him to choose how he wishes to see the story unfold.

For writing the narration for a filmed documentary there are certain rules for timing the voiceovers. At the time of filming, any sounds and dialogue should be recorded on a 'wild track'. In laying the narration over the edited film, leave five seconds free at the opening. Count two words per foot of 35 mm film, or (since most shooting will be on video now) three words per second. Avoid long sentences. Don't use narration over sound effects or heavy music.

Chapter 13 | TAKING THE MYTHIC TRIP

Today, the buzz words in Hollywood are 'mythic structure'. If you talk to a producer or story editor, or to a writer or director, that's what they consider the main story strength for a guaranteed hit. Of course, we all know there are no guarantees – and so do the production companies. But Hollywood is always looking for an angle, and 'mythic' is the mantra of the moment. We will analyze what two of the authors responsible for the current interest have had to say, and see where it can apply to your work.

Joseph Campbell's Hero

It all started with a scholar named Joseph Campbell who wrote a book, *The Hero With a Thousand Faces* (1949), proposing the aspects of what he termed the Hero's Journey as the basis of mythological story-telling from ancient times until today. His concept of bringing mythic archetypes into modern thought was based on the writings of the Swiss psychiatrist, Carl G. Jung.

At the beginning of the 20th century, Jung had already psychoanalyzed people's dreams and sourced their roots in universal archetypes (characters or energies common to every culture). Jung believed these *archetypes* reflected different aspects of the human psyche and had their origins in the dream life of all races and religions. He drew a strong parallel between the dream figures his patients reported to him and archetypes stretching back to ancient mythology. He propounded the theory of the *collective unconscious* – intuitive ideas that are instinctively shared by all the peoples of a given time and culture, with broad similarities among human cultures throughout time and place. Jung's idea was that for mental well-being, humans needed the reassurance of satisfying and repeated patterns and so they developed these 'story' patterns in myths.

Joseph Campbell's contribution was to apply this Jungian 'power of the mythic archetype' to ancient heroes and to modern life. His book pays a great deal of attention to Eastern cultures, and while he did not directly

attach his ideas to film writing, he named and catalogued the various obstacles encountered by the hero on the *Journey of Life*.

Campbell affirmed that mythology serves as a meaningful pattern for all men and women searching for their place in the human formula. The mythic archetypes communicate with our primal ego and illuminate the way past the thresholds of our own personal life journey, allowing us to discover where our private ogres hide in wait.

The Greeks invented the art of mythological story-telling with their pantheon of gods, goddesses and a host of interacting human personalities. Campbell formalized Jung's ancient prototypes into characters that reflect the psychological truth beneath all modern human relationships.

Vogler's Mythic Structure

While Campbell's book may seem a far cry from the movies, his student and interpreter, Christopher Vogler, wearing his guru hat at a rakish angle, applied Campbell's ideas specifically to screenwriting.[1] Vogler used the mythic structure to create characters who are both unique persons and universal archetypes. He formulates a pattern for the Hero's journey, believing the audience can more easily empathize with modern-day characters who reflect archetypes.

Vogler lists as universal the questions: *'Who am I? Where do I come from? Where do I go when I die? What is good and what is evil? What must I do about it? What will tomorrow be like? Where did yesterday go? Is there anybody else out there?'* You can see that each of these questions could be (and has been) the theme of a story written by a writer who has never heard of the mythic structure – because it's what good screenwriters and novelists have always asked themselves.

Vogler traces the Hero from his *Ordinary World* through the phases of *The Journey*. His formula carries the Hero from the *Threshold of Adventure* to his *Final Return*. A Hero has a special attribute that gives him dignity and power and makes him a leader of men.

Naturally, he is never more alive than when facing death. Vogler says the Hero may at first refuse the *Call to Adventure*, but ultimately, he must accept it (or we would have no story).

Archetypes

Campbell has named and described the archetypes and Vogler has used them. Assuming the Hero accepts *The Call*, the first encounter of his Journey is with:

The Mentor

A Merlin-like character whose bond is strong and advisory – the bond of parent and child or teacher and student. The Mentor is a helping or protective figure, often a wise older person – a Fairy Godmother or Cosmic Mother image offering supernatural aid. Dante's Beatrice, the Virgin Mary, and Merlin are all epic defenders of the Hero. In fairy tales you will find the Wizard or Hermit of the Wood representing the benign, protecting power of destiny who supplies the priceless amulet of advice.

One of the functions of the Mentor in mythology can be as inventor or scientist, to teach and train and give gifts, if only of wisdom. The Mentor performs a special function of providing a conscience for the Hero. The eccentric woman biologist raising humanoid plants in *Minority Report* (played by Lois Smith) is Tom Cruise's Mentor. Spielberg slowed the film's frenetic pace, allowing one scene in which Lois Smith gave a star performance.

Other recent film examples include: Alfred, *Batman's* long-time butler. Mr Wolf (Harvey Keitel) is the Mentor who comes to the aid of the two killers in *Pulp Fiction* when they find they have an unexpected dead body on their hands.

There are also *Dark Mentors* who lure the Hero away from his goal and into danger. Willem Dafoe's 'baddie' in Spiderman is a Dark Mentor, because he pretends to be a helpful friend to Peter Parker, the *Spiderman*. The Mentor role serves a story function and it may be spread between several characters. Or the Mentor may be the Hero's own conscience. Vogler points to Jiminy Cricket as Pinocchio's conscience.

Starting on his *Journey* the Hero meets:

The Threshold Guardian

This is a character who tries to prevent the Hero's progress. He may be a character defending the Villain or may be just a force of nature, like a flood or a volcanic eruption. The Guardian's function as *Obstacle* may be large or small, but the purpose is to make it difficult for the Hero to cross the *First Threshold* and *Encounter the Tests, the Allies and the Enemies*.

The Herald

The one who brings tidings and give warnings and can be a challenging force for either good or evil. The Herald's dramatic function is to alert the Hero to the possibilities of the future – good or bad – and to motivate him to action. It need not be a person; it can be a thing – like a letter bringing news that starts the Hero on his adventure. The Herald creates the initial turning point in the story, so he/she/it is employed in act one.

The Shadow

Can be an anti-hero's darker, hidden nature as with the character of Hannibal Lecter (Anthony Hopkins) in *Silence of the Lambs*, Francis Dolarhyde (Ralph Fiennes) in *Red Dragon*, or Dad Meiks (Bill Paxton) in *Frailty*. By giving a villain a certain layer of vulnerability the writer can humanize him. For example, the *Shadow* could also be the dark, repressed side of the Hero himself; the Mr Hyde side of a righteous man like Dr Jekyll. We can empathize with him to a degree. Sometimes the Hero manages to overcome his personal Shadow on his Journey.

The Trickster

This character can serve the function of the clown. Tricksters can 'take the Mickey', provide comic relief, and undermine the status quo. This can be a clownish sidekick, such as Sancho Panza in *Don Quixote*, or Joe Pesci's character Leo Getz in the *Lethal Weapon* films. But the Trickster can also be a Hero – such Stanley Ipkiss (Jim Carrey) in *The Mask*, the *Marx Brothers*, or even Bugs Bunny.

Shapeshifters

Archetypes who go through unexpected changes from the Hero's ally to foe, or vice versa; or they may be the Hero, undergoing a transformation over which he may have no control. Female examples include Catherine Tramell (Sharon Stone) in *Basic Instinct*, Alex Forrest (Glenn Close) in *Fatal Attraction* and the deranged fan Evelyn Draper (Jessica Walter) in *Play Misty For Me.*

Male *Shapeshifters* would include Martin Burney (Patrick Bergin) in *Sleeping With The Enemy*, Aaron Stampler/Roy (Edward Norton) in *Primal Fear*, Jack Nicholson as *Wolf*, Verbal Kint (Kevin Spacey) in *The Usual Suspects*, and all the many versions of *Dracula*. To journey safely, the Hero must see beneath the outer camouflage and be armed.

Other Archetypes

The ego's search for identity brings the Hero into contact with other archetypes: *Demons, Scapegoats, Masters, Seducers, Villains, Lovers, Friends, Foes*, and so on. Vogler has given names to all.

If you study fairytales you will find many other variations on the archetypes, including the *Wicked Stepmother* (Villain) and the *Fairy Godmother* (Mentor) all of whom are reflected in modern story-telling to some degree. Certain archetypes will prove to be part of the Hero himself. If so, he must integrate the myriad parts of himself into one whole entity to become complete.

Campbell points out that while most popular tales represent the Hero's role as a physical one of conquering his enemies, the mythologies of the major religions show the Hero's victories to be moral and spiritual issues. The archetype represents the ego – that part of each person's consciousness that is individual and separate from all other men or women including, as he points out, the mother who gave the Hero birth.

The Journey

The Call To Adventure

Campbell cites the first stage of the mythic journey as being when Destiny removes the Hero from his spiritual centre of gravity and separates him from his society, placing him in an unknown realm of danger, eventually dangling the possibility of Reward. This Call to Adventure can begin by chance – an unexpected happening, good or bad. It is the initial turning point, whatever the story. The Hero can be struck down by illness and must begin the road back through self-discovery (as in *Regarding Henry* and *The Doctor*, outlined in chapter 10). It can also be a threat to one's life (as in *The Player*) by the elements or another person.

Refusal of the Call is Campbell's next step. The Hero refuses to give up all that is familiar in exchange for the terror of the unknown. In *Four Weddings and a Funeral* it is Charles's (Hugh Grant's) refusal to get involved with any of the women chasing him.

SEPARATION: ACT 1

This is pure Jung. He calls it the inability of the infantile ego to outgrow the protection of the father and mother who were the Hero's Threshold Guardians.

If the Hero refuses to advance into the adventure he will be faced with calamity. He must move forward and progress to the wider, unknown world.

The Approach: forces the Hero to cross the First Threshold into the unexplored and be met by violent enemies and the mysteriously seductive *Sirens of Desire*. These Threshold Guardians of the boundaries of the next stage of the journey are dangerous to deal with and are always a risk to the Hero. He must face the polarities of life and death, beauty and ugliness, good and evil – and all that binds him to Hope and Fear. He must actively perform deeds of defence and acquisition. If the Hero is competent and courageous, the dangers can be overcome.

The Ordeal: The Hero makes The Approach to the *Innermost Cave* and prepares for the *Supreme Ordeal*. He is afraid but that does not deter him.

Vogler calls it mythic, and the element of experiencing fear but overcoming it in order to survive is instinctual and buried in the human psyche. It is reflected in the initiation rituals of all cultures from indigenous peoples deep in the jungle to rituals of initiation into a street gang, a college fraternity, or a secret society. The urge to prove oneself worthy seems to transcend many cultures and demonstrates the human compulsion to belong – yet to be singled out from the herd.

Vogler's Hero encounters other archetypes on his way:

DESCENT: ACT 2 (A)

The Road of Trials: Vogler's Hero has moved into a darkly incomprehensible landscape and is forced into a succession of tests, ordeals and almost superhuman tasks to achieve his goal. But this is only the beginning and perilous adventures still lie ahead. It's dragon-slaying time, escape from the enemy.

Meeting the Goddess: The battles with all the ogres have been won and the Journey reaches its epiphany at the Hero's meeting with the Universal Mothering/Lover figure, a nourishing and protective presence, the incarnation of perfection. In the language of mythology the archetype Goddess/Woman represents the symbol of life – the totality of all that can be known until death. As lover, she is the door to sublime sensual adventure.

Winning the Boon of Love is the Hero's final test. There will be battles, defeats, conquests, moments of illumination, glimpses of the future, little failures and, finally, success. But it's not quite that simple. First there will be more barriers to pass until 'Boy gets girl and lives happily ever after' – metaphorically speaking. Vogler describes the Hero's progress, should he meet instead the *Woman as Temptress*. She can lead him away from his goal with temptations of the flesh.

Atonement with the Father for the sins of the flesh is required to bring the Hero back to sanctity. He can rely on the Wise Woman or Mother/protectress as Mentor to act as intermediary between himself and the Father. But he must have faith that the father will be merciful because there is also an ogre aspect to the *Father* of our childhood, akin to the Wrath of God. This could mean the Hero abandoning his own ego. Sean Maguire, the Robin Williams character in *Good Will Hunting* who guides Will Hunting's abilities to develop himself, combines a Father image with that of a Mentor and also Herald since he shows Will the way forward.

INITIATION: ACT 2 (B)

The Hero's Refusal to Return to his old way of life – when the world he has encountered offers him delights he never knew – can delay him. But other powers may arrive in the form of Rescue from Without, which will force his return via The *Magic Flight*.

When he has passed the last terrors of *Ignorance*, and free of all fear, he is beyond the grasp of change and has achieved the *Apotheosis* where human beings lose the restrictions of *Self*. He has reached the *Ultimate Boon*.

RETURN: ACT 3

The Hero's feet are now firmly on the *Road Back* and he is ready to face the final *Obstacle* he must overcome to return *Home*. The Hero must transcend the infantile self-obsessed attitudes of his previous life and discover a fuller and spiritually richer self. He has made a transition into a state of rebirth. In a sense he has been swallowed into the unknown. (The mythological symbol is the worldwide womb image of the *Belly of the Whale*.) Part of him has died; part of him is reborn. With the annihilation of his persona and initiation into a world wider than 'family' the Hero's Journey is turning inward in a life-centring, life-renewing act – he is 'born again' through self-revelation.

A stronger and wiser person, he brings back the *elixir* or *trophy* guaranteed to put his former world right (think of Jason and the Golden Fleece). It can be merely wisdom. What he does is necessary for the good of others as well as himself. He is ready to receive:

The Reward – Seizing the Sword. Don't take these images as realistic; the sword could be some particular kind of knowledge or Hitchcock's MacGuffin – or a real prize may be won; but that is not what is important. The prize will be the inner changes in the Hero. The Hero is the activator of his own path of life, and his journey of discovery and choices on the path create the story, during which he grows and learns.

Crossing the Return Threshold brings him back to the everyday world of his friends, family and former life – but he is not the same person who began the Journey. He has now become the righteous *Master of the Two Worlds*, secure in his understanding of Self, and has been given the *Freedom to Live*. The Hero is a more perfect man, a king among men, and will encounter no more obstacles.

The Hero's Journey.
(Mainstream Structure approx 120 minutes)

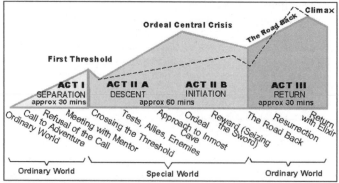

A composite diagram of the mythic Hero's Journey showing Major Dramatic
High Points in a story with a Central Crisis and (in dotted) a Delayed Crisis.
The Hero's Journey model contains twelve stages passing from Ordinary World
(Act I) via the First Threshold, through Special World (Acts II A & B) and
returning to Ordinary World (Act III) via the Road Back to the Climax.

The above graph incorporates elements of several of Vogler's diagrams of the Hero's Journey.

Echoes of this concept can be seen in such diverse films as *The Return of Martin Guerre* (1982) – although there is a duality in his identity, Spencer Tracy as John Macreedy, the one-armed stranger who comes to town in *Bad Day at Black Rock*, or Clint Eastwood in essentially the same role as the Preacher in *High Plains Drifter* – their purpose is to bring the town to their knees and make the community 'do the right thing'.

Many of the archetypes sited in Campbell's and Vogler's Mythic Structure are predictable and would be of minimal help today. Every protagonist in modern story-telling encounters helpers, obstacles, and challenges. The mainstream three-act format with its beginning, middle, and end, its antagonists, protagonists, and subplot characters is little different from Vogler's mythic structure because essentially, his is simply the same truth, given a new set of name tags. You do not have to understand the mythic structure to be aware of the basic disciplines of story-telling. Nor can a writer who wants any depth to his characters ignore what Jung described in terms of human motivations, emotions and desires. These ideas have always been the basis of good characterization, even if finding them is often instinctive.

Nothing is rigid in story-telling. Science has transformed the world of symbols. The gods no longer support the old ways and there is no hiding place for them from the telescope and test tube. The gods are dead, and modern man has forgotten the symbolism of the myths. The mysteries have lost much of their force.

For a writer, the important thing in studying Vogler and Campbell's archetypes is to decide what personality trait and purpose they serve in the dramatic structure of your own story-telling. In creating your story, what preparations can your hero make to defend himself against each crisis? And do the obstacles you put in his path progressively become more difficult to overcome? Is he physically entering the villain's lair or is it an emotional upheaval he must conquer?

If you read Jung and Freud you will probably learn much more about the human condition and how it applies to creating characters. But since 'Mythic' is today's Hollywood spin, you should be familiar with the concept. Perhaps it will help you make producers understand what writers have been trying to tell them all along!

CHAPTER 14 | ADAPTATIONS

The Novel

Certain subjects and types of stories are inherently not filmic – and that includes most novels. The novel is a form that descriptively dramatizes the inner conflicts of the protagonist(s), not necessarily in dialogue or in physical action. A novel can delve into a character's thoughts or weave through long detailed passages that take pages to communicate, say, the look of a bazaar in Marrakesh – which would take 15 seconds on the screen to absorb. The novelist can also digress on ideas unrelated to the narrative, such as the chapter 'The Whiteness of the Whale' – a meditation on human associations with the colour white – in Herman Melville's novel *Moby Dick* (1851).

The experience of watching a movie, while emotionally stimulating is, by contrast, generally non-intellectual. We can have a visceral reaction to seeing a particularly gory murder (such as in *Red Dragon*) or someone being catapulted out of an aeroplane, but it does not intrude on our analytical mind.

A novel can deal with a large cast. Only epic films can do that, even with computerization (such as in *Gladiator*). Some novels have too many subplots to encompass in a film. It might work for you in a structure like *Pulp Fiction* where you're weaving four separate stories (none of them sub-plots) together, but with a heavily multi-plotted story structure, some characters and plot lines may have to be eliminated for the screenplay. A novel's subplots work in film only if they mirror or counterpoint the main plot and do not wander off on a tangent.

A novel needs to translate thought into action in order to become a film.

Stepline the event structure. Begin by listing those parts of the story that can be behavioural, not philosophical.

Look for the strong through-line – the backbone of the story – and see which characters can work for you and which are unnecessary. You might have to *morph* several characters into one, eliminating or combining some threads of the story-line.

If you later meet the novelist, don't expect him to be delighted. He has put everything in there because he wanted it and he probably thinks you're a philistine for destroying his brainchild. If it's your own novel, be ruthless with yourself in translating it for the changed medium. The truer the novel or stage play is to its own form, the worse it will generally be as a movie. Don't stick to the original structure when it interferes with the visual story-telling. Remember, most of the audience won't have read the book or seen the play. They came to be entertained. Being 'true' to the book can be a disservice to the book – to the extent that people will judge it by your work – and a disaster to the film.

Adaptations From Novels

L.A Confidential: This 1997 Oscar-winning script was written by Curtis Hanson (who also directed) and Bryan Helgeland, from James Ellroy's complex book. This screenplay is considered a tour de force of adaptation, having honed the rambling novel into a tightly packaged thriller. The movie has been closely compared to *Chinatown* for its starkly stylized realism soaked in period authenticity. This is a tribute to the research of the novelist and the film's costume and set designers who created the visual style and ambience of the period.

The story out-noirs film noir with its focus on three cops who travel through a corpse-strewn land of sleaze. To succeed, all three protagonists have to commit morally questionable acts that often put them uncomfortably close to the villains, so although there are clear-cut heros, the dividing line between their acts and those of the villains are often blurred. Kim Basinger's Oscar-winning role of a Veronica Lake lookalike prostitute shines a light on the connection between reality and make-believe.

As an exercise, read the novel and then get the film out of the video shop to see how the adaptation was constructed. This entails you making a list of the scenes in each and comparing the story-line structure and the characters with the book. A lot of work? Yes, but a quick learning curve.

In *Harry Potter and the Philosopher's Stone* (2001) Steve Klovis's screenplay could not bring everything in J K Rowling's book to the screen. It concentrated on only the most memorable moments. The film left out two supporting characters – Peeves, a troublesome ghost, and Piers, a troublesome boy – and the film works without them.

Trainspotting (1995) was based on the bestselling novel by Irvine Welsh, and directed by Danny Boyle. The novel, a savage black comedy about four Edinburgh lads as they descend into drugs, petty crime and near oblivion in the drug culture, was considered nearly unfilmable but was brilliantly adapted for the screen by John Hodge. Ewan McGregor's horror excursion through a toilet bowl brilliantly illustrated the visual stretch that a film can give to a book.

The English Patient (1996) was based on Michael Ondaatje's novel, adapted and directed by Anthony Minghella's. This World War II romantic drama unfolds in two main time frames, jumping back and forth between past and present. The screenplay simplifies and alters many elements of the book but there are plenty remaining for a rich, complex story that offers hope after tragedy. Set in Tuscany, the nurse (Juliette Binoche) stays behind in an abandoned monastery to care for the burned, dying patient. The thief who quizzes the patient dredges up the patient's passionate memories of his lost romance, and so the flashback story and present story are really separate entities but totally entwined. Visually the film opens areas of the story sketchily suggested in the book and operates on a highly charged emotional level.

As an exercise, read the novel, and see what parts were expanded that were barely touched in the book, and what parts of the book were not developed in the film.

The Stage Play

If you don't know your medium, you shouldn't be writing in it. Film actors use their eyes and faces to express thought. Stage actors must use their bodies and voices and can replace the CLOSE-UP with a speech – which theatre audiences expect and are prepared to listen to. A stage actor's speech can even be delivered directly to the audience – Shakespeare is full of 'asides'. There are few occasions in film in which an actor breaks the invisible wall and talks directly to camera. Some screen actors – without the close-up to bring them into focus, can be physically stilted and awkward on stage. The great Anthony Hopkins, on stage in the London production of *M Butterfly* (1989), had no eye contact with his audience and his performance suffered for it. His marvellous gift is communication through his wonderfully expressive eyes.

The only tool for the writer or actor on stage to build tension and conflict, or wit and humour, is through dialogue. To become a film, a play needs to open up the action and the visuals and in a lot of cases, to tighten the dialogue. To widen the vistas of a play visually, find other places for the characters to inhabit.

Expand locations and settings – get them outdoors for some fresh air! Take them for a walk for goodness' sake! Find logical locations where these characters would exist when not being imprisoned behind the proscenium of a stage.

Adaptations From Stage Plays

Glengarry Glen Ross (1992), David Mamet's screenplay, based on his own play, is a drama about four real estate salesmen who sacrifice their principles for greed. Although Mamet didn't much expand his play from its 'office' stage setting, the fine writing, the stars and direction keep it brilliantly alive. This could have been claustrophobic in lesser hands, but it could have been even better if Mamet had opened up his stage play. Director James Foley kept his focus tightly on the brilliant all-star cast.

Mr Roberts (1955), one of the big hits of its day, was brilliantly adapted by Joshua Logan and Frank S Nugent from Logan's stage play written with Thomas Heggen, which in turn was adapted from Heggen's novel. Setting the film on a real battleship at sea gave it a perspective the play could not hope to achieve.

The Caine Mutiny (1954) was adapted from Herman Wouk's Pulitzer Prize-winning novel and his subsequent stage play, and also features a naval setting during World War II.

I think that the lengthy speeches worked better on the stage and make the film heavy and tiresome, and even the fabulous Bogart wasn't enough. Audiences don't go to the cinema to be lectured. Stanley Roberts, who wrote the screenplay, did not open it up enough and was too faithful to the original, perhaps because the book had won the Pulitzer Prize. A lesson to be learned.

The Importance of Being Earnest (2002) is certainly one of the best recent adaptations – the memorable 1952 version was really no more than a filmed record of a theatrical production and the 1992 American version with a black cast was a disservice to both cast and play. Writer/director Oliver Parker opened up this latest version in highly creative ways. Parker said, 'Wilde had such a radical mind, I wanted to capture some of the iconoclast, the wit, freshness and spontaneity of the writer.' [1] His main criteria for adapting the play was to translate the energy and appeal of 19th century wit for the 21st century. 'Oscar Wilde is never more profound than when he is at his lightest. How would he have written it today?' Parker was 'brave enough to reinvent it, setting the film some 10 years later than when the play was written in 1895 – to the first decade of the 20th century so that he could use elements of early jazz to instil it with contemporary energy. He researched the fact that the Prince of Wales and fashionable aristocrats of the period wore tattoos around this time. Without violating historical reality, Gwendolen has 'Earnest' tattooed on her backside and Jack has 'Gwendolen' tattooed on his.

The opening scenes set in the bustling streets of London instil the film with vitality from the start. Seeing much of the action in Cecily's imagination gives it the fantasy resonance of *A Midsummer Night's Dream*. When they have tea, it's in the garden. A stiffly theatrical drawing room scene now has the two 'Earnests' arguing their way through a field of bluebells, gathering flowers for their ladies. This is an excellent adaptation of a period stage classic.

Casablanca (1942) was based on a play, *Everybody Goes to Rick's*, by Murray Burnett and Joan Allison. The screenplay by Julius J and Philip G Epstein and Howard Koch wasn't finished when they started shooting, and the casting was last-minute, but if ever a stage play translated well to the screen, this was it. As with many stage plays, it never got opened up visually, except for the last scene at the airport. But the director Michael Curtiz kept his camera focused tightly on his electric stars, and entrances and exits of characters kept the pace rolling along to become an all-time masterpiece of film-making.

Other well-made adaptations include *The Madness of King George* (1995, adapted by Alan Bennett from his own play *The Madness of George III*) and *Dangerous Liaisons*, 1988 (adapted by Christopher Hampton from his own play *Les Liaisons Dangereuses* and Choderlos de Laclos's novel).

Historical And Biographical Material

To dramatize real-life historical events or a person's entire life for film, think of your subject matter as fiction. Look for the most dramatic moments and focus on those. You cannot possibly tell a whole life or the entire French Revolution in the space of 90 minutes or two hours. However, in telling a 'present time' story, you can judiciously flashback to certain events in your 'back story' to reveal the salient points the audience needs to know.

George Clooney's first effort at directing was a biopic, based on the 'unauthorized autobiography' of Chuck Barris, *Confessions of a Dangerous Mind* (2002). 'It's tricky to make a character who goes around killing people as a hitman for the CIA empathetic to the audience', Clooney pointed out[2]. His answer was the right one. He and writer Charles Kaufman went for the essence of the character, and Sam Rockwell played that, rather than giving an impersonation of Barris.

A writer with the proper research behind him can use his artistic imagination to interpret social history, humanize the cold, hard facts, bring the characters into perspective giving us a deeper understanding of their actions. Only drama or the novel can bring to life the people and their relationships through scene-playing and dialogue. Dramatization can illuminate the period of history and the people in it as no straight biography can (unfortunately, it's hard to sell historical novels today).

Research can supply you with ammunition. What games did your subject play? How did the women apply makeup? What was different about how and what they ate? Did the clothes they wore make them walk, sit and stand differently? (Actors concentrate on physical details like this.) Were their manners different from ours? How did they speak? How can you 'translate' their dialogue so that today's audience can understand them and yet not lose the sense of period? Some words have changed meaning today. Find a way of saying what must be said, choosing words that are understandable but also fairly correct for period.

I have selected several examples because they illustrate a variety of ways of approaching the problem.

Frida (2002) is the biographical tale of two Mexican painters, one of whom became internationally famous. The consequences of Frida Kahlo's (Salma Hayek) horrible, crippling accident and her tempestuous relationship and marriage to Diego Rivera (Alfred Molina) are the forces driving the film. Her affair with Trotsky is the weakest link. The screenplay was written by actor Edward Norton and Rodrigo Garcia. It is not Norton's first venture into scriptwriting and he shows a firm grasp of handling the two complex lives. The script started with a flash forward and was poignant, inventive, succinct and exceptionally focused. Dotted with historical figures it is a good example of handling biographical material in a dramatic way. Directed by Julie Taymor, it had high energy, pace and remarkably beautiful visuals.

Riding in Cars with Boys (2001) was based on Beverly D'Onofrio's autobiography (with literary licence) about her trials as a single mother, with a screenplay by Morgan Upton Ward (who was also an executive producer). The film focuses on the frustrations of a bright young woman about to go to college who gets pregnant, destroying her life as she knew it. Enough to put any young girl on the pill.

Erin Brockovich (2000) used Susannah Grant's tight, penetrating script about a real-life case of criminal corruption by a utility company gave Steven Soderbergh a chance to add an Oscar to Julia Roberts' credits with the type of biographical story that concentrates on *only one period of a real person's life.*

In *Catch Me if you Can* (2002), Jeff Nathanson's script was based on Frank W. Abagnale Jr's autobiographical memoirs (written with Stan Redding). One of the all-time great conmen, he started his career in the 1960s at the age of 17 when he ran away from home. In a satellite-link interview with BAFTA members,[3] Steven Spielberg pointed out that in doing a biopic, you must use your creative imagination to keep the focus on your characters. 'Frank was disenfranchised from his family when they divorced and he ran away,' Spielberg said. Frank had been very close to his father and fantasized meetings with him. To keep the tension of that relationship alive, Spielberg and Nathanson added scenes in which Frank actually meets his father for brief interludes in which he seeks fatherly approval (it's the *Atonement with the Father* right out of Campbell's mythic structure – see chapter 13). These scenes deliberately have a sense of unreality about them. They could be real, and then again, maybe not. When Abagnale is finally caught, he demands to see his father, only to learn that he is dead. For all that, the story has an upbeat ending and in true mythic mode, he returns to his world (and jail) a changed person.

For all adaptations, from whatever medium, go back to the three basic arenas of conflict – inner, personal, and society and environment – and devise ways to visualize these. Make a stepline of the event structure, the key turning points of the book, play, or other source material. Keeping the spirit and meaning of the original, your task is one of reinvention and developing the more visual aspects of the story.

Chapter 15 | GENRES

What is meant by genre? Theme is not genre – the theme of a story is the central concept, its one clear, cohesive, unified controlling idea that makes the story worth telling. The type (genre) of your story is defined partly by its subject matter, but more by the actions of your characters and the way you write their parts – for instance, if your setting is in wartime, the genre will probably be drama or thriller, but with a different focus and approach to the dialogue, it could also be a historical romance. Once you decide on your genre it will bind you to the creative discipline of forms and conventions that are particular to that genre.

In Michael Tolkin's 1992 BAFTA acceptance speech on receiving the Best Adapted Screenplay Award for *The Player*, he said: 'The problem with the studios is that they are drawn to genre, because genre can be easily broken down into components. And these genres are easy to pitch and are attractive to actors.'

Tolkin wrote both the novel and screenplay of *The Player*. The opening sequence of that film, an elaborate homage to the long takes of Hitchcock's *Rope*, comes to rest in a story editor's office on the lot of a major Hollywood studio. The scene sends up *genre* and *the pitch* and makes the point that if the writer has a star attached, he has clout.

EXEC.
OK, Give me your pitch.
WRITER
Does political scare you?
EXEC.
Political doesn't scare me.
Radical political scares me.
Political political scares me.
WRITER
This is politely politically radical. But it's a…
EXEC.
Is it funny?
WRITER
It's funny.
EXEC.
It's a funny, political thing.

WRITER
It's a thriller, too.
EXEC.
It's a thriller.
WRITER
It's all at once.
EXEC.
And what's the story?
WRITER
Well, I want Bruce Willis and I think I can get him. It's a story about a bad guy Senator.
EXEC.
Sort of a cynical, political, thriller, comedy.
WRITER
Yeah, but it's got a heart. He has an accident and becomes clairvoyant.
EXEC.
So it's kind of a psychic, cynical, political, thriller, comedy.
WRITER
Yeah. Sort of like Ghost meets Manchurian Candidate.

Aside from sending up the Hollywood focus on genre, this scene sets out who the characters are, who's got the power, and includes the initial turning point in the form of the postcard with a death threat that the executive's secretary brings in to him. In the first nine ironic minutes (including the credits) the audience knows exactly what kind of man the executive is, the world he inhabits, what crisis is facing him – and you're off on your story. This is extremely tight screenwriting.

Genres have conventions, but the conventions of genres continue to evolve and change with the problems and changes in society. Some are rigid, others more flexible. The genre limits what is possible in the story-line. It creates parameters. This should stimulate the creative process, not deter it. You are still telling stories about people. If they are in outer space, we may call it sci-fi, but it's still about relationships, human or otherwise.

Mixing genres can often cause confusion, so it's important that you identify your genre early on and always write in one in which you're comfortable. Genres are there to be reworked and transformed by the writer, depending upon his skill and originality, but there are genres that don't always mix successfully. Putting a special effects sci-fi ending to an otherwise realistic story – as in Tarantino's gorefest script *From Dusk Till Dawn* (1996, from a novel by Robert Kurtzman), which was described as 'Splatter-Action Horror Genre' – is an uneasy blend. The story is about two crooks who take a family hostage and end up for no logical reason under attack from bloodthirsty vampires, Hells Angels and the 'Undead', who also happen to be strippers. Why? Setting up the parameters in the beginning so that this might eventually be believable would not have been impossible. As it is, you don't 'suspend disbelief', and for a scriptwriter, that's a problem.

Drama, romance, fantasy, sci-fi, action adventure, crime, comedy, black comedy, romantic comedy, western, documentary, and so on – a genre itself can become a cliché (which is after all, only a truth repeating itself too often), but it's increasingly difficult to avoid them. How do you reverse genre clichés? By altering the conventions and adding something new. However, your story must be justified – you can break the old conventions in order to do something more important, to achieve a certain end result, but you must know why you are doing it. You can bend the genres to suit your mood but if you extend the boundaries too far, distributors tend to think it no longer fits the genre and will have trouble knowing how to market the film. There is a danger here, so walk a fine line. When pitching a story to a producer, a subdivision will help set it in his mind.

Below are some genres and subdivisions:

Comedy

There are so many types of comedy, but you would be safe in calling the following just 'Comedy':

His Girl Friday (1939) and *Some Like it Hot* (1959) are fast and witty with all the stops pulled out.

The Producers (1968). Mel Brooks wrote and directed this classic showbiz tale about a down-at-heel Broadway producer (played by Zero Mostel) and his neurotic accountant

(Gene Wilder) who try to produce a play that will guarantee them a box-office failure and a financial coup. They come up with *Springtime For Hitler,* but it ends up being a huge success and ruins them.

A Fish Called Wanda (1988). A zany British comedy (which included two American actors to get good US distribution), John Cleese's screenplay from a story by him and Charles Crichton (who also directed). Big BO internationally.

O Brother, Where Art Thou (2000), takes a mythic journey based on Homer's *The Odyssey* in the Coen brothers' deft comic tradition, with George Clooney as a modern day Ulysses, updated to a jailbird on the run. You could also classify this one in the next division:

Comedy/Fantasy

The Nutty Professor (1963). Triumphantly written, directed by and starring Jerry Lewis, this was remade for Eddie Murphy in 1996 with four writers reworking Lewis's script.

Michael (1996). Heavy-handed tale of an angel come to earth. Great idea that somehow didn't come off – no fault of John Travolta's who handled the humour and his wings quite well. Screenplay by Nora and Delia Ephron with Pete Dexter and Jim Quinlin, from their story.

The Mask (1994). This stunningly imaginative mix of computer animation and Jim Carrey's rubber-faced antics was based on a cartoon character. But the story offered two important elements: the special powers of the Mask were totally justified from the start and there was a nice character twist on the good girl/bad girl image. This film would also fit into the next category.

Sci-Fi/Action/Adventure/Comedy

The Fifth Element (1997). Luc Besson directed and co-wrote with Robert Mark Kamen this slick satire of futuristic thrills. The script, Bruce Willis and Gary Oldman make the 23rd century believable. It is a close runner to *Blade Runner.*

Comic Strip/Fantasy/Sci-Fi

This genre (not animated) has been the mammoth hit of the 1990s and into the new millennium. As the computer graphics get better, the genre will be even more successful. Mostly, the stories are allegories of good and evil. Steven Spielberg calls sci-fi 'the sugar that makes the medicine go down ... people will listen to you (because) it stimulates the imagination before it hits the intellect.'[3]

Judge Dredd (1995) brought the cartoon character to life as portrayed by Sylvester Stallone.

Men In Black (1997) is one of the most successful of the current wave of bringing comic-strip characters (as created by Lowell Cunningham) to the big screen. Ed Solomon's script has hip, dry humour. Good actors, Tommy Lee Jones and Will Smith, and 100 digital effects artists and another 50 for alien make-up effects made this and the sequel *Men in Black II* (2002) smash hits.

Spiderman (2002). 'With great power comes great responsibility' – so says Peter Parker's uncle and it becomes the ethos of the character. David Koepp brought this fantasy comic strip to believability because he created a back story to justify his character's situation (a genetically engineered spider's bite that turned Peter into something more than a spider and less than a man).

Then we have the hugely successful franchises of *Superman* (1978, through to Superman II, III, and IV in 1987), which really began the modern series of comic-book adaptations, and *Batman* (1989, 1992, 1995, and 1997), as well as *Dick Tracy* (1990), a colourful flop, and *Punk Girl* (2000).

Cartoon/Animated/Comedy

We see physical pain, but it doesn't really hurt. From *Tom and Jerry* and *Mickey Mouse* we have graduated to *The Grinch* (2000), *Monsters, Inc.* (2002), *Antz* and *A Bug's Life* (both 1998), and all the many similar animated films – perhaps overlaps with the next category:

Animation/Adventure/Comedy

These pictures take a lot of time to make. *Toy Story* (1995), *Toy Story 2* (1999), and *Shrek* (2001) all use computer-generated animation, while *Chicken Run* (2000) used the claymation technique (stop-frame camerawork and plasticine models) and came from the successful Aardman Animation studio in Britain. It was four years in the making, with an excellent script by Jack Rosenthal and Kerry Kirkpatrick.

Computer Game/Comedy

Teenage Mutant Ninja Turtles (1990), and *Lara Croft: Tomb Raider* (2001) both came from computer games. These interactive computer games can take up to five years to make, and in a recent BAFTA seminar, the games makers said they are 'desperate for writers who understand the medium'. Although there are not many films in this genre yet, as computer games become more sophisticated, and action films such as the *Matrix* series draw ever more heavily on the visual vocabulary of computer games, there are sure to be increasing numbers in the future.

Supernatural/Comedy

Ghostbusters (1984). Dan Aykroyd and Harold Ramis parlayed this into a slightly less successful *Ghostbusters II* in 1989.

Detective/Fantasy/Comedy

Who Framed Roger Rabbit (1988). Screenplay by Jeffrey Price and Roger S. Seaman (adapted from a novel by Gary K Wolf). This mixed animated characters with live ones. This had been done before (for instance, in a dance sequence with Gene Kelly, and in the 1971 film *Bedknobs and Broomsticks*), but this was the first time it had been used in a complete film, with the protagonist (played by Bob Hoskins) interacting with the animated characters throughout.

Comedy/Social Drama

Nurse Betty (2000). The parameters of believability are made elastic and although they don't snap, ask yourself, would the soap actor really believe her? The hole in believability is covered by making the soap actor think she's 'acting' to get on his show

10 (1979). Blake Edwards' film worked mainly because of Dudley Moore's performance.

The Full Monty (1997). One of the hits of that year, it was written by Simon Beaufoy (although two New Zealand writers claimed the story was purloined from their produced stage play, and brought a lawsuit). A desperate, out-of-work steel worker forms a club act with six other unemployed workers, designed to out-raunch the Chippendales. This sprightly tale gains depth and meaning by its poignant look at the emotional ineptness of these men trying to preserve their self-respect in a post-industrial wilderness. The desperation underlying their lives and relationships with their women is allowed to remain low key, so the story doesn't wallow in bathos. Nor does the script sink into farce. But the subtle vista of the men in the dole queue, haunted by their rehearsal of dance routines, slyly beginning to gyrate to a radio tune was unforgettable. I *hope* it was in the script.

Black Comedy

The King of Comedy (1983). Scorsese's cringe-making satire on showbiz (De Niro and Jerry Lewis), now a cult film, it was a BO failure at the time.

Black Comedy/Fantasy

Death Becomes Her (1992). Martin Donovan and David Koepp's cleverly acerbic script, phenomenal special effects for its day made this dark comedy a real dark horse. Open ended, but the short, sharp resolution scene offers a hint at the future as various parts of the women fall off and tumble down the stairs.

Oddball/Comedy Drama

The Royal Tenenbaums (2001). Wes Anderson (also director) and Owen Wilson created an extraordinary tale of an outlandish family in New York with the empathetic but rogueish Gene Hackman as the penniless father trying to rejoin his dysfunctional clan. What makes a story like this work is keeping everything and everybody believable within the eccentric parameters. A must-see.

Action/Comedy

True Lies (1994). The action is imaginative and the plot is funny. Logline: *A James Bond style secret agent saves the world in time for*

dinner with his unsuspecting wife and kids. Then (or we'd have no story) something goes wrong. James Cameron's script was based on a screenplay by three other writers. Lots of work went into it. But it's all there on the screen.

Comedy/Thriller/Road Movie

Midnight Run (1988). George Gallo's brilliant screenplay is a classic. One to study for scene construction – and who has the power (see chapter 5).

Thelma and Louise (1991). Oscar-winning script by Callie Khourie, this set a trend for a host of road movies. The ending is unexpected and created one of those images (like *Bonnie and Clyde*) that stick in the collective consciousness to become mythic.

Comedy/Mystery

The Pink Panther (1964). Inspector Clouseau's introduction to the world of gentle anarchy. However, this is not always a successful genre.

The Cat and the Canary had an uneven sad but persistent history. John Willard's play was adapted three times as the definitive haunted house film. First, in 1927 in Germany, then remade in 1939 with Bob Hope. Although critics applauded Hope's performance and it won Paulette Goddard a contract at Paramount, the film was not a huge success at the box office and story was, and was unsuccessfully remade in 1979. For some reason Willard's play was revived a few years ago, and it also flopped as a stage production. Maybe by now somebody's got the message.

Crime/Comedy

This genre does much better with the use of satire. *Analyze This* (1999) and *Analyze That* (2003). Billy Crystal and Robert De Niro could do no wrong with dialogue that fairly sings. Director Harold Ramis worked closely with Peter Tolan and Kenneth Lonergan adapting their story to create this screenplay.

Thriller/Black Comedy

Pulp Fiction (1994). Writer/director Quentin Tarantino's midstream-structured low-life world of greed and self indulgence trivializes violent crime with detachment. But it is a brilliant and intricately constructed film (see chapter 14).

Tragi-Comedy

This category seems to be amply represented in European films: *Life is Beautiful* (1997), writer/director Roberto Benigni's prize-winning film about the concentration camps of World War II. (see 'Comic Relief' in chapter 4).

Kolya (1996). A warm tale of the relationship between an old Czech man and a young Russian boy. Made by a father and son, directed by Jan Sverák, written by and starring Zdenek Sverák.

Musicals

The old-fashioned musicals of the kind that were most popular in the 1940s were long gone until *Chicago* (2002) revived them. It may have started a trend.

Musical/Comedy/Drama

Everyone Says I Love You (1996). Woody Allen examines a broad spectrum of romantic entanglements as the characters fall in and out of love and sing about it.

Love's Labour's Lost (1999). Kenneth Branagh's little-appreciated musical update adapted from Shakespeare's play – and you can't fault the original writer.

Musical/Biography

Evita (1996). Alan Parker (who also directed) and Oliver Stone unsuccessfully adapted the highly successful stage musical with not much concern for clarity. Since they were dealing with a historical subject, it would have helped to be more lucid. Madonna was much better than the critics liked to admit.

The World Of Romance

Screen romances are no longer just between a man and a woman. Gay and lesbian love stories have entered the feature film and TV market. Shakespeare said in *A Midsummer Night's Dream*: 'The course of true love never did run smooth'. Although this is not totally true, as far as story-telling goes, without it there'd be no conflict and no story. Whether the lovers overcome obstacles or not, distinguishes a happy ending from a tragic one.

Romantic Drama (Tragic Ending)

UK filmmakers tend to go for the downbeat negative endings. Blame it on Shakespeare's *Romeo and Juliet*. The weepie with the lovers dying or at least parted in the end.

Brief Encounter (1945). Noel Coward's one-act play *Still Life* adapted for the screen by Coward with David Lean (who also directed) and Anthony Havelock-Allan is considered one of the finest of British films. Two ordinary people accidentally fall in love but ultimately don't do anything about it in the morally restrictive 1940s. Today, they'd probably both leave their mates and run off – and maybe come to a sticky end. Is this a reflection on British society? Here are two American classics in the tragic genre.

Love Story (1970). Written by Eric Segal from his own novelette, this is pure classic romance. Two students marry, she dies. British film critic Alexander Walker, who was not always right, called it '*Camille* with bullshit ... bypassed the brain and assaulted the tear ducts'. American and British audiences paid no attention to such opinions and it was a huge success.

The Way We Were (1973). Arthur Laurents adapted this from his own novel, opening up all the right bits. The girl doesn't get the boy, so this romantic drama is a weepie with a memorable title song sung by Barbra Streisand.

There is no subject that is beyond the writer's reach. It is all in the way you handle it.

Y Tu Mamá También [And Your Mother Too] (2001) – a Mexican film which won its writers, Alfonso and Carlos Cuarón, Best Screenplay at the Venice Film Festival, is a tale of innocence, discovery, sexual awakening and death. Two young lads invite a beautiful and mysterious older cousin Luisa to go to a holiday beach. Earlier, Luisa has been to see a doctor and the audience has the impression that she may be pregnant. Nevertheless, she leaves her unfaithful husband, telling him she will never see him again, and goes with the two boys. To their surprise, she sleeps with each of them. Then she sends them off as men, not boys, leaving her on the beach with a fisherman's family. Then we discover that from the beginning she knew that she was dying of cancer.

It is only at that point that the story layers unfold. We realize why Luisa told her husband she wouldn't see him again and went off with the boys for a last taste of life. The audience will accept the emotional experience of a sad ending to a light comedy drama because the humour is not forced. The film has a lot of warmth, and comes out of believable human relationships, not jokes.

Romantic Comedy (Happy Ending)

Because the world is in chaos, audiences want reassurance that things could turn out all right. Forgetting their problems in a cinema, they can find a thimbleful of hope. Generally, preview audiences in the United States have a negative reaction to downbeat endings (and therefore, so do producers). American romantic comedies almost always have happy endings, therefore.

It Happened One Night (1934). One of the early great romantic comedies. Robert Riskin's script based on a story by Samuel Hopkins Adams, was meant for a little picture but Frank Capra and the stars made it big.

Bridget Jones's Diary (2001). A secretary seeks love choosing between the cad and Mr Nice Guy. Adapted from a hit book, the film was a bigger hit. *Sleepless In Seattle* (1993). Nora Ephron again. This unusual story structure kept the two lovers apart until the very end of the film. Not all the reviewers thought this worked. It was illuminated by a brilliant performance by Tom Hanks. The story recalls Leo McCarey's *Love Affair* (1939, screenplay by Delmer Daves and Donald Ogden Stewart from a story by McCarey, Daves, and Mildred Cram) in which the lovers, Charles Boyer and Irene Dunne, plan to meet at the top of the Empire State building and are kept apart by a cruel twist of fate – until the end. In 1957 Leo McCarey successfully remade it with Deborah Kerr and Cary Grant under the title *An Affair to Remember*.

Annie Hall (1977). Written by idiosyncratic Woody Allen (who also directed and starred) and Marshall Brickman. Allen's neurotic New Yorker meets Diana Keaton's kooky Midwesterner and earned the writers one of the four Oscars (including Best Film).

Romantic Comedy/Drama

The Apartment (1960). Billy Wilder's satirical view of office life in New York (he often wrote with I.A.L. Diamond) and the poor soul (Jack Lemmon) who loans his apartment to his boss for his assignations, could be called Comedy/Drama but which ever category you put it in, it's an Oscar-winning classic.

One Fine Day (1996). Terrel Seltzer and Ellen Simon's original screenplay echoed the romantic comedies of the 1940s and 1950s – updated for the cellular age. Romantic leads Michelle Pfeiffer and George Clooney couldn't save a good script thanks to lacklustre direction by Michael Hoffman, who is no Billy Wilder.

Chocolat (2000). Adapted from the novel by Joanne Harris, screenplay by Robert Nelson Jacobs, directed by Lasse Hallström. Into the stifling provincial life of a small French village in the 1960s comes Juliette Binoche and hooks the local women on her chocolate shop and philosophy, flaunting the rules of the disapproving Mayor. A riverboat gypsy (Johnny Depp) introduces romance. A BO winner proving the world is still ready for a little light romance.

Drama

This category covers a multitude of the seven deadly sins.

Glengarry Glen Ross (1992). David Mamet's screenplay (discussed in chapter 14).

Wild At Heart (1990). David Lynch wrote and directed this film from a novel by Barry Gifford. It traces the surreal flight of Nicolas Cage) and his girlfriend Lula (Laura Dern), who are on the run. Not much plot but lots of fireworks.

Crash (1996). Sometimes called David Cronenberg's daring masterpiece (not to be confused with the 1977 horror film of the same name), and based on J G Ballard's cult novel, this is an adult look at the hi-tech future of sexuality with the need for stimulation fulfilled by car crashes. Not for the faint hearted.

Historical-Romantic Drama

Gone With the Wind (1939). The all-time most popular Hollywood movie adapted from Margaret Mitchell's massive tome. David O Selznick had a raft of directors, and of writers working on the screenplay, of whom Sidney Howard got the credit. Ben Hecht, Jo Swerling, and Oliver HP Garrett, (among 13 other top writers of their day) didn't. In the end, Selznick was said to have written a great deal of it himself.

Also Cleopatra (1963), The Last of the Mohicans (1992), Shakespeare in Love (1998), Doctor Zhivago (1965), and many more. As you can tell from this list, films in this genre are frequently epic in scope, so this is an expensive genre for a beginning screenwriter to indulge in.

Fantasy Drama

Naked Lunch (1991). David Cronenberg adapted and directed the notorious cult semi-autobiographical novel by William S Burroughs, an explosive paranoiac exploration of the 'power corrupts' philosophy – translated into drugs and sexual abuse.

Being There (1979). Screenplay by Jerzy Kosinski from his novel. Peter Sellers plays the gardener, a minimalist character whose mental disability insulates him from the influences and effects of those around him, but who almost becomes President. He walks on water at the end which destroys the story's own parameters and propels it into fantasy.

Social Drama

Although now generally the provenance of TV movies many fine films come from this genre.

Unhook the Stars (1997). Gena Rowlands is directed by her son Nick Cassavetes. A middle-class suburban widow feels a lack in her life and cuts all ties from her children. She embarks on an uncertain destiny. Open-ended because her journey is just beginning.

Playing by Heart (1998). Writer/Director Willard Carroll's tale of three couples (Sean Connery, Gena Rowlands, Angelina Jolie, and others) who separately grapple with their problems – all ingeniously coming together at the end with a twist. A neatly woven midstream structure.

The Doctor and Regarding Henry (see chapter 10) are both social drama.

Romance/Drama/Thriller

Sunset Boulevard (1950). One of the truly noteworthy classics – and all about the Hollywood of its day. The great Billy Wilder directed and co-wrote with Charles Brackett and D M Marshman Jr. William Holden as the luckless script hack is found dead in the pool at the opening. The entire film is told is flashback with Holden's voiceover to elucidate the action.

Thrillers

A wide genre.

Rashomon (1950). Akira Kurosawa's masterpiece, set in 11th century Japan. Four witnesses to a rape and death offer different interpretations of the same events. It is not about truth but about human fallibility, dishonesty, and selfishness. This weird and wonderful thriller is a landmark of film history.

Play Misty For Me (1971). Clint Eastwood (also the director) has a one-night-stand with a deranged fan (Jessica Walter) that leads to sheer terror as she becomes a stalker – a forerunner of the psychotic love interest of Fatal Attraction. Dean Riesner and Jo Heims scripted it from Heims's story.

Fatal Attraction (1987). In the decade after Eastwood's film this story echoed the theme of the jealous 'female from Hell'. Director Adrian Lyne did justice to James Deardon's screenplay which raised the hair on the back of your neck and killed any taste for rabbit stew. This was the third highest grosser of the year.

Action/Thriller

What matters is keeping the audience guessing and worried. They know the hero will survive – but how? What are the obstacles? How will he overcome them? Disaster and conspiracy are good themes. Sometimes these stories develop in more than three acts because of the many peaks of the action structure. From the end of the act two crisis, action must fill the third act until all climactic action resolves. This can become monotonous and ordinary – even the wrong kind of funny – if the story does not follow a second strand and the pace of the action does not accelerate and involve the protagonist in heavy decision making. This popular genre requires no deep characterisation – merely pace and surprise. It must crack along relentlessly.

Clear and Present Danger (1994). Harrison Ford had another smash hit with this, a formula mainstream structure with a multi-track story-line of some substance. The themes are political with a covert war on a drug king. Tom Clancy wrote the book while Donald Stewart, Steven Zaillian, and John Milius worked on the screenplay; top writers all. Philip Noyce directed.

The Fugitive (1993), was based on the highly successful TV series that ran for 120 episodes in 1963–67. Writers Jeb Stuart and David Twohy did not cling to the TV plots and director Andrew Davis created some spectacular visuals with the train crash and Harrison Ford's dive into the dam. Tommy Lee Jones's character was relentless.

Under Siege (1992). Another Andrew Davis film with highjacker Tommy Lee Jones stealing the picture as well as a US battleship, but having to face the cook, Stephen Seagal, who is as wooden as his stirring spoon. To keep up the incredible pace the editing rarely holds on a shot more than four beats. There are unexplained gaps in logic, as when the villain lingers with a pistol long enough for the hero to escape. The original screenplay by J F Lawton lacks motivations – but it did well at the box office.

Under Suspicion (1991). This genre is heavily dependent on the actor. Liam Neeson was neither hard-boiled nor tough enough for an action detective, and the audience laughed at the ending. Clint Eastwood, Arnie Schwarzenegger, Bruce Willis (who made *Die Hard*, one of the best-ever action thrillers), Sylvester Stallone, and Mel Gibson are the masters of this genre. The leading actor in Action films of the moment, Harrison Ford, calls himself 'a pragmatist with perfectionist leanings'. This is the type of hero you will be writing for in this genre.

Heroic Bloodshed Drama

John Woo's gangster melodrama, *Hard Target* (1993), was his Hollywood début, though he approached eight producers before he could get it made. He creates balletic violence and can have 30 corpses on the floor in two minutes, so reality is not an option. The killer is always hard boiled, and the good guys hope for a better tomorrow. This is really not the writer's provenance. All the writer can do is set up a series of action sequences, which, hopefully, offer something new.

Psychological/Thriller

Basic Instinct (1992). Written by Joe Eszterhas and directed by Paul Verhoeven, the open end leaves the audience unsure if she is the killer.

Jacob's Ladder (1990), written by Bruce Joel Rubin and directed by Adrian Lyne, is discussed in 'The Writer's Working Method' in chapter 4.

Film Noir

These are characterized by their focus on the dark side of their characters' personalities, motivated by greed and revenge, with plenty of double crossing.

Build My Gallows High (1947; released in the United States as *Out of the Past*). Daniel Mainwaring (writing as Geoffrey Homes) broke the rules about having a flashback within a flashback – but it worked. Robert Mitchum as the hard-edged ex-private eye who finds that his past has caught up with him. Brilliant 1940s filmmaking, it was remade in 1984 as *Against All Odds* – not as good as the original.

Double Indemnity (1944). Another classic Billy Wilder. He co-wrote the script with Raymond Chandler, based on a short story by James M Cain. Barbara Stanwyck seduces Fred MacMurray into killing for her. A much-used theme since.

The Big Sleep (1946). Writers William Faulkner, Jules Furthman and Leigh Brackett turned Raymond Chandler's Philip Marlowe into the perfect vehicle for Bogart and Bacall. It's still better than the 1978 remake, although Robert Mitchum was excellent.

Noir Thriller/Political Satire

The Manchurian Candidate (1962). Writer George Axlerod and director John Frankenheimer gave us the most sophisticated political satire ever to come out of Hollywood, starring Laurence Harvey. One critic said that 'the movie went from failure to classic without passing through success'.

Disaster

Your movie may be *about* a disaster but you don't want it to be a disaster.

San Francisco (1936), gave us an earthquake, then *Volcano* (1997), *Volcano – Fire on the Mountain* (1997), and *Dante's Peak* (1997) brought three eruptions in the same year. But the 1970s were the great decade of the disaster movie, kicking off with *Airport* (1970). *The Poseidon Adventure* (1972) was a calamity at sea but not at the box office. *Earthquake* (1974) made good business out of destroying Los Angeles, but *Meteor* (1979) did less well in nearly destroying the Earth. On a smaller scale, *Hotel* (1967) engulfed us in flames but its follow-up, *The Towering Inferno* (1974), was perhaps the most famous fire in a big hotel – Irwin Allen based his film on two books and got three Oscars. Disasters can be a great success.

Murder Mystery

Whodunits is a genre much used for TV as well as films. It may be fluff, but if you're writing one, treat it as a masterpiece. Flashback is often used in the mystery genre to keep the pace moving forward while letting us know the back story.

Murder on the Orient Express (1974). Paul Dehn's screenplay from Agatha Christie at her best, with Hercule Poirot at his most flamboyant (played by Albert Finney, who was nominated for an Oscar). The perfect classic murder mystery, with the 'dénouement' scene a must. Unfortunately, many other inferior versions exist.

Suspense

This is the common catch-all term for a group of genres. As the protagonist learns something, the audience learns it too. How will it turn out? The film generates empathy through the audience's curiosity and concern. It includes:

Suspense/Thriller

Dead Calm (1989). Terry Hayes's taut script from the novel by Charles Williams never lets up the pace for one second. Nicole Kidman and Australian director Phillip Noyce made their names in this first-class Hitchcockian panic-making thriller on the high seas. This is a lesson on how to keep the audience reaching for their life belts.

Crime Thriller

The Usual Suspects (1995). Kevin Spacey appears to be an ineffectual hood. The audience thinks the wrong man is the protagonist (see 'The Writer's Working Method' in chapter 4).

Reservoir Dogs (1991). Writer/director Quentin Tarantino's stylishly lurid melange of crime caper and homoerotica distils the essence of evil in an unrelentingly abrasive and violent blood bath. It was a runaway hit, much to Tarantino's surprise, and set a slew of copy-cat filmmakers on his trail.

Supernatural/Drama

The Innocents (1961). Adapted from Henry James's *The Turn of the Screw* by William Archibald, Truman Capote and John Mortimer, Jack Clayton directed. Beautifully photographed in black and white one wonders if it would have been so chilling in colour. As it stands, it's terrifying.

The Sixth Sense (1999). Writer/director M Night Shyamalan has created a classic ghost story about the little boy who sees dead people and the psychologist (Bruce Willis) who tries to help him. The twist ending was echoed in *The Others* (2002), in which Nicole Kidman finds out that what she's breathing isn't oxygen.

Gothic Horror/Fantasy

Sleepy Hollow (1999), adapted from Washington Irving's *The Legend of Sleepy Hollow*, screenplay by Andrew Kevin Walker and Kevin Yagher, has been described as 'The Ultimate Tim Burton Movie'.

Biographical And Historical Material

This is a category in which for a writer, *focus* is essential. How much of a person's life do you tell? Is it a 'warts and all' exposé? Or is it a whitewash? The fiction writer of novels is free to invent his characters and their choices. He can choose the beginning and middle and where to end his story. The biographer, whether in book form or film, must stick to the facts. But that has nothing to do with the way you tell your story. (See chapter 14.)

Historical/Thriller

K19: The Widowmaker (2002), based on a true incident during the 1961 trial run of the USSR's first nuclear ballistic submarine, K-19. The sub's reactor failed; which could have lead to a nuclear war. At the BAFTA preview and Q & A session with the two stars and producer/director Kathryn Bigelow, the latter, a director with a good track record (*Strange Days, Point Break, Near Dark, Blue Steel, The Weight of Water*), told how she came upon the story watching a National Geographic documentary developed from previously classified material (no-one mentioned the writer's name, Christopher Kyle). She took five years trying to interest anyone in making a film seen from the Russian point of view. One producer asked her, 'There are no Americans, so who are the good guys?'

It looked like the end, then news events did her a favour. In October 2000, a month after the tragic sinking of the Russian sub *Kursk* and a few months after the release of *U-571*, her project suddenly surfaced with two A-list actors, Harrison Ford and Liam Neeson. Coming just before the expected Screen Actors' Guild strike most major Hollywood players wanted to get a film into production quickly. Paramount Pictures and producer Nigel Sinclair of Intermedia picked it up and she had a green light (proving the old showbiz adage that timing is everything).

Variety reported that after Harrison Ford 'went poring through the best scripts Hollywood has to offer he chose Christopher Kyle's screenplay' (Kyle was the co-writer of *The Weight of Water* and *Alexander*). Ford, famous for playing the Cold War hero Jack Ryan in two earlier films, was enthused by the idea of playing a Soviet Captain on the other side of the Iron Curtain, whose efforts are intended to thwart war, not cause it. Ford said, 'I grew up thinking the Nazis spoke with a British accent because British actors always portrayed them. I wanted an American audience to realize this

was a Russian experience. The story was ... about men who feel it is a moral obligation of military leadership to gain and keep political advantage by expending men's lives. It is a metaphor in the story to ponder.'

Neeson said he was always attracted to material in which someone makes a stand for honour and human dignity. With each scene Neeson asked himself, 'What is this scene about? What are we trying to tell? Where are the dynamics in the relationship between the two men and where do the explosions come?' – these are, of course, exactly the kind of questions a scriptwriter should be asking himself.

According to *Variety*, Russian survivors were enraged about being portrayed as incompetent alcoholics. This detail was softened in the script and character names were changed to prevent lawsuits. (With a budget of $80 million, the film took $34 million in its first 38 days in America. Ford's fee was $25 million after which he would receive 20 per cent of the box office.)

Historical/Biographical

Sergeant York (1941). Produced by Jesse Lasky Sr and directed by Howard Hawks, this story of an American World War I hero helped to bring America into World War II. Nominated for 11 Oscars, and his first for Gary Cooper, it is the definitive biopic (original screenplay by Harry Chandlee, Abem Finkel, John Huston, Howard Koch, and Sam Cowan) about the Tennessee backwoodsman who swore off violence when lightning struck his rifle but later single-handedly killed 20 Germans and captured 132 more.

Chaplin (1992), screenplay by William Boyd, Bryan Forbes, and William Goldman, is based on three biographies of Chaplin. This film suffered from too many (and all top) writers. It used the plot structure of a fictitious interview. Anthony Hopkins, playing an inquiring publisher, interviews the aged Chaplin, who recalls only the high moments in his life – revealed in a series of flashbacks. With a magnificent performance by Robert Downey Jr it sounds like it should have worked; but it was a hopelessly flawed film because the plot construction was predictable and, consequently, boring.

The Madness of King George (1994). Alan Bennett's witty screenplay won the Oscar, adapted from his stage play *The Madness of George III* (the title was changed because they were afraid Americans would think it was a sequel). Bennett used his whimsical humour for a serious look at the politics of 18th century England and the Monarchy. Bennett insisted that director Nicholas Hytner (who had directed the stage play) and star Nigel Hawthorne, make the film.

Ed Wood (1994). This quirky gem of a film about the off-the-wall career of a B-movie director in Hollywood in the 1950s (played by Johnny Depp) was a truly brilliant homage to bad taste. Tim Burton directed Scott Alexander and Larry Karaszewski's script from a book by Rudolph Grey – with an Oscar for Martin Landau as Bela Lugosi. It focuses on a fairly short period of Wood's life.

Mrs Brown (1997). Blending fact and conjecture into an unrequited (?) love story of Queen Victoria (Judi Dench) and her Scottish Gillie, John Brown (Billy Connolly). Scripted by Jeremy Brock and directed by John Madden, it is a thoroughly modern film focused entirely on the relationship.

Westerns

The genre was immortalized by John Ford in films such as *Stagecoach* (1939), *Fort Apache* (1948), *She Wore a Yellow Ribbon* (1949), *The Searchers* (1956), *The Horse Soldiers* (1959), *How the West Was Won* (1962) and *The Man Who Shot Liberty Valance* (also 1962) – and the many other films made by this fine director with John Wayne, the greatest Western hero of them all if you don't count Roy Rogers and Gene Autry. In its 'pure' form, today it's a lost genre.

Anti-Hero Western

The Italian director Sergio Leone shifted the genre by filming in Italy, Spain and Germany, making films that were described as 'spaghetti Westerns'. He started a new breed of anti-hero protagonists. The anti-hero is not a villain but rather one who stands aloof from society and the law, with whom the audience can identify and empathize because at some point in our lives we have all been outsiders. The role made a star of Clint Eastwood with *A Fistful of Dollars* (1964), *For A Few Dollars More*

(1965), *The Good, the Bad and the Ugly* (1966) and *A Fistful of Dynamite* (1971).

The Brat Pack Western

Young Guns (1988) and *Young Guns II* (1990). Emilio Estevez portrayed Billy the Kid with a youthful persona closer to the truth. This film, written by John Fusco, gave a grittier reality to what the old West was really like.

Tombstone (1993). Kevin Jarre's script was in the classic tradition but was weakened by the absence of a strong through-line. The hero's quest was a negative: *not* to be a lawman. Jarre also started as director but was replaced in the middle of shooting by George Pan Cosmatos, who got all the credit. The film was highlighted by an outstanding performance by Val Kilmer as the consumptive Doc Holliday.

Comedy Western

City Slickers (1991). Scripted by Lowell Ganz and Babaloo Mandel from Billy Crystal's story. Crystal and two chums suffering from middle-age 'angstipation' go West – only to be roped in by the enigmatic Jack Palance (who won the Best Supporting Actor Oscar). A comedy must-see.

Blazing Saddles (1974). Mel Brooks wrote this with four other writers and directed. With crude gags, hilarious antics, and use of bodily functions for laughs, perhaps it was Brooks' best work after *The Producers*.

Fantasy

Jurassic Park (1993). Michael Crichton and David Koepp's excellent script from Crichton's novel could not have given Steven Spielberg a bigger success. But it is the computerized animatronics that make this picture and its sequels so popular.

Barbarella (1968). Directed by Roger Vadim, made in Rome, written by Terry Southern and seven others from a comic by Jean-Claude Forest. The idea of depersonalizing sex was slightly shocking for its time and when Barbarella (Jane Fonda) went in the 'machine' for an orgasm it became a cult film.

Fantasy/Comedy/Adventure

Back To The Future (1985) and its sequels *Part II* (1989) and *Part III* (1990). Bob Gale and Robert Zemeckis wrote this ingenious screenplay and Zemeckis directed all three. The first satirizes the 1950s when a boy travels back in time to make sure his parents get properly hitched. In *Part II* (1989), the past, present and future were a little over-plotted. *Part III* (1990) finds its setting in the old West. Michael J Fox and Christopher Lloyd were ace.

Action/Fantasy

There's a crossover here with **Comic Strip/Action**. *Waterworld* (1995) was considered Kevin Costner's most expensive failure. In the first draft of *Alien* (1979), the writers hadn't decided whether the protagonist was male or female. But Sigourney Weaver broke the convention that a woman couldn't play an action lead. However, *Blue Steel* (1990) with Jamie Lee Curtis and *Impulse* (1990) with Theresa Russell both failed.

Action/Adventure

Action cinema and the Theme Park are veering dangerously close together. This type of story requires lots of false endings. We need to go with the flow and have our emotions swept along on the mounting tide of events. A common device in action/adventure and spy/adventure films is to show, before the real story starts, an action sequence in which the hero performs an impossible feat which usually has nothing to do with the present story. It's almost a trailer – a pre-initial turning point that sets up what type of character the protagonist is. It is unrelated to plot *but not to character*. Most of these films today fit into:

Action/Adventure/Fantasy

Raiders of the Lost Ark (1981). Spielberg and Lucas triumphed with Lawrence Kasdan's action-packed script that set them and Harrison Ford (and a few other filmmakers) on a series of adventure films, with a nod towards mythic prototypes. There is a major reversal in the action at least every 15 minutes in this genre to keep up the pace.

In *Raiders* the opening sequence (unrelated to the main plot but telling us a lot about the hero's character) finds archaeologist Ford in a cave beset by spiders and deadly traps, getting the treasure – nearly being killed by a giant stone ball – losing the treasure and escaping from a hoard of blowpipes in a sea plane. This action sequence gets the audience's attention before the story actually begins.

Harrison Ford has the right face for this genre and few actors can carry it off so successfully. His perplexed but essentially emotionless expression allows the audience to project an emotion onto him – while he calculates his next move. Ford is called by critic Iain Johnstone 'an actor always in search of less'.

Although this genre is expensive to make, the successful ones are among the most commercially successful of all films, so they are a regular feature on production schedules. Some other notable titles include *The Dark Crystal* (1982), *Jumanji* (1995), *The Mummy* (1999), and *The Mummy Returns* (2001) – see the discussion of this in chapter 5.

Cops And Robbers /Action /Thriller

Lethal Weapon (1987). Richard Donner directed Shane Black's original screenplay. Believability is not the criteria in this wildly action-packed adventure between buddy-cops played by Mel Gibson and Danny Glover, who have very different ways of looking at the rules. Great fun, and Black doesn't give the audience time to think about plausible reasons for anything because at that pace, the script can get away with a lot. Also *Lethal Weapon 2* (1989), *Lethal Weapon 3* (1992) – the best of the sequels, and *Lethal Weapon 4* (1998).

Satirical/Science-Fiction/Thriller

RoboCop (1987). A Detroit cop of the future, now a cyborg, head-hunts the sadistic villains who attacked him. Dutch director Paul Verhoeven did a masterful job creating the sharply observed look at society in Edward Neumeier and Michael Miner's screenplay. *RoboCop 2* (1990) and *RoboCop 3* (1993) were not up to the first one.

Spy/Adventure

All the James Bond films of the past and future: *Dr. No, From With Russia With Love,* and the rest.

Sci-Fi/Action/Adventure

The secret of sci-fi is that you have to make the future look like somebody actually lives in it. These stories offer a prescient peek at the possibilities, which requires an attention to detail in your 'research'.

Because market research said it would attract nobody over eight years old, *E.T.* (1982), the highest-grossing movie ever until *Titanic*, was originally put into 'turnaround' (which means a script that has been refused by all potential buyers or its option hasn't been picked up). Once your script is in turnaround the chances of selling it are bleak, unless it's repackaged at a lower budget or you've suddenly interested a major star/director. Fortunately, Steven Spielberg picked up *E.T.*.

The 1920 version of *Dr Jekyll and Mr Hyde* used colour filters and special make-up to change the actor's appearance. *King Kong* (1933) and Ray Harryhausen's monsters in *Clash Of The Titans* (1981) or his famous skeletons in *Jason and the Argonauts* (1963) all used rubber models and stop-frame photography. Computer graphics-generated images have improved facial movement and skin textures and revolutionized this genre for films like *Jurassic Park*. Modern techniques of 'morphing' make things and people look real in a seamless transformation. But animation lets you know they are created, imaginary beings.

Speaking about this to my friend Ray Harryhausen, he told me that he feels that while the new methods have gained a great deal, they've lost the charm of the old-style monsters, who were less intimidating because you knew they were not real. I'm afraid today's audiences want to be intimidated.

AI (2001). Spielberg's dark twist on the tale of Pinocchio's quest to be a real boy, set in a world of robot outcasts, was based on a story by Brian W. Aldiss. Other fine examples of the genre include *The Fifth Element* (1997), *Aliens* (1986), *Blade Runner* (1982), *Solaris* (1972), *The Terminator* (1984), *Terminator 2* (1991), and *Invasion of the Body Snatchers* (1956).

Thriller/Horror

Silence Of The Lambs (1991). See the discussion of this in relation to flashbacks in chapter 4. The theme involves the conflict between masculine power, feminine vulnerability and sexual humiliation.

Cape Fear (1962). Robert Mitchum as an embittered, psychotic ex-con terrorizes the family of the lawyer who sent him down (Gregory Peck). James R Webb wrote the screenplay from John D MacDonald's novel. J Lee Thompson's use of light and shadow in the classic black and white version was formidable. A taut, menace-packed screenplay and film.

Cape Fear (1991). This time around Martin Scorsese and writer Wesley Strick brought this masterpiece of menace to the screen with Robert De Niro playing it slightly over the top – and Nick Nolte as the father. Scorsese created stunning images of a family threatened and an unforgettable bat-like opening shot of De Niro hanging upside down. Time did not diminish the story but the end was a bit too *Friday 13th* – with the villain seemingly indestructible.

Horror

This is a very hot genre, and if you can write in it well, you're a winner. Horror is simply what scares you, fills you with dread, instils paranoiac fear, and if you're susceptible, gives you nightmares. Stephen King's stories have been the basis of many horror films, such as *Carrie* (1976). Lawrence D Cohen's script based on Stephen King's book offered a false ending when Sissy Spacek kills the villain. The horrifying last scene sees his hand pop out of his grave.

The Shining (1980). Also based on a Stephen King novel, Diane Johnson and Stanley Kubrick co-wrote the script, and Kubrick directed. Surprisingly, the critics panned it on release. They were wrong. The story is really quite simple but it is frightening and visually unforgettable with brilliant performances from Jack Nicholson and Shelley Duvall. Even with a great script, stars make a difference.

There were 13 feature films on the subject of *Dracula* between 1931 and 2001, all preceded by Murnau's terrifying 1922 version, *Nosferatu*. The compelling fascination with Bram Stoker's Dracula tales, however badly the films have been made, seems to be as eternal as the vampire himself. It has to do with our fear of mortality and death. Count Dracula is a metaphor for the possibilities of enjoying eternal life whatever the cost. Today there are more than a few fan clubs devoted to the tales of the vampire and his true inspiration, the Walachian ruler Vlad the Impaler (1431–1476), and devotional trips are made to Transylvania. Bela Lugosi's interpretation was brought into modern focus by Christopher Lee who made the role his own. Countess Dracula was immortalized by Ingrid Pitt, whose fan club grows every year.

There were twelve *Frankenstein* films made between 1931 and 1994 about the melancholy man-made monster, including Kenneth Branagh's valiant but flawed attempt, *Mary Shelley's Frankenstein* (1994). Even with Robert De Niro as the monster, it didn't come off. The world has moved on and old monsters no longer frighten us. Modern science-fiction and comic-strip characters on the big screen have put Frankenstein's monster on the back burner. Today he is more a figure of caricature and fun than a genuinely spooky menace. If you can think of a really frightening monster (or menacing tale) there is a market for it. People still like to be frightened.

The Exorcist (1973). The screenplay was adapted by William Peter Blatty from his own hit book. Called 'the most talked about and reviled horror film of all time', it's all about possession, and once seen is hard to forget. I had lunch with Blatty at the home of my friend Tippi Hedren when his film first came out. I asked him if he believed in possession and he said he did. 'How could you tell if someone was possessed?' I asked. He said that they twitched. Since he had been twitching all through lunch, I asked no more questions!

Other examples of this perennially popular genre include *Halloween* (1978) any of the many sequels – the ninth in the series is due for release in 2004, *The Amityville Horror*

(1979) with four feature sequels, and *A Nightmare On Elm Street* (1984) and six sequels – see the stepline breakdown of the original film in chapter 11.

Psychological/Thriller/Fantasy

Lost Highway (1996). Is it film noir? I don't think so. Barry Gifford and David Lynch wrote and Lynch directed this mystifying story with a spineless plot and characters who change into other people. But then reason and logic are often bypassed in Lynch's films; weird and impenetrable – but if you're a *Twin Peaks* fan, you'll be riveted.

War Drama

The Deer Hunter (1978). Screenplay by Eric Washburn from a story by Michael Cimino (who also directed) and two others. A look at the Vietnam war – with its unforgettable and chilling Russian Roulette sequence.

Full Metal Jacket (1987). Based on Gustov Hasford's novel and co-written with Michael Herr and Stanley Kubrick it brought the young innocents straight from boot camp to become killing machines in Vietnam. It was shot in England on sets and outdoor lots but that didn't stop it from delivering its message.

Black Hawk Down (2001). The screenplay was by Mark Bowden, Ken Nolan, Steven Zaillian, and it was directed by Ridley Scott. Based on a true account of elite US soldiers sent into Mogadishu, Somalia in 1993 on a mission that went terribly wrong.

War Drama/Horror

Apocalypse Now (1979). Writer John Milius worked with Francis Ford Coppola (also director) on this epic Vietnam War film that updated an idea from Joseph Conrad's novella *Heart of Darkness*. It was re-released in 2001 with the director's cut.

Chapter 16 | ON WRITING COMEDY

Someone once said, 'Language was invented because we need to communicate. Humour was invented because we need to complain.' If you have what comedy writer Melvin Helitzer calls 'the gift of glee' this chapter will give you a few signposts for writing comedy for films, for sitcoms already on the air, for creating sitcoms of your own, and writing for stand-up comics.

The Serious Side Of Being Funny

Although this is the world of laughs, the least funny thing in the world is creating comedy – it is hard work. In a WGA interview, top American comedy writer Larry Gelbart said he was surprised that producer/director George Abbott at the first reading of the future stage hit, *A Funny Thing Happened on the Way to the Forum*, told his cast of star comedy actors, 'I've just got one thing to tell you guys, don't let me catch any of you trying to be funny.' Gelbart acknowledged the golden rule of comedy: play it as though it's serious drama.

The only approach to comedy for the theatre and for films is to take it seriously. Sitcoms are written especially for laughs – nearly every line must be funny.

Writer/director Cameron Crowe, who started his writing career as a journalist said, 'You can write comedy and you're not laughing. Two weeks later you laugh. The reverse also happens and you say, why did I think that was funny?' He suggests that finding humour in the most personal things is the best. Crowe wrote his first screenplay from his novel *Fast Times at Ridgemont High* (1982), and went on to write and direct *Say Anything* (1989), *Singles* (1992), *Jerry Maguire* (1996), and *Almost Famous* (2000).

The Essence Of All Comedy: Something Goes Wrong

And the rules for writing it – as the protagonist tries to respond to the initial turning point – are the same as for drama:

only the situations are different. It is logical story-telling that highlights the funny and ridiculous side of the events, and the characters' choices of action. Comedy is far funnier when it skirts the edge of disaster; when, if it weren't funny, it would be a tragedy. That is why Laurel and Hardy are still so funny today. They are always on the edge.

According to psychologist Patricia Keith-Spiegal there are eight major categories in which we can classify what makes us laugh: **Surprise, Superiority, Biology, Incongruity, Ambivalence, (Emotional) Release, and Configurational and Psychoanalytical Ideas.** I will consider each of these in this chapter.

Comedy also has a faster pace than drama. Since people are more interesting than things, a writer gets better comedy values from the human element. *Chitty Chitty Bang Bang* (1958) might seem to be a story about a flying Edwardian motorcar – but it is actually about the people involved with the car. So was *The Love Bug* (1969) and its successors – it was still about the people, although the cars in both cases were given an anthropomorphic outlook. You might classify the humour in both those two films as based on **Surprise** and **Incongruity.**

One way of exploiting these elements is to put your protagonist into a world he cannot adjust to. In the French farce *Les Visiteurs* (1993), the plot deals with two 11th-century knights who have been catapulted through time into today's world. They cannot relate to objects, people, or anything else because nothing in the 20th century is within their frame of reference. Everything must be perceived in a totally new way.

In *Big* (1988) a 12-year old boy is magically turned into a man (Tom Hanks) and must live in a man's world, relating to everything with a child's mind. It is not farce, but gentle comedy drama. Both films are examples of Incongruity.

Styles Of Comedy

These are generally broken into the following categories: **Slapstick/Broad/Farce (both Drawing Room and Bedroom), Gentle Comedy, Black Comedy, and Satire.**
Farce has always been the province of the stage and is sometimes referred to as a 'comedy of manners'. In the English theatre the concept was refined in 17th century Restoration comedies (written from the 1660s onwards), which were mainly built on the theme of hypocrisy – presenting socially unacceptable behaviour within the highly restrictive society of the day, with its firm rules of conduct. This could be classified under Incongruity.

Bedroom Farce was a 19th-century development based on the idea of the love triangle, with convoluted variations on the theme of adultery and misunderstanding; attempts at extra-marital relationships carried to the point of the ridiculous with lots of people hiding in wardrobes and under beds. Usually the adultery is never consummated because the stories are not about sex, but sexual frustration. The former isn't funny; the latter can be.

Many films today and most animated cartoons are based on farce. Farce is heavy on intricate plotting with maniacally ingenious, perplexing situations. It is a world inhabited by the half-witted antics of a white-faced, babyish Harry Langdon, Stan Laurel, Benny Hill, or Jim Carrey; a world of catastrophic encounters and misunderstandings. Characters do not act in a normal or expected manner. In a moment of crisis when forced to make a decision, they will always choose the wrong path, skirting disaster but ludicrously funny.

Humour As A Social Comment

Humour can be used to criticize. That's one reason humour is often used for political pressure – to deflate one's opponent. Humour can make us feel secure in our prejudices and our failings. In a TV interview John Cleese said: 'My comedy is about envy, greed, lust, malice, narrowness and stupidity'.

Sigmund Freud wrote that a lack of humour is a sign of mental illness. Medically speaking, laughter is a function of the nervous system, an emotional, not intellectual response to something we have seen or heard. It is certainly biological. If you have come into the cinema with a lot of problems on your mind watching the comical antics in a film can relax you, give you a sense of well-being and make you forget your troubles for a short time. When you sit in the dark watching a film with hundreds of other people, you can vent your tensions, stress, and feelings of hostility in a socially acceptable way. When the lights come up you feel refreshed and more able to cope with your personal problems – at least for a while.

Why do different people laugh at different things? Because some things we empathize with while some do not touch us since they are outside our frame of reference. A joke about a yak in the middle of the Siberian desert might not seem funny to us living in a

THOSE TWO WRITERS HAVE A FUNNY WAY OF SCREWING IN A LIGHT BULB.

YES. ONE WILL SCREW IT IN ALMOST TO THE END. AND THE OTHER WILL GIVE IT A FINAL AMAZING TWIST.

Rooby

densely populated city, but yak riding on a city bus might cause a lot of laughs.

We identify with our own culture and our own inadequacies. If we are embarrassed by something we have said or done or if someone has played a trick on us, we often laugh in a self-depreciating manner. Watching a comedy, we can safely laugh at the stupid behaviour or fears of a character. We may smile at a witty line but we will laugh at a joke. Or - How many actors does it take to change a light bulb? Only one. They don't like to share the spotlight.

The Comic Persona
Uninhibited, Anti-Social, Childish Behaviour

Comedy writer Art Gliner said, 'We're young only once. But with humour – we can be immature forever.' We watch with glee the protagonist's regression into an infantile state of mind in *The Young Ones* with Rik Mayall and Adrian Edmondson, as they do things we might secretly wish to but would never dare.

Stan Laurel was the master of the childish point of view, and long ago my next-door neighbour told me that his favourite gag in all the films he made with Oliver Hardy was where Stan is leaning against the wall of a house. Ollie comes up.
Ollie: Why are you leaning against that wall?
Stan: I'm holding it up.
Ollie: Don't be ridiculous. Come away from there right now!
Ollie pulls Stan away and the wall falls down on them.

This is a visual gag, but based on their characterizations. Neither Laurel nor Hardy's characters have any understanding of normal behaviour. Laurel is dim, and bewildered, an innocent, child-like protagonist who can't cope with the physical world in which objects seem to have a life of their own and always defeat him. His lack of physical competence means that his wimpish exterior masks a source of danger to the normal people around him (the same idea is central to the character of Frank Spencer in the sitcom *Some Mothers do 'Ave 'Em*).

Visual Comedy

The type of humour that Laurel and Hardy excelled in depends heavily on visual comedy. This is not entirely up to the writer, although the writer may dream up the situations. The qualities of a visual comedian can be understood without dialogue; this is the art of each individual comedian. It's not what they say, it's what they do. Timing is the fine art of the true visual comic, as it is when the comedy is verbal. Their forté is mime and illusion. Doing normal things in an eccentric, overcomplicated way or having a comic walk, like Chaplin. The skill of the performer in visual comedy is in executing the action.

Generally, it requires the performer to have an easily recognizable personality and comic image that immediately defines his attitude to life. Visual comedy comes from extremes. Some of the devices comics use to make us laugh are in dress and make-up. The clown persona involving funny and distinctive clothes were perfected by Chaplin, Keaton, and Laurel and Hardy among others.

If a performer has physically comic features it helps create his character. Jim Carrey and Rick Mayall don't have a comic appearance. Since both men are basically good looking, they create their characters by exaggeration, and people who write for them have to understand their particular talent. Both Carrey and Mayall have also played straight roles with success, but this would be more difficult for Rowan Atkinson or Robbie Corbett to do since they each have a 'comic face' to begin with, and can look funny with no effort.

Lucille Ball was beautiful, but had a comic expression, brilliant body language and impeccable timing. Victoria Wood is not funny to look at, so her comedy is also based on what she says, not what she does. Jo Brand is comic looking, but it is her attitude and humorous comments (the writer's domain) that make her funny. Ruby Wax has an eccentric look, and is fast with the wisecrack but, like Wood and Brand, is not fundamentally a visual comic and relies on her jokes and her style of delivery, which is essentially a monologue. Unless they write their own material, these are the type of comics you can submit material to and write for. Most such comics employ a team of writers.

Comic Tenacity

The 20th century French comedian Jacques Tati's character acts without thinking of the consequences. His inability to cope produces anger which in turn produces irrational action. Rowan Atkinson's character Mr Bean rejects logic, so naturally the illogic of incompetence leads to comic disaster. The tenacious comic character keeps on repeating an action long after a normal person would give up, refusing to believe they won't succeed.

The Stooge

In writing comedy, the butt of a joke is called the target. Every series needs *one dumb character.* The protagonist to whom we feel superior must have a target to whom *he* feels superior. His target must therefore be stupider than the protagonist or the audience.
- In *Cosby* his son is the target
- In *Fawlty Towers,* Manuel the waiter has that honour
- In *Blackadder,* Baldrick takes the pratfalls
- In *Absolutely Fabulous* it's the moronic Bubble
- In *Friends* Joey is the stooge

For a stand-up comic, however, the least offensive target is himself, ridiculing his own shortcomings. Ben Elton always uses this with a twist of the logical expectation:
I even got a threatening phone call from Information.
I once joined a Key Club and they changed the locks.
The only thing I ever got on a silver platter was tarnish.

But insults also work against superior authority. Belittling those above us in authority and bringing them down to size has wide audience appeal.
Artificial hearts aren't new.
Politicians have had them for years.

Elements of Comic Writing
Finding Comic Situations

For a TV sitcom think in terms of five laughs a page. I'm afraid it's the same old list of questions and knowing what to ask, starting with 'what if'? Writing comedy requires much more *lateral thinking* (a leap sideways from normal linear thinking and behavioural patterns). If you find that difficult, then comedy writing is not for you. Because it is difficult, comedy writers are generally the highest paid.

Look for the most absurd step – something way beyond 'too far'. Try to see ordinary every day events and ideas in a different way. Ask yourself what a normal person would do in the situation you have created, and then work out what is the very antithesis of that. Always go for the lateral outer limits.

Audience Identification

What you want is to be universally understood. Choose the most typical setting in which the incident can happen and a prototype person for it to happen to. Create a familiar image for quick audience comprehension. In a fast-moving comedy there is no time to work out complexities or absorb needless details. Your audience must understand and focus instantly. They are ready to see the absurdity in an otherwise normal situation. Therefore, the situation must initially be normal to the audience. This also means simplifying dialogue – the least number of words, the most impact for the joke.

Conversely you could choose the weirdest setting in which to place an ordinary type of person, such as in *Red Dwarf*, in which David Lister, a curry-eating slob, lives aboard a spaceship.

Area of the Story

The premise itself should be funny and it should also be timely. For example, a reversal of roles offers humour, but it must be in tune with the times. In the 1960s *The Mary Tyler Moore Show* was about a woman trying to make it in a man's job. This wouldn't be funny in itself today because women working in such situations has become commonplace. But the reversal of roles was successful for Joe McGann in in the TV series *The Upper Hand* (1988) when he played a man trying to make it in a woman's job – as a housekeeper. Today, even that scenario is probably not uncommon enough to provide a comic situation.

Satire

A comedy writer must be cynical and probing to pull the mask off hypocrisy. Your focus may be on an individual character but you can be attacking the foibles in an institution or a specific sector of society. Some comedy film titles show the focus on the social structure: *The Ruling Class* (1972), *Down And Out In Beverly Hills* (1986), *Police Academy* (1988), and *Best in Show* (2000) – not so much a film about dogs as about how the characters relate to their dogs.

Believability versus Reality

In comedy, realism and believability have a warped point of view. Reality is not necessarily important to the comedy writers' world, as long as you maintain believability by staying within your created parameters – as with any other genre. The truly comic character lives in a world of his own, beyond the limits of our society. If you met the character Jim Carrey became in *The Mask* you would feel too scared to laugh because in real life he would be more frightening than funny. The screen distances him from reality. The incongruity and biological impossibility of the character give him his platform for humour and Carrey's physical comic dexterity.

For TV characters in a series you must also have a believable reason why they see each other so often. They must have normal daily contact. Neighbours, fellow workers, etc. A clear-cut example is *Drop the Dead Donkey*. The Newsroom is their base. In *Cheers* the bar is their base. In *Men Behaving Badly* they are flatmates.

Broad Comedy and The Comedy Sketch

A sketch is a one story-line scene with a punch line, lasting up to three minutes. This type of comedy is not subtle. The sketch is the mainstay for 'variety' TV. In England, French and Saunders, Victoria Wood, Benny Hill, and Harry Enfield are some of the performers who use the form. In America *Saturday Night Live* was sketch-based. *Seinfeld* developed from sketches the actor had been doing in stand-up comedy. The sketch doesn't suit normal sitcom where your time frame is short but it can

work in a film. In the late 1960s the Monty Python team perfected the idea of a series of sketches flowing from one to the next without punchlines.

Talking to various comedy writers, I was given different approaches. Some outline the entire sketch on paper, and others start with a rough idea in their heads and write it moment to moment as it flows. Like all story material, it has a beginning (the protagonist wants something), a middle (something goes wrong), and an end (the protagonist gets something he doesn't expect). The end payoff must develop from within the material of the sketch.

In choosing a subject, find one you like that your audience can relate to easily. The theme can be outlandish, e.g. Superman comes home to his wife for dinner. What would every step of such a story be like? Would he fly in through the window? What excuse would he have for being late? Would she greet him with 'How was your day, dear?' What would they eat? Carry the concept to extremes. Try writing this as an exercise – or any other idea you have.

A Block Comedy Scene

This term refers to a sketch set within the framework of a story that is funny all on its own. You can stop a story-line in a film to insert a block scene if it is true to your theme and characters. Marx Brothers films had only about 15 minutes of actual plot in any one of their movie story-lines. The high jinx grew out of the characters' foibles and idiosyncrasies, carrying them into a series of what amounted to vaudeville sketches. One of their most famous was when they (and almost everyone else aboard the ship) climbed into a tiny stateroom in *A Night at the Opera* (1935).

The Humorous Point Of View

Truth must be grossly exaggerated. Expand the believable into the ridiculous. Any subject will do but some may have more impact for you, personally. According to the pundits, men worry more about sex, and women worry about money. Both lead to frustration.
Woody Allen joked: I finally had an orgasm and the Doc told me it was the wrong kind.
Oscar Wilde said: When I was young,

I thought money was the most important thing in life. Now that I'm old, I know it is.

You should be able to find your subject matter almost anywhere. Salaries, taxes, buying a house, investments, gambling, credit cards, school days, school fees, driving a car, having a baby. Human emotions like love, greed, hate, any of the seven deadly sins or the Ten Commandments are all good subjects for ironic satire. It's your 'take' on it that can make the subject funny rather than serious.

The Surprise (Shock) Element

The shock of a protagonist opening a wardrobe, out of which steps a monster, can be funny or scary, depending on the story and the creature. The shock element works for both comedy and horror.

The other kind of shock – the shock value of a tasteless joke – is more dangerous. Jokes are expendable. Is it too easy? Is it too tasteless? Relying on shock value is good for horror, but bad for comedy.

Incongruity And Reversals

Ronald Wolfe (who has written dozens of sitcom favourites, starting with *On The Buses*) in his very useful book *Writing Comedy*[1] points to the reversal gag as being one of the most important tricks of the trade. It is the reverse of the expected happening that gets a laugh.

Place your protagonist into a world he is unfamiliar with and has to adjust to, for instance:

• The unintentional transvestite: *Tootsie* – Dustin Hoffman pretends to be a woman and gets stuck in the role. *Mrs Doubtfire* – Robin Williams pretends to be a woman and gets stuck in the role. Same situation, different plot.
• The child masquerading as an adult: *Big*
• The adult who never grows up: Stan Laurel, *Bottom*, *The Young Ones*.

Role reversals do not always work the same way, however. If you make the woman the aggressor it tends to become action rather than comedy: *Lara Croft*, *Tank Girl*, *Charlie's Angels*, *The Fifth Element*, and *Nikita* are anything but comedy.

Realism and Exaggeration

Pairing two logical but unconventional ideas often works. John Cleese in *Fawlty Towers* played a hotel manager – someone whose business it is to be polite – as rude and overbearing. Or Cleese's Monty Python sketch about the 'Department Of Silly Walks' – where the humour comes from the idea of a serious, bureaucratic government department for a childish impossibility. Think of opposites: a chef who's always on a diet; a taxi driver who gets car sick; a singer whose boyfriend is deaf.

Look for the paradox, the unexpected juxtaposition of the reasonable and unreasonable – but to be most effective it must have a core of truth.

Find the thing your character doesn't want to happen and exploit it. Or take an every day problem, where we expect a clichéd resolution, and switch the ending to the unlikely. In *I Love You to Death* (1990, written by John Kostmayer), Tracey Ullman's character tries to kill her husband, played by Kevin Kline, but he just thinks she's being nice to him. They live happily ever after.

Sounds Funny

Certain words, odd speech rhythms, certain foreign words or accents can get laughs. Funny character names got laughs in 17th and 18th century Restoration Comedy where they also defined the attributes of the character: Mrs Bracegirdle, Mrs Malaprop, Mr Moody, Sir John Modelove, Mrs Sackbut, Sir Jealous Traffick, Mr Brainworm, Mr Downright, Sir George Wealthy, and so on. This device is woefully out of fashion in writing for today's market and can lose you a commission. Avoid it even if you're tempted. The *Monty Python* team were able to revive it by pushing the idea to absurd lengths, coming up with surreal names such as Raymond Luxury-Yacht, Ron Obvious, and Ernest Pythagoras.

Homonyms can provide another sort of humour based on the sound of words. *Why did the blonde want to make a baby with Ralph Lauren? So it would have designer genes.* Or, *I know a transsexual who only wants to eat, drink and be Mary.*

Planning A Sitcom Series

Plotting TV Series Characters

The basic difference in writing comedy characters is that they need to be *one-dimensional* for quick audience understanding and identification. In designing them, give each one an exaggerated but consistent idiosyncrasy and stick with it. 'Lock in' on your character's behaviour.

Don't give the same idiosyncrasy to more than one, and each must be in opposition to the others. Let the audience see the flaw as soon as possible. Avoid the expected turn of events. Look for the unexpected. These are the elements on which you can build the comedy. Once you establish certain facts about your characters, they will lead you to other facts. The characters' actions will be based on the behavioural patterns you set.

In creating the characters for hit British TV series *The Fast Show*, writers/actors Charlie Higson and Paul Whitehouse looked for their humour not in jokes with punch lines, but in the characters themselves. They decided to give one character ('Bob Fleming') a permanent cough. Looking for the worst possible scenario, Paul's lateral question was 'What's the job most likely to be thrown into chaos by someone with a cough?' Since on TV a person is never allowed to cough, they made the character a TV presenter.

In their search for odd juxtapositions they chose an aristocratic landowner with a crush on his elderly gamekeeper, newsreaders with no grasp of world affairs, or two salesmen whose sexual innuendo disturbs their customers. The physical sight of these characters and their catch phrases has grown into the consciousness of their audiences. Whitehouse's tag line, 'Suits you, sir' and Arabella Weir's, 'Does my bum look big in this?' are now well-known quotes.

In *Frasier*, the eponymous psychiatrist is conceited and cannot keep a girlfriend, his brother Niles is a hypochondriac, Roz the radio producer is always on the lookout for a man, the father Martin is solidly home-spun, and the laconic Daphne is the object of Niles's lust. When Niles finally won her in one of the later episodes, the humour largely went out of that subplot, though the writers compensated by giving a much greater role to Daphne's abrasive mother.

In *Men Behaving Badly* Gary is pompous, overbearing, and always wrong but his girlfriend Dorothy always sees through him. Tony is the stupid, naive daydreamer.

Absolutely Fabulous shows a complete role switch from what would normally be expected: a straight-laced daughter, delinquent mother, dipso best friend and a grandmother oblivious to everything.

The Odd Couple (successful as a play, a film, and a TV series). One character is ultra neat; the other is a slob. The humour derives from the abrasive interaction of their two idiosyncrasies.

Plotting the Story

As with drama, never think of your characters as 'them'. Each character is a separate entity, who will react to events and information in unique ways. Also as with drama, there must be a *conflict* in the plot. The protagonist must desire to achieve something and the story deals with his journey towards his goal. The obstacles lead him into frustrating situations.

Roughly outline your story. Don't be too specific at the start; just put down the broad strokes. Who is the protagonist? Is there going to be a development of the relationships during the series? In *Love Hurts* as the relationship progressed, the series turned from a sitcom into comedy drama. This was probably not the original intention.

Does your series maintain the status quo? In *Absolutely Fabulous* the far-out characters all return to whatever they were by the end of each episode. Even Bubble who gets 'brains' in one episode, at the end returns to being an airhead (it was all a dream). Joanna Lumley's character counterpoints that of Saunders.

Which characters counterpoint your protagonist? What are their flaws? Their foibles? You can cover a wide spectrum of points of view through your cast of permanent characters. What sort of situations would your protagonist be involved in?

Start with your premise: a one-line statement of theme. What is the story about? Deal with people, not things. *M.A.S.H.* took a humorous look not at war itself, but by a group of unlikely comrades caught up in a war. Likewise, politics is not your subject – rather, somebody involved in politics (as in *Yes, Prime Minister*). You can make a comedy about institutions (such as the police in *The Thin Blue Line*) but it is always focused through the people.

Pick a subject that you know something about. Be able to pinpoint the weaknesses and pitfalls. What sort of characters would inhabit that world? Explore the situation thoroughly before beginning writing. Ask yourself the five big W and one H questions (see chapter 2).

Don't overcomplicate the plot by including too many characters or story-lines. Impose conflicts on your protagonist – and design characters that get in his way. Laughs come out of character traits and defects when they are put to the test, or even, since this is comedy, when faced with the simplest problems.

In comedy, unlike drama, your plot can be resolved more easily by fate or chance. You can use plot construction shortcuts and jump into things with little or no explanation. This would not go down in theatre or film, where you want some in-depth understanding of your characters.

Plot Jokes

Don't reach out for a joke in sitcom – that's for sketches or stand-up. Make it come out of the situation or the characters' peculiarities (that's why they call it *situation comedy*). Predictability can be funny. An audience can anticipate what a character will do in a given situation, and they will wait for it to happen.

Take for example the banana skin gag. Generally, you should always let the audience see the banana in advance. Then when the protagonist slips on it, it will justify what they knew and he didn't. But the unexpected opposite is also funny: the audience has seen the banana skin and is waiting for the protagonist to slip on it. But this time he neatly steps over it and the man behind him slips. Or he misses it completely and the audience is slightly disappointed, then he turns around and walks back – and *this* time he slips on it. Or he trips on something else and falls into an open manhole. There are many permutations. Find them.

However, the reverse situation – in which an audience has not been prepared by seeing the joke set up – can also be true. In *One Foot in the Grave*, for instance, Victor Meldrew in

his armchair hears the phone ring, reaches down to the ground without looking to pick it up, and instead picks up a small dog, which he attempts to 'answer'. Neither he nor the audience knew it was there, so preparation was not part of its impact, but it became a visual sight gag nevertheless.

The Format: Structure and Length

A half-hour show is a two-act structure. Syndication in the US requires a one-minute trailer before act one. Get your initial crisis and plot moving by page two. To be credible, only one character role reversal is permissible in a story (unless everybody is changed in the same way by some magical device and then is returned to normal at the end).

For an American half-hour comedy series you have 23 minutes of script. It's 26 minutes for the UK (these figures are approximate). Do not overwrite your script: if you do it will only be cut by someone else, who will almost certainly have less sensitivity in deciding what to cut than you would. And remember that in writing for a sitcom series in the US, there can be as many as 20 collaborators on a script. You'll have to fight to keep your bum on that seat at the conference table.

The Pilot

The first episode of any series takes too much time setting up the premise to be a good example of what the show will become after the audience begins to know the characters. Therefore in filming a pilot, very often the producers will not choose the first episode. The actors will generally give better performances in the first episode if it is shot after they've settled into their characters.

Open or Closed Ending

You must set up specific behavioural patterns and character interrelationships early, which will remain consistent throughout the series.

A running story-line that continues through the series is called an open end. There is a continuity of character relationships but nothing is resolved at the end of each episode. Like the soaps, we have to tune in for the next instalment. This also works for two, four or six part dramas that only resolve the plot in the final episode. *Sex and the City* is in essence open-ended since most of the women's problems are ongoing. But some plot lines are resolved in each episode and some minor characters dispensed with.

By contrast, series like *Bilko*, *M.A.S.H.*, *Cheers*, and *Frasier* are said to be closed-ended because each episode finishes with story points resolved and the characters maintaining their established relationships, which remain more or less constant throughout the series. Don't force a character to behave in a certain way that is against his prototype without a good reason. It must be believable. If a character changes his prototype idiosyncrasies in an episode, he must revert to type to put back the status quo for the rest of the series. In one episode of *Lovejoy*, Ian McShane's antique dealer fell in love with Lady Jane (his financial backer), but by end of the next episode he had reverted to his original on-off relationship with her.

Location

Where is your series set? What are the arenas of action? One or two regular locations are okay for a series but avoid too many sets. This is not a feature film and TV works on tight budgets and short shooting schedules. Your series, which may be highly original and an idea the broadcaster actually likes, can be thrown out because you've put in too many sets.

Most successful series are based around one permanent set and no more than two locations per episode at the most. *Frasier, Sex and the City, The Vicar of Dibley, Two Pints Of Lager and a Packet of Crisps, Fawlty Towers, My Family, Steptoe and Son,* and *Fat Friends* all have one main set with an establishing shot for an exterior and at the most, a couple of locations.

Scenes and Dialogue

If the scene isn't funny and doesn't seem to gel with the characters you've created, cut it or rewrite it. How many laughs are in it? Tape one of your favourite sitcoms and choose one scene. Count how many laughs there are per scene. You will be surprised.

Dialogue is crucial in comedy. In stage directions, write only a character's attitude (cheerfully, sadly, and so on), but *only when it*

is not obvious from the line itself. Keep the dialogue tight and pointed to the laugh, avoiding wordy sentences. Do not tell actors how to do a physical action, especially comedians. Each has a specific way of working with an established, consistent persona. They may use a lot of body language and visual humour. When working on an entrenched series you will have to write specifically *for* the traits, mannerisms, and style of speech that have already been established. Don't decide you know better than they do.

Overstatement or understatement are excellent devices for writing comic dialogue. You must 'point' your joke so that the words fall in a way to highlight the humorous idea or word in the sentence. There is a certain amount of instinct here, which you have to feel. The way a sentence is worded can get a laugh or lay the groundwork for one.

Submitting Material

To write material for an ongoing series you must be familiar with the star's own idiosyncratic type of humour. Each requires specifically designed material. The star always has to make an entrance, so give them the proper arrival in the script. Stars have a built-in audience acceptance and empathy and they know what works for them. They are leery of material of a type they have never tried before.

If you're trying to write for a current series, send the story editor or the producer a script, but *not* for that series. Show them something else you have written, even if it was not produced (as long as you have registered it or have sent yourself a registered copy – see chapter 7) You can, however, also submit along with it a short synopsis – a one-page story idea for their series. Write a few pages with some situation jokes.

Stand-up Notes

Writing for a stand-up comic is not an easy assignment. You must be very familiar with the style of the performer. If you think you've got the comic touch, there will always be work for a writer who can come up with funny jokes or a funny script.

Thematic Umbrellas and the Magic of Three

This refers to jokes on the same basic subject. You can build on a theme – such as mother-in-law jokes, marital problems, the workplace – which lead to the big laugh, but never more than three times on one theme.

One of the hard-and-fast rules that every comedy writer will tell you is that there is a certain magic about repeating a funny word, thematic joke, or humorous bit of action three times. The first time may get a chuckle. The second time, the audience can laugh out loud in remembrance. The third time they will roar with laughter (you hope). But don't try for the fourth because your gag will lay an egg. Why? That's the magic.

If you have three gags under one umbrella, tell the funniest last – for the same reason that you would escalate the action in drama. For example, if you have three bar jokes, which one would you put last?

A girl walked into a bar and asked for a double entendre. So the bartender gave her one.

A skeleton walked into a bar and asked for a pint of lager and a mop.

A man walked into a bar, and said, 'Ouch!'

The Punch Line

The first part of the sentence is a cliché; something we all know. The second part is given an unexpected twist: Then the cliché works as a plus. Abe Burrows gives an example in *There's No Business Like Show Business*: Yesterday they told you you would not go far. Last night you opened – and they were right! Be sure your gag is timely. Jokes about 'free love' are outdated in an openly promiscuous society.

Make Lists

I was fortunate to know one of the most famous comedy writers in America was Morey Amsterdam. He wrote for every major comedian including Jack Benny and Bob Hope and played the part of the agent on *The Dick Van Dyke Show* in the 1960s. His joke files filled a small box room with neat filing cabinets holding thousands of jokes. On the nightclub circuit Morey prided himself on being able to tell jokes without end on any subject the audience could throw at him. It is true he was a walking encyclopedia, but he made the point that it is vital to keep a file of jokes, funny situations, ideas, word play, and so on. Anything that comes your way that strikes you as funny, file it away. This goes for all writing. Keeping files can pay off; news clippings, pictures, anything that starts your creative juices bubbling.

Comedy Writers' Terminology

When sitting around a writers' table going over gags, you must know the terminology.
The Target: The butt of a joke.
A Topper: One joke that tops the other.
Hide the Joke: Let the point come as a surprise.
Running Gags: If it's a gag that deals with a character's idiosyncrasy, it can run through the series. If it's in the story plot of one episode, remember that it should only occur three times.
Sight Gags: A visual action or image that is instantly funny without words.
Curving the language: Altering the meaning. '2,000 years ago, they had only one means of locomotion — one thing that got them to move quickly from one place to another. Fear!'(Carl Reiner/Mel Brooks recording: *The 2,000 Year Old Man.*)
'Joke' Jokes: Inserted for a quick laugh. 'This town is so impersonal, if it weren't for the muggers, you wouldn't meet anyone.' These are a mainstay of stand-up writing, but for sitcoms, unless it ties into the story or character in some way, it will stand out as a cheap laugh.
Striking Gold: Finding something that works as you're writing that you hadn't planned.
Milk It: Carry the gag or routine as far as you can until it stops being funny (remember the magic three!).

Chapter 17 | SELLING YOUR SCREENPLAY AND THE PRE-PRODUCTION PROCESS

Knowing The Trends

What's hot and what's not? A sense of the Zeitgeist – literally 'the spirit of the times', more loosely something that's 'in the air' at a certain time – is the one thing the novice screenwriter rarely has. Information about what certain producers might be looking for at the moment is valuable but hard to come by. In principle, they are looking for subject matter that's filling the newspapers, but unless you have a script on a similar theme that is ready to go, it's already too late because of the time a project takes in development. As Stephen Frears pointed out in a recent interview, 'All films take two years to get on the screen. And if the script isn't good (meaning it doesn't catch his interest) I wouldn't know where to start.'

So how does anyone find out what the studios or directors are looking for? It is not easy for the writer who prefers to sit at his computer. You must develop networking skills, and try to build up relationships in the business. If you can interest a powerful agent in your script, he may guide you.

In one sense, knowing what a producer is looking for is easy: he wants a project he thinks will be a box-office draw. Most films lose money. The cost of a Hollywood film at the moment can be anywhere from $30 million to $100+ million and a picture must gross four times its production cost to break even. A major studio should make $300 million overall profit a year to stay in business. Heads of production companies receive on average up to 100 scripts a week. The larger film companies aim to make 15 commercially successful pictures a year. The head of production's job is to figure out which 15 should be made. The reality is that a company would make more money by banking their cash and collecting the interest and not making movies at all. But they don't do that. So how do they hope to win? Because one box-office success can pay for most of the flops.

In the United States since the terrorist attacks of September 2001 and the war in Iraq there has been a wariness about subjects dealing with terrorism or certain internal problems in the country. It also made it more difficult to sell a script with too much violence or overt sex. *Black Hawk Down*, which had been made before that attack, used negative material and turned it to a positive by thrusting a hero into a defeatist situation, giving him a major challenge. It caught the Zeitgeist at the time.

Kim Vecera, head of production at Fox Studios, Australia, finds few submissions of material that are 'robust, demonstrate strong filmmaker vision, are uncompromising in their point of view and are of popular appeal'. She receives instead material that is 'well ploughed and lacking in originality...without taking into account audiences, the craft of writing, or theatrical realities ... The vast majority are just not theatrical features ... (and are simply) small character pieces, or television, or linear narrative stories that have no interweaving of story.' She notes that a lot of good ideas get lost in the execution because they are 'dealt with simplistically ... and don't carry the level of sophistication needed to sustain a 90-minute feature.' Although she is looking for films with a strong sense of Australianness she is trying to reach an international audience and adds, 'that is what everyone is looking for'. [1]

That should give you an idea of what producers are looking for, not just in Australia but everywhere. They want films with the widest possible audience appeal. Today's marketplace is constantly searching for more spectacular material.

In November 2001, *Shrek* was the top box office grosser followed by *How the Grinch Stole Christmas*, *Cast Away* (Tom Hanks), *Rush Hour 2* (Hong Kong superstar Jackie Chan), and *The Mummy Returns. Lord of the Rings,* followed closely by *Harry Potter* were the winners in 2002. Fantasy and mythic story-telling made their mark.

To most studio heads, box office means big star names. They will happily pay $20 million to someone like Julia Roberts. Stars are commodities, franchises – some, such as Bruce Willis or Mel Gibson, are even like brands, in that their name indicates the genre of the film (an 'Arnie movie' will always be a high-octane action thriller). But there are other types of franchises. The studios and independent producers looking for the magic ingredient hope to find it in comic strips, interactive video games, or adaptations of plays or books, because these things all have what the marketing people call 'brand recognition' – and with recognition, they hope, comes a built-in audience.

Nobody can outguess the public. 'Guaranteed commercial successes' do not necessarily pay off. All the money in the world, all the brand recognition from a hit TV series and all the female empowerment of three shapely babes could not save the pop culture disaster of *Charlie's Angels* in 2000. The original budget was $92 million. In the end it cost $135 million and took $124 million in the United States after 80 days (though it did make another $45 million or so overseas). Star and co-producer Drew Barrymore agreed to hire a pop promo first-time director named McG (real name Joseph McGinty Nichol). They started with a flimsy story and subsequently hired 18 writers to save the script. It never had a third act and it certainly wasn't saved. Interestingly, a sequel was approved (*Charlie's Angels: Full Throttle*, 2003), also directed by McG, yet it didn't manage to improve on the financial performance of its predecessor.

End of Days in 1999 starred Arnold Schwarzenegger. It is the story of the Devil's search on Earth for his bride. Sound good? The studio insisted that the writer, Andrew W Marlowe (who also wrote *Airforce One*) have the Devil (Gabriel Byrne) appear a few minutes into the movie. Marlowe worried that the audience would be ahead of the protagonist and would be waiting for him to catch up with what they already knew. But, unable to convince the producers, Marlowe made the changes to his script (if he hadn't, they would simply have hired someone else to do it). To Marlowe, the suspense and tension on the story evaporated – and he was right. The film took half of its $100 million costs.

Bill Mechanic, head of Fox for seven years, made *Fight Club* in 1999, an off-beat story of bare-knuckle fighting he thought could be a winner. After all, the book by Chuck Palahniuk was a bestseller. It was brought to him by producer Laura Ziskin. Though not a subject calculated to appeal to a wide audience, they thought if they could keep it fairly low budget, it could make a profit. Most actors will take a cut in their exorbitant salaries if they see a good story with a great part for themselves. Brad Pitt agreed to star, but only at his full salary. The other actors were not going to work for peanuts if Brad wasn't. *Fight Club* suddenly became a high budget film – which altered the stakes. But Mechanic didn't retreat.

The first commandment for a producer is that the budget of the film must be right (though this is not just the producer's concern – the writer must be aware of the cost implications when presenting his screenplay). When *Fight Club* lost a packet in the United States, Rupert Murdoch fired Mechanic from Fox for making it. Surprised that he could be fired for such an indiscretion, Mechanic instantly found a home at Disney as an independent producer. He now says, 'most movies don't work [financially], so producers should only make the pictures you truly believe in'. He added, 'failure and success are a thread away'.

What do the filmmakers think? Ridley Scott asserts: 'Any great film is always driven by script, script, script. When you've got a great script, that means you've got great characters. That's the fundamental thing. That's the hardest thing of all to develop.' Peter Guber (producer of *Batman*) said, 'At the end of the day when you get done with all the fancy production design, all the great cinematography, when you have finished with all the great actors, a superb director, when you have finished with the great locations and all the capital all the hohas and brohas and the marketing, what's up on the screen is the script. Plain old-fashioned words. It all starts there and it all ends there.'

For a beginning writer to get the 'green light' and have his film made in the current market, he must think commercially. Keep your cast and sets down to a minimum unless you are writing a *Gladiator* and can get it to the right high-powered producer with access to large amounts of money. It's hard to sell 'casts of thousands' today – yet they still get made (with the aid of computer graphics). If you have the right subject and the right producer, there is always a chance.

Mechanic was not without his successes. While he was still at Fox, he heard rumours that the Farrelly brothers, Peter and Bobby, had a script called *There's Something About Mary*. The studio was buzzing about this story that pushed the boundaries of taste and Mechanic demanded to see it. Tasteless it may have been, but it was funny and it made $370 million in 1998. As the saying goes – if the audience want 'tasteless', give them what they want.

Video games are another popular source of movie ideas, because they are popular with the same male teenage demographic group who make up such a large part of the movie-going audience. For the making of *Lara Croft: Tomb Raider*, in 2001, since there was no narrative associated with the original source material, the original scriptwriter had to invent a story from scratch. The director, Simon West, didn't like the script and the British writer hired to do a rewrite threw it all out on the grounds that the characters were not British enough. Ten writers contributed, and all their work was rejected. In the end, out of all the scribes only Patrick Masett and John Zinman are given screenplay credit. West decided to abandon traditional story-telling. He didn't want any surprises or plot twists. 'Those things are too 20th century', the director announced. Consequently the film has no plot and has characterless characters. Since the video games are plotless and characterless, it didn't seem to trouble the target fans (it made well over $150 million on an $80 million budget).

Submitting Your Script

In the United States, if you submit a screenplay or a treatment to a producer you must belong to the Writers' Guild of America (WGA) and submit through a registered agent. The agent, however small, will supposedly know the market and which producers have the best development deals going for them. He will target them one by one, to give them an exclusive viewing period.

The decision to buy a script can sometimes be made simply because the producer knows it's a hot property (because he knows somebody else wants it) rather than because of its merits. Some agents equate this with selling a used car, or selling a painting to a blind man. Producers all say they want something new and fresh, but what they really want is something like somebody else's latest blockbuster, only different. The word is that if you have a great script it will be found. But don't count on it.

The producer has a reading period in which to come back to you and your agent. This can be from one to three weeks. If he is interested, he must exercise an option. The option can be from $10,000 to $15,000 against the balance of a six-figure fee paid in stages and paid in full by the first day of filming.

In Britain, as a new writer you could get a development deal from a production company for, say, £5,000 to develop your original idea or treatment. You could also get much less. However, if the producer does not pay an agreed sum or an option, the material must be returned to the writer. You can make a great deal of money on a percentage deal but, for this, you need a good agent.

Many student and novice writers join writing programmes of one kind or another. A growing number of universities around the world have departments devoted to screenwriting. USC and UCLA in Los Angeles has excellent film and screenwriting departments, as does the New York Film Academy. In the UK the National Film School and the London Film School (formerly called the London International Film School) include scriptwriting seminars and lectures. I have listed some at the back of this book. There are all sorts of mail-order courses advertized on the Internet and in writers' magazines. Courses that you can attend personally are generally conducted in groups of from six to twenty student writers. The Arvon Foundation is one of the better ones in England. There are too many would-be gurus out there with little background as writers, so it's important that you look for courses and lecturers with a track record.

In workshop groups, a common practice is to have a few in the class read your script. Everyone in the group, including the instructor, will offer suggestions. You can learn a lot and you can also get many contrary opinions, which is not in itself a bad thing. It shows you how very differently the same character or situation can strike another person.

It is also possible for somebody else in the class to, perhaps unconsciously, dig it out of their memory a few years later thinking it is their own. Being a writer can make you slightly paranoid about your work being stolen. You have to know where to draw the line. No doubt in your working life, you will have ideas stolen. I certainly have. However, if you have one good idea, you are most likely to have many more – it's the person who stole it who has a problem with ideas, if that's a consolation. But take the proper precautions. Likewise, a producer to whom you show a script or treatment may also make a copy, and a year or two later you could find that your story has been ripped off. So how can you prevent it happening to you?

How to Protect Your Property

As mentioned in earlier chapters, before showing your screenplay or treatment to anyone, always post a dated, registered copy to yourself, and when you receive it back in the post, mark *on the outside* the name of the enclosed script and the date. File it away *unopened*, and always keep a record of all your submissions and the names of people you think may have read it. Remember to use a gummed envelope that must be moistened to stick down, so it cannot be opened without tearing the envelope. It is good to seal it with sealing wax.

Doing this means that, if you later come to believe that some aspect of your material has been stolen, you can show proof (so long as the envelope remains *unopened*) that your material predates the material you believe to have been stolen. You can also register your script or treatment with the Writers Guild of America, even if you live outside the United States and are not a member of the Guild. This is not copyright registration, however – in the United States copyrights must be registered with the United States Copyright Office, in Washington, DC, who charge a non-refundable fee that is currently $30 (see www.loc.gov/copyright). In the United Kingdom there is no registration process:

all works are protected by copyright law automatically. If you put the copyright insignia © on your script after your name it will signify to anyone who reads it that you own the copyright, but it does not in itself constitute any sort of registration, or have any legal status.

Registration does not establish proof of originality, merely the date when the material was registered. It can prove that you were there first. You can download the forms and rules for submission from the Writers Guild of America website (www.wga.org) and get the current registration costs. Post them two copies, one separately sealed in an envelope inside. They will number and file the unopened copy. The other copy will be numbered and stamped with their seal and returned to you in your self-addressed envelope. The WGA will keep your sealed copy on file for five years at which time you must renew the registration – if your screenplay has not yet been optioned or made and you still want to protect it.

Several years ago when I was on the Executive Council of the Writers Guild of Great Britain (www.writersguild.org.uk), I tried to set up a registration program similar to WGA's, but those then in charge considered it too much effort and not legally binding.

The legality lies in proving your dated script registration is on file, giving your original story priority. You will also have to prove the suspected plagiarist had access to your material, which may not be easy.

Bernie Corbett, the General Secretary of the Writers Guild of Great Britain informed me that the WGGB has now given a slight nod of approval to a few private companies registering scripts in the UK. The Writers' Copyright Association UK (www.wcauk.com) provides an online service and the Screen Vault offers to store your sealed copy, which would appear to be more effective than one registered online. But be wary of websites offering to register your scripts that do not have Guild approval. There are lots of people out there ready to take your money.

At the time of writing the WGA are in the process of changing the current credit designations for screenwriters. Their website has the current screen credit manual and television credit manual, representing the guidelines used to determine writing credits. If you are a member of the Writers Guild of America, they will arbitrate any dispute for you.

If an unknown writer sends a manuscript to an agent and later sees a similar story on film, it may well be a coincidence. In any event, one cannot copyright an idea. Ideas circulate. Themes, even general plots can be borrowed. Furthermore, you don't need to buy someone's life story to use it as long as you can access the facts from publicly available sources like newspaper reports.

You could, however, get sued for using dialogue, complicated story-lines or exact wording from a copyrighted work. That's why producers often buy the rights to a story that's been in the news just to avoid legal hassles. But even if you can prove that your plot is in someone else's film, you must also prove that the film company had access to it. For that reason, few people sue, and studios and agents are leery of unsolicited manuscripts and submissions from strangers. They generally mail them back unopened out of fear of litigation. So unless you have a 'in', don't send without an agent. It's still safer to send a screenplay than a treatment, particularly when you're starting out.

The Pitch

Steven Spielberg said, 'If a person can tell me the idea in 25 words or less, it's going to make a pretty good movie'. A story like *Big* or *What Women Want* are good examples. Reducing the idea to a couple of sentences in this way is called a logline. The logline for *Kindergarten Cop*, for instance, might be: *A tough cop, in order to find a mother he thinks is involved in embezzlement, has to take over a kindergarten and teach the class.*

Imagine you've actually got an appointment – with or without an agent – to make your pitch. You've got maybe 15 minutes in a producer's office and you were lucky to get that. The quality of your pitch can make the difference.

Stories that can be pitched in a paragraph are called 'high concept'. Pitch the concept, not the story. Focus on communicating your idea in the most exciting way you can. Make your pitch in no more than ten minutes. Tell it as though you just saw it happening and as

visually as you can, expressing the idea, the theme, the quest, the type of people – who the protagonist is and what he wants and how he goes about getting it. Give them only the broad strokes. Don't get bogged down in details. If there is real interest and the producer and his team start asking questions, it could take 40 minutes. If they ask you something you hadn't thought about yet, don't be afraid to say, 'I don't know yet'.

The first question you will be asked is, 'What kind of a film is it? What genre?' Offer some suggestions of other films it is like in some way, to give the producer a way of understanding what you're getting at. Suggesting actors who could play particular roles, especially the star protagonist, is another way of helping the producer visualize your idea, and of sparking his interest. If you know the producer has a commitment with some star, try to make your story fit that person. Remember that above all else, you are there to sell your project.

Unless you strike it lucky and sell to the first person you pitch to, your story must be pitched many times over. If you have written the script already, start with the pitch anyway. Get them hooked on your idea.

The pitch is all a question of simplification and it breaks down to the old question: What if? Here are some sample loglines to give you an idea of the kind of thing you need to get across about your story. The super-condensed version could be the basis for the movie's advertizing tagline.

Driving Miss Daisy: The 20-year relationship between a black chauffeur and his ageing Jewish employer (or) black chauffeur changes white bigot's mind.

Back to the Future: A teenager travels back to 1955 to get his parents together before he ceases to exist (or) Teenager finds future in his past.

Tootsie: An unemployed actor disguises himself as a woman to get work (or) Actor in drag becomes a better man.

Ghostbusters: Three entrepreneurs set up a business to get rid of ghosts in Manhattan (or) Paranormal hit-squad in Manhattan.

From Dusk Till Dawn: Gunslingers meet bloodsuckers in a horror-comedy.

Alien 3: (If you have a star attached, you pitch the name with your story – but only if the star is committed to the project.)

Pursued by acid-salivating monsters Sigourney Weaver meets her match on an all-male prison colony planet.

Harry Potter: The books have sold millions. As far as a producer is concerned, that's logline enough.

One-word titles like *Jaws, Alien* (pitched as *'Jaws* on a spaceship'), *Twister, Gladiator, Speed,* or *Titanic* all tell the audience what they can expect.

Reading is not a strong point with many producers – they have to read so many scripts that the activity quickly ceases to be pleasurable in itself. One producer at Columbia told me, 'When I open a script, I read the first page. If that sounds interesting, I flip to the middle somewhere, and read another page. If I'm still interested, I flip to the last page and if it grabs me – then I go back and read the whole script.' So be sure you grab your producer on the first page.

The Reader's Report

Producers will often first pass a script on to a reader and ask for a report, as a way of weeding out the dull or incompetent ones. This is called coverage and in theory, every script that comes into a studio or production company in the US or UK through proper channels (i.e. not unsolicited) is covered.

One of the assistant script editors at Tri-Star noted that the studio liked their reports written in a straightforward style, very dry and with no personal opinion, no off-the-cuff 'cute' remarks, and definitely no casting or marketing suggestions, which are up to the executives to decide.

The reader will write a half-page synopsis of the plot with comments on its strengths and weaknesses. The reader will usually assess the script by judging its success in conforming to a pre-determined checklist of points, as follows:

1) Concept: Is the concept actually marketable in a trailer? If they show a trailer in a cinema or on TV, can they clip one riveting minute to sell the picture?
2) Overall marketing: Will the story lend itself to marketing for posters, TV, newspapers, and interviews, and are there any merchandising aspects to the story or characters?
3) What is the theme? The logline?
4) What is the hook? The initial turning point?

5) Does it carry the story forward?
6) Who is the target audience?
7) What does the story deal with most?
8) What does the audience need to know?
9) Is this concept original?
10) Does it offer an experience something you couldn't get from real life?
11) Is the technical execution of the script professional?
12) What about the formatting – is it a three-act structure?
13) Is it from a book or stage play or other source material?
14) Can it interest star actors?
15) Does it have a budget? (This may have been done by a former possible production that didn't get consummated.)
This is accompanied by a printed form:

Reader's Report

Title:..
Author:..
Genre:...
Length:..
Log Line..
Story Line..
....

'Elements Attached':...............(Star/Director)

Rating:.........(Excellent/Good/Fair/Poor)
Characters:..
Dialogue:...
Setting:..
Production Values:...............................

☐ RECOMMEND
☐ CONSIDER
☐ PASS

Reading between the lines, the reader's recommendations could be interpreted as:
Recommend: means 'I'd put my money on it'.
Consider: means 'You back it'.
Pass: means 'You couldn't pay me to see it'.

The completed report will be returned to the executive who submitted it for coverage. Mike Medavoy, head of Tri-Star from 1990 to 1994, said that he read every coverage beginning with the logline and then read the short paragraph accompanying it that describes the film.

Since most writers would prefer that the producer read their script rather than the soulless reader's report, those with a little clout try their best to short-circuit the readers and get as close to the Head of Production as they can. 'Avoid the underlings' seems to be the message. All of this is good advice when you are established but it is of little use to the beginning writer unless he has some very good contacts. If you do have contacts, don't be shy about using them in the nicest possible way.

If your script is accepted it goes to the next stage. Remember, the script is a point of departure for the film.

The Pre-Production Process

Writer Roger Simon says, 'A lot has been said about the studio development process and not any of it good ... Each studio has 25 to 30 junior executives and every time you 'take a meeting' there are six or seven new people you've never seen before with yellow pads taking down your every word.' Simon advises avoiding the development process if possible. Naturally, if your agent can get you in to see the producer directly you may bypass the reader's report and the development process, but that happens rarely with new writers.

In the development process, committees tell you what's wrong. You could be told that 'this is a brilliant script except that we hate the leading character'. Often the criticism will be that the character is not 'sympathetic enough', or that he is not in enough jeopardy. So the writer has to suck out the leading character and replace him with somebody more acceptable to the committee. Naturally, this affects every scene – and the entire body of the work.

The British writer Christopher Isherwood, who worked in Hollywood for many years (his play I Am A Camera was the basis for the musical Cabaret) said: 'Compromise is inseparable from making motion pictures in a big commercial way. But compromise demands great strength of purpose. You have to be quite clear in how far you will give way. Be open-minded in considering other people's suggestions – and you have to judge every instant if the point at issue is vital or not. You can get lazy – and corrupted by the money. One can argue dispassionately if one is ready, if necessary, to throw up one's job; not in a tizzy of temperament – but because one can

honestly retreat no further. Most of us, once in – don't want to throw up our jobs.'

Working With A Producer

Once you've got the job (and this is equally true in television) your producer will want to meet with you to thrash out any ideas he has for changes he wants you to make to the script. Never try to do this on the phone: you need to meet face-to-face to sense clearly what it is your producer is really trying to say to you. You need to take notes or use a pocket tape recorder (ask first) and then try to make the changes he wants. If you have a valid reason why his ideas won't work, then state your point of view clearly and rationally – ideally being more articulate than he is. After all, you're the wordsmith. You might win your point.

Never lose your temper, no matter how sorely tried. If you see that you are losing, go home and figure out a way to give him what he wants – impossible as it may seem – without destroying the core of your work. Use lateral thinking to come up with an ingenious solution. Successful filmmaking is based on building up good relationships with the other players. If you don't, you'll find another writer replacing you – and you can be pretty sure of not working for that producer again.

Still, you must not allow fear of rejection to deter your strong sense of direction about your work. If you think the producer is going to hate something and you'd better change it before it is even read – then you're dead as a writer. Never try to outguess the rejection or the negatives. But do listen to the suggestions when they are made from the top. The producer (who is, or might soon be paying you) is not always wrong. You need a thick skin and must be able to 'go with the flow' because you're also going to take a lot of knocks from the development people, the actors, the director, and the critics when the film finally gets made (if they remember to mention the writer at all).

Getting the Green Light

A script that has had a negative response and literally been turned down can sometimes become the flavour of the month if it suddenly has a star attached or some news event has made the subject matter timely (as happened with *K19: The Widowmaker*, discussed in chapter 15). The political landscape in the producer's office changes with a new set of criteria.

Let's say you've got a green light. What next? I'm afraid you have no control of how many writers the producer can call in after he has bought your script. The first draft (or the draft you hand in, though that probably won't be your first!) is the writer's creation and whatever he hopes it will be had better be on the page at that point. The next draft begins the metamorphosis from what was in the writer's head and thoughts, into the director's head and thoughts. So lucidity is one of your best weapons.

If it's a treatment you've sold, you will be contracted to hand in your first draft screenplay by a certain date and must be available to do the first revisions (see below).

Directors work in different ways. Relationships vary; the writer might become good friends with the director or the relationship might become so abrasive that there has got to be a split. If that happens, remember – it is the writer who will be considered dispensable. Director Sydney Pollack likes to hang out with his writer while making a film, in what he refers to as an 'odd forced marriage'.

Pre-Production

Once the shooting script has been agreed a shooting budget is worked out. This includes all the things about which the writer will not be asked his opinion, unless he's very famous, which includes actors, director (with whom he may already have been working), the cinematographer, production manager, designer, location scout and all the equipment – cameras, film stock, lights and so on. If the producer doesn't already have all his funding, he will try to finalize it now. Many a production has come unstuck part way through filming because the promised money didn't appear when the bills needed paying. But the writer/s may still be on call when director and actors come on board with fresh ideas.

Categories of Revision

A script may go through many different stages

and different levels of revision. These have all been carefully defined by the Writers Guild of America (WGA) in order to determine what credit each writer in the process should receive.

Revisions: According to the WGA Minimum Basic Agreement this means: 'the writing of changes in dialogue, narration or action, but not including a rewrite'. It includes changes in scene structure or omitting or adding a minimum number of scenes, strengthening a character's part or omitting characters, or polishing dialogue in accordance with suggestions by producer, director, actors – or all three. Sometimes these suggestions might conflict. Find out who has the power (who pays you) and follow his dictates first. If necessary you will need to get him to pacify the others. He can have a cut-off on your services at this point. Or he can call you in for a rewrite. Another writer could be called in 'just to punch up the dialogue', which may mean that, or more cynically may mean throwing out your entire script and doing a total rewrite.

A Rewrite: This means major changes in the plot, story-line, or interrelationship of characters, and this service receives a separate fee. It is a WGA ruling that the original writer is allowed to do the first draft rewrites with the director. Rewrites are usually assigned in stages – there will be a first set of revisions when you get one person's input, a second set when another person's comments are received, and so on. One of the chief duties of the rewrite is to tailor the script to the star, who is now on board. The actor is consulted because he knows what he will be good at doing or saying. Further rewrites may be made by a writer(s) on their own screenplay, or these may be assigned to a completely different writer.

A Page-One Rewrite: is a complete rewrite of the script (i.e. 'starting from page one') using only the original story-line. When the producer asks for this, somebody is not happy with your dialogue, characterization, or even the way you have developed your plot line. All they presumably like is your original premise, and maybe not even that. In that case it in unlikely to be you who will be asked to do the rewrite. Some writers struggling to survive in the Hollywood jungle advise, 'take the money and run, because at some point you're going to be asked to leave the stage'.

Collaborations and The Third Approach:
Often you can be assigned to work with
another writer or perhaps with the director.
Good personal relationships are primary, and if
there is bending over backwards to be done,
this is where you will need a flexible spine.
When working with a collaborator, making
creative decisions about story plot, characters,
or dialogue, I have always found that, if you
cannot agree on a necessary change, you
should look for a third way to do the scene.
Remember all those lists you made? Go back to
see if there is another possible solution to this
problem – an option you can both accept. Such
mental stretching forces your creative juices to
flow, and you usually end up with a better idea
than either of your original solutions.

Determining Credits

When the final shooting script is finished
and you compare all those additional
contributions to your script, you can ascertain
how much of your original material is left.
Unless someone else rewrites 33 per cent or
more of the screenplay the original writer gets
a solo credit. Any additional writers to a
project will have to contribute 50 per cent to
get shared credit of 'Written by Mr X and
Miss Y'. Writers who add some dialogue or
story changes of more than 30 per cent but
less than 50 per cent, which are actually used
in the finished film might or might not get

any credit, depending on the producer and
arbitration. Naturally, additional writers try to
add as much as they can in order to get that
precious credit. If your script is sold to an
American producer and if there is a dispute
over credits, it can be arbitrated through the
WGA. Your agent and the other writer's agent
wil arbitrate on the financial aspects involved.
Two of the writers of *Lethal Weapon 4*, Miles
Millar and Alfred Gough, only secured their
credits after arbitration.

'Screenplay By': This means that the writer
has written the screenplay adapted from
another medium – book, play, article, etc. –
not his own original story.

'Screen Story By': When a rewriter has
created a screenplay substantially new and
different (subject to arbitration), the original
story will get this separate credit. This means
the final screenplay is based on another
writer's screen story or screenplay.

'Written By': This is a stronger credit and
means that the writer has written both the
original story and the screenplay. If it is from
his own book or play, it could also say it is
based on his book.

When the final screenplay is filmed, a cash
award can be paid to the writer with either
shared or sole credit as 'Screenplay by' or
'Written by'. This is called a Production Bonus
and can be a considerable sum if based on a
percentage.

CHAPTER 18 | THE PRODUCTION AND AFTER

Most often today, after having sold a screenplay or story, the writer sees only the producer and his junior executive assistants during the development period and into the pre-production days when, if he's lucky, he'll get to see the director. Once into production he is most often kept away from the director – not to mention the art director, costume designer, and actors. The concept of that fabled teamwork goes out the window.

Logically, the director is meant to interpret the writer's vision, but more often he discards what he doesn't want in favour of his own inspiration. If you find yourself actually invited onto the set, be aware of the protocols: if you have a burning need to offer a suggestion, approach the director only (no matter who the suggestion is for). If you were to offer a suggestion directly to, say, the cameraman, that will be considered to be 'crossing the line' and you will not be invited back again.

Actors have different points of view about writers. At the four-day Forum International du Cinema et de l'Escriture in Monte Carlo in October 2002, the panel of speakers included Christopher Lee, who stated, 'For actors, everything begins with the written word. Without it, we'd have nothing to do.' But Tim Roth's opinion differed: 'A writer is really the last person you want to see on the set, even the great ones. While we're collaborating on a screenplay, I always tell them "this is the time to enjoy yourself, because once [the director says] *Action*, it's over."'

Although the writer is the original creative artist and all the others are interpreters of his work, making a film is not a question of democracy. Roth is not the only one who would prefer the writer to disappear once the script is finished. Once into production the writer's work is at the mercy of producer, director, and stars. The producer can always hire another writer to rewrite you, if the director doesn't do it himself. That is why so many successful writers today turn their hand to directing. The two-hatted writer/producer or writer/director has a better chance of making the film he wants.

The screenwriter cannot retain total control of his work. Writers such as novelist William Nicholson (*Gladiator* and *Shadowlands*) said 'The writer is valued and important, but if someone else on the team comes up with a good idea or a suitable line, it goes into the script ... don't get precious, get writing.' Nicholson is respected and sought after by producers because of the quality of his work. There are many others. Joe Eszterhas is one of the highest paid writers in Hollywood and producers have a great respect for writers who can command from $200, 000 to over $1m for a screenplay. Money talks.

Who Does What?

I have listed below (in the order in which they generally become involved) the main people who will be part of making a film once it has been green-lighted – and how you may meet them.

Pre-Production

Executive Producer(s): The person who buys the script or idea from the writer(s) and finances (via backers and distributors) the film. A good producer is proficient at financial and logistical planning. He's ultimately responsible for all decisions concerning cast, director, and crew, and he supervises the production, distribution, and theatrical release. There can be several producers and separate production companies involved, depending on how many different sources the money is coming from.

Line Producer: The person who handles the day-to-day problems and reports to the executive producers.

The Production Office: The producer will initially have set up his production office and hired his production staff. Sets and costumes are being designed, locations chosen, crews hired and shooting schedules are laid out on large charts in his office. Storyboards are drawn and posted for all relevant departments. Obviously, the more that can be fixed and worked out before first day of shooting, the better.

Screenwriter: This may or may not be you,

but if a writer's services are wanted on set, it will be someone with a forte for quickly producing strong dialogue. More fundamental problems of story construction and characterization will be assumed to have been fixed by the time filming starts.

Production Designers: Designing the sets and the overall look of the film falls to a team of production designers.

Unit Production Manager: The PM is responsible for the day-to-day running of the production office, scheduling, budgeting, and handling permits. He reports directly to the line producer.

Production

The actual work of shooting a film is like laying the wood and setting the firelighters for a conflagration.

Director: The director is there to stoke the fires and keep the flames burning. He needs a solid team of people behind him. He is the person whose creative talents interpret the screenplay visually and who works with cast and crew to bring it to the screen.

First Assistant Director: The 1st AD's responsibility covers cast and crew and the shooting schedule. Assists the director on each shot; 2nd and 3rd ADS are also required on most films.

Continuity (or Script) Supervisor: The highly accurate memory of the script continuity person is imperative. Continuity must ensure that shots will actually cut together in editing. Takes photos and notes of props and action, entrances and exits, clothes and hair to make sure these details match the previous or following scenes (possibly shot on another day) where they need to.

Casting director: Aside from the stars, and with the approval of producer and director, the casting director chooses actors and works out their contracts with their agents. Extras are hired through special agencies.

Actors: The creative talent who interpret the roles under the guidance of the director. Stars are another matter. They also have a lot of input into the script since the BO is dependent on their being shown off at their best. They usually come with an entourage of minions. If they happen to like your writing, you may have struck it lucky. They could ask to see more of your work.

Principal Photography

The minute the cameras begin to roll, the money pours out like a severed artery. Now comes the work of physically making the film.

Director of photography: Working closely with the director, the DOP (or DP or Cinematographer) is responsible for the photography and instructs Camera Operators, including the Lighting Cameraman and the grips and gaffers, on placing the cameras. On small films or documentaries, the DOP may operate the camera and act as Lighting Cameraman.

Camera operator: As the title suggests, this person operates the camera under the instruction of the director or DOP.

Camera Assistants: Changing film stock, filling out camera reports, slating shots and cleaning camera equipment are the duties of the assistants.

Focus Pullers: If the lens is not properly in focus it can destroy a shot.
The director normally rehearses actors and crew, blocking the action (to work out who will be standing where, and from that the position/s of the camera/s) before shooting the scene. Stand-ins replace stars while the lighting is set. For action scenes, more than one camera will be used. Low-budget films may use only one or two cameras for a scene because of the time taken in lighting each new camera angle.

Whenever the position of the camera is changed it becomes a new shot. Each scene will be made up of many single shots. When the director calls 'That's a take', he is finished with a shot. The same take re-shot is a retake. There are many reasons why they may need to retake a shot. The actor may fluff his line, the lighting may not be quite right, or the focus puller may have his lens out of focus.

Key grip: The grips are a team who set up and adjust camera and dolly equipment for each shot. This person is in charge of the team is the key grip.

Editor: After screening the dailies or rushes (film footage) the editor compiles a rough cut as the picture is being shot. When principal photography is completed the director supervises this initial editing.

Location Sound Mixer: This person is in charge of recording and mixing the sound recorded during shooting away from the studio.

Boom Operator: Assists with the microphone on a crane arm out of shot of camera. On location, extraneous sounds such as cars and planes can slow up shooting.

Any remaining noises to be edited out of the soundtrack, along with extra sounds to be put in (e.g. the sound of feet walking where this is important but hasn't been recorded successfully on set – such as a scene that takes place in the dark) are added in the post-production phase by the Foley Editor. It is increasingly common in feature films for large portions of the dialogue – even the entire script – to be re-recorded in the studio by the actors after filming is over (miming to their own mouths on screen), allowing maximum control in fine-tuning the quality of the sound track.

Gaffer: The gaffer is in charge of electrical work and is assisted by a Best Boy. Assisting the DP, the gaffer creates the correct mood lighting.

Production assistants: Fresh to the business, also called 'gofers' because they 'go for' anything, from coffee to running messages. One holds the clapperboard at the start of the scene: this indicates the scene and take numbers, as well as providing a convenient means of synchronizing the film with the soundtrack recording. At the end of a scene the clapperboard is photographed upside down.

Composer: A film employs a technical arsenal of enticements. After the rough cut or after the final cut the composer writes and records a 'mood' score and chooses the songs to be used in the film. Music can make a difference in bringing a scene into focus. But the over-use of music today in some films (and in too much television drama) drowns out dialogue and is utilized as a cheap metaphor for the story, crudely attempting to choreograph the audience's emotional response. The truth is that producers make money on performance rights for using specially commissioned music, so they have an incentive to use more of it rather than less, in many cases to the detriment of the film.

Sound Editor: works with the composer to place the music in the proper position. All this is under the guidance of the director.

Special Effects and Computer Animation: A writer should be aware of the latest technical advances if you are intending to write sci-fi, in particular.

Post-Production

Now is the time that the director and possibly the producer will work with the editor to assemble the many hundreds of separate shots and scenes. Special effects are put in, sound track and audio effects are added and finally, the rough cut film is assembled. This is screened for all interested parties and from it, the final finished film, re-edited according to their comments, is completed and ready for previews and distribution.

Hollywood films will almost always be shown first to a preview audience (a randomly selected audience with no connection to the production), and their reactions, detailed on cards they are asked to fill in, will be used to judge if any further adjustment needs to be made. The most common reaction of preview audiences is to ask for happier endings and the tying up of what may have been deliberately ambiguous loose ends. Changes arising out of the preview may be accomplished by further minor re-editing using existing footage, or at the other extreme it may require calling the entire cast and crew back to shoot some newly written scenes.

The Added Expenses

Contingency Bond: (completion bond) If the film has run over its shooting schedule or for any reason has cost more than initially budgeted, the 'bond' is effectively a high-interest emergency loan to cover these additional expenses, allowing the film to be completed and thus ensuring that all the money invested so far is not wasted. It is hard money to come by the producer pays a lot for it, but it is a prime necessity.

CHAPTER 19 | DISTRIBUTION AND MARKETING

The business of launching films into the market place is highly competitive. Good marketing can do a lot towards making a low- to medium-budget film with minor or no-name actors into a huge success. Conversely, bad marketing can be enough to destroy the chances of a big-budget film.

Where is the Market Place?

Feature films usually open theatrically first, in cinemas where they can be seen with maximum visual and sound quality. Their next market place is home video and DVD. Pay TV can follow, and two or three years after first release they are sold to television companies and shown free-to-air to the public. The response to its initial theatrical release will determine what sort of ride a film gets for the future.

The UK has a number of major distributors (affiliated to Hollywood studios) and independent (unaffiliated) distributors who handle non-studio and 'niche' product. The distributor's role often starts before filming begins. They collaborate with the filmmakers, exhibitors (cinema operators), publicists, advertising agencies, and designers. They want to know the genre, may even wish to read the screenplay, and certainly want to know the target market. Sales and marketing strategy is individually geared to each film and developed with the production company in order to interest the widest possible audience. The distributor isn't selling straight to the public although finally his efforts will affect ticket sales. His primary targets are exhibitors, the media and his marketing partners.

Five or six new films open in British cinemas each week. A single distributor may handle around 25 films a year. There are more than 300 new releases each year in the United Kingdom (many of them American) and around 420 in the United States, so it is highly competitive with only a certain number of films getting a crack at prime cinemas for their first release.[1]

In the US a medium-budget film would cost about $35 million to make, with another $10–25 million spent on prints and advertizing. In such expensive waters, most films can't expect to recoup their costs from the theatrical release alone. The major profits for the distributors (and the film companies) come from only a handful of films.

Marketing Angles

Could the film spin off into a television series, as *Stargate* (1994) spawned *Stargate SG-1*? Naturally, the studio wants to utilize every potential for making money from the property. If there is a possibility of it getting awards, should it be released in time to be considered for the Oscars and BAFTAs? (most awards take place between January and March, judging films released the previous year). What were the stars' last films and were they commercially or critically successful? What are competitors releasing at the same time? Is it an 'event' film (blockbuster) or a 'niche' film for a select audience? Does it have an added value as a sequel or franchise that could give it an edge?

The distributor's considerations, some of which the writer should consider, include: What genre is it? What genre have recent hit films been? Is this for a specific holiday release? Does it have a good shelf life? In a sense they evaluate the property like a sack of potatoes, but what they are really asking is: Is it the type of story people will want to go back and see again and again? Could it have a sequel? When are the appropriate screens available? Is it important enough to get reviewed on release? Is there already a buzz about it for any reason prior to its UK release? Has it opened in the US and was it successful there? What classification will it get from the British Board of Film Classification (BBFC)? Distributors previously favoured rating no more restrictive than PG – but this has recently altered slightly in the UK to admit children at a younger age if accompanied by parents.

It's useful for big-budget films, but not essential, to have their distribution deal in place before they start. The distributor's opinion on a film's playability is often considered before it is given the green light for production. But although distributors often read the script up front and appear interested, most will make no final decisions until they see the finished product, particularly from independent production companies. However, in some cases, with producers who have a proven track record, distributors will partner the production company and invest in the film. In the case of certain major films, distributors will even be willing to pay the company an advance against sales. Distributors also pay the print duplication costs. A 35mm print of a two-hour film costs around $10,000, which means a wide release is costly (blockbusters might be released on 3,000 screens at once).

Under English law, two weeks is the maximum booking period for a new release. After that, the exhibitor and distributor together will decide if it should play longer. 'At Cinemas Everywhere!' could mean that the film has opened in 300 cinemas UK-wide, and often on more than one screen per cinema. In 2002 there are actually more than 3,000 screens spread throughout the multiplexes. That is one-third higher than the number in 1982. Exhibitors' investment in new sites and facilities has pushed ticket costs up 50 per cent in the last ten years. Some £727 million worth of tickets were sold in 2001 in the UK, but exhibitors complain that the growth in admissions has not kept pace with the increase in screens.

Even 'Guerrilla' Films Need Friends

Low, low budget independent films find it harder to get international distribution (or sometimes any distribution at all). These independently-made films are sometimes referred to as 'guerrilla films' and are generally made by people with no previous experience in producing who are working outside the system. Those lucky enough to get deferments (agreements to work for no up-front fee) from their actors and crew may actually get their film made. A few will eventually land some sort of distribution, Generally, these films have no stars or even

known faces. The dividing line between high/low budget also affects minimum production costs for various crew and technical staff, extras, and so on. The 'little picture' had better win some festival awards if it hopes to get distribution and earn back its backers' investment.

However, in the hands of experience, there can be some big surprises in the low-budget field. One winner in 2002 really got its break because of Tom Hanks's half-Greek wife, Rita Wilson. She saw a one-woman play written and performed by Canadian-Greek stand-up comedienne Nia Vardalos. Unable to crack acting roles in Hollywood, Vardalos wrote a play about the culture clash when she married into a WASP family. Wilson and Hanks produced the film *My Big Fat Greek Wedding* from a screenplay by Vardalos – with no-name actors and Vardalos herself playing the lead. She was only paid $500 for her screenplay, plus $150,000 to star in the film, but she was given 8 per cent of the profits. The budget was $5 million. Marketing costs added another $25 million. The big distributors turned it down, considering it no more than a made-for-TV film. It has become one of the most profitable independent movies of all time having grossed over $241 million in the US alone by April 2003.

Taking the Plunge

Plenty of former film students have made one – and only one – film. When they can't get film distribution, the hope is that they can unload it directly to a television or video sale. The UK has a thriving home video market worth an annual £1.6 billion across rental and sell-through sales. These are often handled by sister companies to the major distributors and will consider low-budget first time filmmakers.

But unless you are making a film for around £5,000, and can get it into a festival with some positive comment, it's important to hook or at least interest a small distributor if possible before your camera starts turning. It won't be easy, but if it were, everyone would be doing it.

What can your script offer that is new, different, and has commercial value? What market are you aiming at? Talking to distributors up front might give you some valuable advice and direction. It may also be a learning curve. The distributor's cut of profits may seem out of proportion, but it's nothing to the loss the filmmaker and his backers will suffer if he doesn't get distribution.

On a first foray the filmmaker is better advised to take his time in preparation. If you're planning to write, direct and make the film yourself and you've got enough rich acquaintances to have raised the finance, be sure your project is commercial enough to get that magic distribution.

The Post-*Star Wars* World

In the mid-1970s Hollywood film executives were not yet concerned with 'event' movies, special effects, or marketing tie-ins such as Happy Meals and theme park rides. They had not yet settled on the the 'key male 14–24 age-group demographic', because films were still considered to be a medium primarily aimed at adults. Then along came *Star Wars* (1977). There is no question of the impact it had on the American film industry and the flow of blockbusters that followed. It still tops polls as the favourite film of all time. A quarter-century after its release, *Star Wars'* effect in refocusing the whole creative and marketing effort of Hollywood onto the straightforward plots and simplified characterizations that would appeal to an audience of children and teenagers is abundantly clear. At the time of writing, *Harry Potter and the Philosopher's Stone* is in second place to *Titanic* as the all-time box-office winner. The five (so far) films of the *Star Wars* cycle have made more than $1 billion at the box office, with $4 billion more coming from merchandizing and videos – box office receipts were only the tip of the financial iceberg.

Lucas moved away from traditional film techniques in making *Attack of the Clones* (2002), the fifth film in the *Star Wars* cycle, the first major film shot entirely digitally (with the special Sony 24P camera). No film stock was used. The production, complete with virtual sets and special effects, was created electronically in computerized pixels.

Why is it important to you as a writer to know about markets? Because you don't start making carriage wheels when the cars of the future are going to be running on hydrogen. It may not be your job to market the film that is made from your screenplay, but having some overall understanding of how films get sold and what producers are looking for will help you to choose a subject and story that has a marketing potential. That means some producer might buy it.

For Britain and the United States you cannot market a film that does not fit into a specific genre because the marketing people complain that they don't know how to sell it. Therefore production companies are reluctant to buy it. When you pitch your screenplay to the producer remember that he has to market it, so make it easy for him. Clearly state the genre – hopefully a popular one that he likes.

Market research confirms that the most frequent cinemagoers in the UK are now between the ages of 15 and 24 (since so many films are aimed at them, this is perhaps not surprising). But distributors feel that the UK and US audience is broadening as the population ages, and they aim for a core target market for each film. Sometimes they find that a film crosses over and catches a new type of audience.

No one is certain what makes a hit film. Success of one genre or star in a particular type of picture does not mean making a duplicate will be successful. The producers thought that the sequels of *Back to the Future*, *Batman*, and *Jaws* were going to be winners, but they did not reach the BO success of the originals. Producers thought *American Beauty* (1999) would probably take around $30 million at the US box office. Instead it took $130 million.

Ultimately, a movie is often only made when a proven box-office-draw actor agrees to make it. Most actors don't have the courage to do risky material. The brutal truth is that the 'money' doesn't have the courage to back what they consider risky.

Sir Alan Parker said in the 1997 BAFTA Lecture: 'Heretical as it may sound, are the films good enough to be distributed in the first place? If they look like TV films, maybe they should go straight to TV ... we are weakest of all in the impossibly difficult art of screenwriting – and too many films are rushed into production before the ideas and screenplays are adequately formed ...'

Chapter 20 | THE INDUSTRY IN THE 21ST CENTURY

In The UK

Sir Alan Parker CBE, chair of the British Film Council, recently said that the UK film industry needs radical reinvention. 'We can never be the biggest film industry in the world, but we should be right up there near the top of the league, not permanently hovering in the relegation zone ... We need to abandon forever the "little England" vision of a UK industry comprised of small British film companies delivering parochial British films. That, I suspect, is what many people think of when they talk of a "sustainable" British industry. Well, it's time for a reality check. That "British" film industry never existed, and, in the brutal age of global capitalism, it never will.'

Hollywood still dominates the world film market in terms of its global reach: nearly 80 percent of films widely distributed and screened in Europe are American-made. But in America the majority of films from Europe only reach art-house audiences.

Lord Puttnam reported in his BAFTA lecture in June 2002, that, 'British filmmakers are especially well placed to reflect the complexity of our world. Unlike many in Hollywood who unquestioningly believe that they operate at the epicentre of the world, we know from hard experience that we most certainly do not. But as a consequence of our history, we are, or ought to be better placed to create sophisticated but accessible stories which demonstrate a genuine empathy and understanding of the real world.'

Every country needs its own homegrown film and television output to retain and mirror its national identity. Entertainment is more than just escapism, it teaches something about cultural values. A country's films are an affirmation of all the elements that set that culture apart – the customs, social attitudes and mores, the food, dress, language, and many facets that make it individual.

Yet while each country should make films for its home market, if filmmakers want to have a voice outside their own borders, they must aim some of their product at a wider international audience. There's really no mystique to it: the American industry's success is based on appealing to the maximum number of people with a marketable and commercial product, ensuring that their films get distributed and enjoyed internationally.

The Worldwide Marketplace

There is no reason why a good movie cannot satisfy both markets, and European filmmakers are now trying to produce product that can enter this wider trade. In recent years France has made a few films that have been extremely successful abroad, shown with subtitles. Among those were *Les Visiteurs* (1993) and *Amélie* (2001).

Some British films have achieved international recognition while remaining characteristically British, such as *Four Weddings and a Funeral, Billy Elliot, Lock, Stock and Two Smoking Barrels* (US/UK), *The Full Monty* (UK/US), *Notting Hill* (US/UK), and *Topsy Turvy*. You will note that they tend to be in the genre of comedy or light entertainment. In the same category, Australia's *Moulin Rouge,* with one homegrown star and director and several British actors, was a hit at the Oscars in 2002. People in any English-speaking country can relate to the human relationships and problems the characters face in these films, and adding foreign subtitles or dubbing opens the markets worldwide.

Only a handful of British films fit into this international category and the majority of those rely partly or wholly on American finance. Many British and continental films and stories are bought up by Hollywood studios and remade, setting them in America, such as Nick Hornby's novel *High Fidelity*, which was relocated from London to Chicago when the film was made in 2000. In 2002 Swedish writer/director Lukas Moodysson's *Tillsammans* (released in English as *Together*) was bought by UK's FilmFour and the US production house Number9Productions to shoot an English-language remake. The filmmaker said, 'In general I think all these American remakes are a sort of cultural imperialism ... My film is set in a 1970s Swedish commune with vegetarian food, free sex, and more Marx than Coca-Cola. It will be funny to see what an American 1970s commune looks like.'[1]

But there is a silent revolution going on that an English-speaking writer should be aware of. Some European countries are widening their market by producing films in English. The $36 million French film *Blueberry* (scheduled for release in 2004) was shot in Spain and Mexico in English, as was Denmark's delightful *Italian for Beginners* (2000). The Northern Lights/Nordisk Film English-language production *I Am Dina* (2002), the most expensive Scandinavian film ever, cost $16 million and was sold internationally at Cannes. It is part of a growing market coming from Denmark and other Nordic countries. Its director, Ole Bornedal, says that if you want to make expensive films for the international market they *must* be in English.

Zentropa Entertainment's CEO Peter Aalbaek confirms that it is impossible to package a film with a budget exceeding $3 million if you shoot it with Danish dialogue. He points out that it takes international funding, and foreign financiers are not putting money into Danish-language films.

John Malkovich tried to get his film *The Dancer Upstairs* (2002) made for five years but could not raise finance. He had worked with British writer Nicholas Shakespeare adapting the latter's novel for the screen. It is loosely based on the story of the hunt for the Peruvian communist terrorist Abimael Guzman, founder of the Shining Path movement. After a few turndowns from American actors who didn't like the theme of revolutions in South America, Malkovich settled on Spanish actor Javier Bardem to play the lead (the police detective who tracks down Guzman). Bardem did not speak English (though he had received an Oscar nomination in 2001 for *Before Night Falls*) but quickly learned. Malkovich got the film financed in 2002 only when he found a Spanish producer who had a separate company in Spain to make films in English. Because it is not

(mainly) sub-titled it is not relegated to arthouse showings and got a major release.

English–Language Opportunities in Foreign Films

With other markets such as China, Japan, Russia and other continental countries opening to their films, producers can make sales outside their own borders. But European filmmakers are still aiming at the big market. Much of the European talent finds its way to Hollywood. Continental and British filmmakers have historically helped to shape Hollywood from the days of Billy Wilder and Alfred Hitchcock to Wolfgang Petersen and Paul Verhoeven. Talented Europeans can't wait to take advantage of the higher budgets and a wealth of special effects at their disposal, to say nothing of much bigger salaries. None of which helps the development of its own home industry.

Many Scandinavian directors who stayed at home, by contrast, have found a foothold in the American market by using some British actors in their English-language films, though they are perhaps best known for their Danish-language films such as Thomas Vinterberg's *Festen* (1998), Søren Kragh-Jacobsen's *Mifune* (1999), Lone Scherfig's engaging *Italian For Beginners* (with 650,000 sales in Germany alone, and making $4.5 million in the US), and Lars von Trier's *The Idiots* (1998). This group was formed in Copenhagen in 1995 as a collective of film directors who expressed the goal of countering 'certain tendencies' towards 'cosmetics' over content, and stating new rules of chastity for filmmaking. None of these directors work exclusively in the Dogme style, however, and all of them have gone on to make films in English to appeal to a wider market, though ironically with mostly less success than their Danish-language work.

In Britain today, filmmaking is less of an industry and more a question of individual filmmakers or independent companies getting together to finance their film or television projects, with the lucky ones able to snag a good distributor through a major American company. Many of the successful international films that have been made over the last ten years have to a great extent been tailored to this wider market and feature at least one

American actor, or British actors who are well known to Americans. In this way the language barrier between British and American English has become progressively more marginalized.

Movies made by other European countries are filmed in one of the 11 major continental languages, but often with actors from a mixture of countries each speaking in their own language. This means that, wherever the film is shown, some of the actors will be dubbed, which tends to reduce the naturalness of the dialogue. The film will have subtitles for release in English-speaking countries, but it will get only an arthouse booking.

Then too, the story structure is generally not mainstream Hollywood. European filmmakers are increasingly beginning to think that it is not just a language issue but there is a need for a professional approach to writing a screenplay that lies at the heart of the problem. Many are hoping to launch their English-language films into the voracious market and get on the American gravy train. They could use some good English-speaking multi-tongued writers.

And then there are the American films shot in the UK to take advantage of the highly skilled British technicians and cheaper costs to film. *Gladiator* made in 2000 cost $100 million. By the middle of shooting Dreamworks was in trouble. Russell Crowe was not happy with the writer, John Logan, who had written the screenplay with David Franzoni from Franzoni's story. Logan was fired from the project.

The production company, Dreamworks, called in British writer William Nicholson, who read the script, turned down the rewrite job, then reconsidered. He had come up with a way to shape the efficient killer gladiator, Maximus, into a more empathetic character by showing the 'back story' – his love for his wife and child. Nicholson was rewriting scenes as they were being shot, and Crowe was still not happy. He didn't like having to learn entire speeches just as he went before the camera.

'On top of that', Nicholson said, 'producers don't like writers meeting actors'. Nicholson had little to complain about financially – he was paid $100,000 a week for 14 weeks.

Normally if you lose one day's shooting it can cost the company $100,000. But a major feature film involves working fifteen hours a day for at least twelve weeks and can cost around $500,000 a day. Actors are hired on a 'play or pay' basis and if the schedule is not ready for them or the film is cancelled, they must be paid anyway. In some crucial cases, writers can be hired on the same basis.

Producers have other screenplay problems. When Fox screened the first rough cut of the remake of *Doctor Doolittle* starring Eddie Murphy, nobody laughed. The head of Fox, Bill Mechanic, called in 20 top comedy writers and set them to work rewriting the dialogue of the animals, giving the four-legged actors all the punch lines. In effect, it made Murphy the straight man, but it worked.

Is this the age of digging up the old hits and reissuing them as the Director's Cut? Francis Ford Coppola, reissued *Apocalypse Now Redux* in 2001 – a 45 minute longer version of his 1979 film. With a self-indulgent performance by Brando as a mad martinet - it was originally nicknamed Apocalypse Later because it took five years to complete. It was the first film to examine the Vietnam war and cost $70 million, much from Coppola's own pocket. But it made $180 million at the B.O. and Coppola obtained rights to the picture in perpetuity. Its revolutionary sound system won an Oscar for best sound cinematography. It has been called brilliant, bizarre, pulp adventure, war fantasy, complex, unforgettable. Joseph Conrad's *Hearts of Darkness* inspired the plot structure and Eleanor Coppola made a documentary of the same name on the making of the film.

The Digital Future

Orson Welles once said that cinema was one of the few art forms where the artist can never get to a point where he can actually own and control all the tools he needs to express himself. But that concept is changing dramatically in the age of digital technology.

In the 1990s the action genre was the prime box-office draw. This has been bolstered in the new millennium by the new possibilities created by computer generated imagery (CGI), both in rendering the effects of live-action films (such as *Bad Boys II*, 2003) more spectacular, and in creating completely computer-generated animations with no human actors on screen. Yet the digital revolution will have perhaps an even greater impact on the straightforward business of filming a normal story using human actors.

For lower-budget films, the digital video (DV) camera is a godsend to young filmmakers. Although for now the quality is still less than that of celluloid, the DV camera allows for free-wheeling anarchy. For his science-fiction drama *28 Days Later* (2002) director Danny Boyle used seven or eight DV cameras to shoot his empty London streets with actor Cillian Murphy the only human in sight. Because they could film so quickly, the police were happy to hold up the early morning traffic. Scriptwriter Alex Garland called the story a post-apocalyptic genre and worked closely with the producer and director on rewrites. Together they came up with 15 or 20 different ideas for the end, and ultimately shot three endings ranging from bleak to hopeful. The final decision was to go for a mainstream film for a wider market and so they went for the ending offering a note of hope – but had their cake and ate it by showing the original ending after the credits.

The digital field of filmmaking puts a different slant on writing for films today. They still need good stories, and still require balanced and well-written screenplays. Films shot with DV cameras, or using CGI effects (or both) are going to become more and more common, especially since the technology continues to become more powerful, and cheaper, by leaps and bounds. *Jurassic Park* and computer games have widened the interest in animation for the market made up of boys – and men who never grow up.

Some 478 films were released in the United States in 2000 and by the summer of 2001 eight films had been released that were filmed entirely digitally (that is, on video). The next step in this direction would be the use of digital projectors, in which the source of the projector's image is not light from a bulb shining through film stock but a video file, either streaming live online or stored on a local server. This would complete the circle by making every element of production – filming, editing, sound recording, and screening – digital. In July 2001 *Jurassic Park III* was presented in this way in a few specially equipped cinemas, becoming the first film to be streamed to two screens simultaneously, and the first to use the new format – Digital Theater Interim Master (DTIM) – that allows films to be played on a variety of digital-cinema equipment.

The last link in the digital chain – projection – is likely to be the longest to take hold, for a number of reasons: it would require investment in new equipment by the exhibitors, yet the financial benefit (in saving the cost of duplicating prints) accrues to the distributors. Unlike changes to the filming and editing process, it doesn't directly affect the budgets of production companies, and unlike previous technical advances such as stereo sound, widescreen picture formats, and colour film itself, it won't be a major draw for audiences, since its success is defined not by how much an audience notices the difference between it and a film-stock projection, but by how little. Nevertheless, since it will represent such a big saving in costs for the industry as a whole, it is a change that will almost certainly happen eventually.

Be that as it may, the effect of digital technology on the process of making films, if not exhibiting them, will be profound, with quicker shoots and reduced production costs lowering the bar for entry into the filmmaking business. Steven Soderbergh, who shot his first digital film, *Full Frontal* (2002), in just 18 days, said that digital technology 'will turn the industry upside down. You can go direct to the bank and you don't need a major studio. The costs and labour will become minimal' (compared with today, when the US industry spends $700m a year on prints.)

Why Does This Matter to the Writer?

All changes in product dictate the future of film production – and that starts with the script. What it will mean to the writer is hard to tell as yet. It may mean that, as costs fall, more films are being made as previously uneconomic 'niche' films become financially viable.

At the big-budget end of the market, technical advances will be a means of pushing up 'market share' against competing forms of entertainment. In the same way that cinemas began to empty when television came in, the TV is taking second place to the cinema today. Fewer people are willing to sit at home and watch the box when they can see something more exciting and spectacular on the big screen. This will mean there will be more opportunity for film writers with a visual imagination and an inventive story mind.

Francis Ford Coppola said recently, 'It is very hard to have innovation in a film when you're dealing in an industry that wants all the films to be the same: to be a franchise – like Coca Cola – something they can be assured will sell over and over again, even though it's the same formula. The cinema should not be Prometheus chained to a rock with all the vultures eating off his liver. The cinema should be free.'[2]

The world of commercial cinema is unlikely to become as free as Coppola and other filmmakers would wish, or as friendly to the work of an *auteur*. The desire of production companies is to have a hit film and make money, so that they can make *another* film – and they never think the writer is the best judge of that. Maybe you can prove them wrong.

Sir Alan Parker, while decidedly happy making films for the Hollywood factory, still devotes himself to the British film industry. At the time of writing, he is Chairman of the British Film Institute and of the Film Council. He made *The Life of David Gale* in 2003 with Kevin Spacey, the kind of serious story that 'it's difficult to persuade the studios to do ... Personally, I've never been offended by the American filmmaking machine ... and I think that [the British film industry] should embrace it.' Parker hopes that the Film Council – whose brief is to distribute Lottery-funded financial help to worthwhile projects – will help the British to ease out of the cottage-industry approach, which he sees as a dead end. 'One of the things I hope we have done is to put the industry on a more professional footing ... Now, I believe if you have a decent script, the money's there.'[3]

If you have a good script it will definitely get interest from an agent because really good material is in short supply. The big agents will want to package it with one of their stars. While it is true that if you have a 'hot property', an agency's wish to tie it to a particular actor might limit the script's progress, it could also be a plus. It is a good idea to find out which agent handles the star you have in mind and try to submit your script to that one.

The information of how to write and present your screenplay is all between the covers of this book. When your screenplay is ready to be sold, put your mind to networking and you may just hear of the right door to open. Others have done it. Two actors (Matt Damon and Ben Affleck) did it. Some of my former students are doing it. You can do it, too. It takes talent, perseverance, hard work, and yes, luck. But it's my belief that you can make your own luck with the proper preparation.

If you think you're a writer, get to work.

Appendix 1 | GLOSSARY

General Terms

LONG-FORM TV: MOWs and Mini-series.

MOW: Movie of the Week (90 min/120 min movie made for TV)

MASTER SCENE SCREENPLAY: Correct format for submitting a script to a Hollywood film company. Scenes are not numbered and transition directions are not used (see also CUT TO: below).

BO: Box Office

INDIE: An independent filmmaker or film company.

Abbreviations and Headings

EXT.: Exterior

INT.: Interior

SFX (FX): Special Effects

POV: Point of view

VO: Voiceover (narration over action)

OS: Off Screen (also Off Stage)

FADE IN: Used at beginning of script.

FADE OUT: At end of script. For TV also at commercial breaks.

FLASHBACK or FLASHBACK SEQUENCE: - Scenes set in an earlier time-frame to the present story.

MONTAGE SEQUENCE: A series of short shots edited together to form an impressionistic sequence or to suggest different events happening simultaneously. A famous example of montage is the two-minute sequence leading up to the distant sound of the train whistle in *High Noon* (1952).

CUT TO: These transition headings are added to the shooting script when the director is aboard. It makes for easier reading of a Master Scene Screenplay without them. They are placed between all scenes in a shooting script on the right side of the page.

SCENE NUMBERS: Generally added at the shooting script stage, although it is fine to use them in your first draft (particularly if you have script software that renumbers automatically during revisions). The numbers go on both sides of the slug line. Don't confuse these with page numbers, which are placed in the upper right-hand corner of each page.

SLUG LINE: tells us where the scene is located. It is written with the following punctuation. American producers are sticklers for such things.

INT. DARK OFFICE — NIGHT.

ACTION: The description of the action that is happening at the moment:

The office is dark. There is a man in the doorway.
We cannot see his face in the shadow.

TRANSITIONS: These terms (and similar) are generally not used in a first draft script and are reserved for the discretion of the director. CUT TO/FADE TO

BLACK/DISSOLVE TO/WIPE TO/CROSS FADE (a dissolve between two scenes).

INTERCUT: For a specific shot or sequence within a scene. e.g. for a close-up of a newspaper or letter,

such as:

> MARY: Come here and look at this!

> INTERCUT: Close on the letter in Mary's hand.

BACK TO SHOT: or CUT BACK TO: to return to the scene you were cutting away from (which will be filmed in continuous time, and the INTERCUT edited into it).

SHOOT DATE: The start date of principal photography.

A WRAP: The completion of the last shot on principal photography as in, 'It's a wrap'. ('WRAP' was originally an acronym derived from the command 'Wind, Reel and Print').

LOOPING: Re-recording dialogue (or adding background voices) after filming is finished. Looping tends to destroy the energy of an actor's reading, as does dubbing somebody else's voice, as happens with translations.

Concerning the Script

STORY: Literary or dramatic material indicating characterization of the principal characters, and sequences and action suitable for use in, or representing a substantial contribution to a final script.

THROUGH LINE: Central story-line, which begins in first 15 minutes of the script from the initial turning point and continues to the end.

THE SPINE: Same as THROUGH LINE.

INITIAL TURNING POINT: (Sometimes called the INCITING INCIDENT). The first moment in the protagonist's life when events bring him to a crisis. Generally occurs in the first 15 minutes of script.

ORIGINAL TREATMENT: Original story written for motion picture purposes in a form suitable to be the basis of a screenplay.

TREATMENT: Screen adaptation of a story, book, play, or other pre-existing material.

SCREENPLAY: The director's version of the final script with individual scenes, full dialogue, and camera set-ups. There can be many numbered drafts.

TELEPLAY: A screenplay intended for television production.

THE PITCH: Telling (pitching) the story to the potential buyer to sell it or get a development deal. You should be able to pitch an idea in 15 minutes.

A PACKAGE: The script plus actors, or director, or finance.

REVISIONS: Changes and polishes to screenplay. Usually, from the shooting script, any further revisions will be put on coloured paper: pink, blue, and yellow for first, second or third revisions respectively. This is an aid to the director in knowing which draft he's working on.

A POLISH: WGA's Minimum Basic Agreement says: The

writing of changes in dialogue, narration, or
action, but not including a REWRITE.

REWRITE: Major changes in plot, story-line, or
interrelationship of characters. This receives a
separate fee. Rewrites may be made by writer(s) on
their own screenplay, or by a new writer brought in
by the producer. Usually assigned in stages: i.e. first
set of revisions, second set, etc.

ELEMENTS: Any extra 'clout' the writer can add to his
PITCH presentation – such as having interest from a
star or an established director – would be elements in
the package.

People On The Set

See 'Who Does What' in chapter 18 for a list of people
involved with the production process and their job titles.

Writer's Signs And Aids

These are for hand-correcting your printed script for aid
in making later corrections on the computer. I always
put any additions or remarks on the right-hand margin
for easy spotting, and if there are subtle changes you
might miss in copying them into the computer, put an
arrow or line on the margin to catch your eye. I also
make corrections in pencil so if I change my mind,
I can erase. These are not for a finished script.

¶   Paragraph sign (very useful for books but
      also useful for separating shots in writing
      ACTION)

R̶   Crossing through means change from capitals
      to lower case

<u>r</u>   Underlining usually means italic, but in a film
      script it means change to capital letters.

↔   Arrows to make a space, or cut a space

ﻉↄ   Connect sentences: The boy stood on ﻉ
      ↗ the burning deck and all around

Stet.   Ignore corrections. Go back to the original

↓   Move down

↑   Move up

number to re-line a speech: 1) Now 4) to come to the
3) for all good men 5) aid of their country. 2) is the
time

                             don't

▲   an upside down V insert: When in doubt ▲
forget to write.

APPENDIX 2 | SOME SCENE EXERCISES

Here are two exercises for writing a social drama scene.
Write a scene of (approximately) three pages. The
situation and attitudes of the characters are suggested
only, but not the dialogue.

Exercise One

Back Story

Walter, a junior executive in a bottling plant, and Gwen
have been married ten years. They have a nice house in
a suburb of the city (*you choose the city*). When Gwen
discovered Walter had been having a long-term affair
with his secretary, Cathy, she demanded a divorce.
Walter has moved in with Cathy (*where?*). Gwen has
refused to let him see their five year old son, Charlie.
When Gwen finds out that Charlie has leukaemia, she
does not tell Walter. But when Walter ran into the
family doctor he discovered the truth. He has telephoned
Gwen and demanded to see her. Reluctantly she has
agreed to see him.

The Scene

It is 10 pm when Walter arrives at the house. Gwen and
he haven't seen each other for seven months. (*How and
when does he arrive? Where do you begin the scene?
Outside? At the door? Does he let himself in?*) He
demands to know why she has kept his son's illness
from him. (*Does he contain his anger?*) Gwen feels that
he doesn't care about them any more, so it is none of
his business. Walter insists on seeing his son. But Gwen
says Charlie is too ill to be woken. Their attitudes are
abrasive.

Walter tells his wife there are new cures. Leukaemia
is not necessarily fatal any more. Gwen is still too hurt
and angry to accept his help.

During the scene we discover that he has actually
broken up with Cathy. (*How and when does he reveal
this information?*) For the last three months he has been
living alone *(where?)* Does he explain what he has
learned about himself and that the reality of living with
Cathy was not the same as the sense of intrigue that
nurtured the affair?

You must choose how to resolve the scene. The scene
should have tension, anger, abrasiveness, and leave us
wondering 'what next?' since this is not the end of the
film. Does their pride keep them strangers? Is Gwen at
fault here? Will the element of danger bring them
closer? Can they get together and start over? Is it
hopeless? Which of them is the most understanding of
their own failures and weaknesses? Is this going to be a
'happy ending' film – or are we in for a weepie?

Exercise Two

Back Story

An older woman who was a great beauty in her youth
has lost her looks through illness and age. She is very
rich, having been given a huge settlement from the
husband she divorced 20 years ago and invested her
money wisely. Since then she has had many lovers, but
they've all disappeared – a few with some of her wealth.
She has not seen her daughter since the girl was 12.

You decide why the couple divorced and why the
wife hasn't seen the child. The daughter, now 20, has
come to see her mother in a previous scene and they
have started a relationship. The daughter works on a
magazine.

The Scene

The daughter brings the father to see her mother,
unannounced. He has lost all his money and has spent
two years in jail for tax evasion. He is a lonely, broken
man. The daughter begs the mother to help him and

maybe take him back – since he has no place to live.

What is the mother's attitude? How does she react to this broken man? Does she say yes or no to her daughter's proposal? How does he feel? Is he a willing participant? Is he ashamed, embarrassed, arrogant, proud?

Try writing one solution to the above scenes and then take the opposite point of view, and write a totally different scene. Which one works the best dramatically, and why?

These are only loosely plotted scenes. Make up some of your own, choosing a key emotional situation. Don't worry about a whole story for this exercise. Just take a dramatic situation between two people, and write it. It could even kick off an entire story idea for you. Try to be analytical about your own work. One of the best ways is to put it on the shelf for a few days or weeks and come back to it with a fresh eye.

APPENDIX 3 | FESTIVALS AND MARKETS

According to Steven Soderbergh, 'Making a film is the best entry-level job into show business. But it is like booking myself into a 10,000 seat arena and playing a guitar that I can't play and charging $10 a head. Just because you can get a film made doesn't mean you *should* get a film made.'

Film festivals are where to go with a film if you have made one. And the lower production costs made possible by digital cameras have opened this door a little wider. A festival can also be the place to take a finished screenplay (properly copyrighted – see 'How to Protect Your Property' in chapter 17) because you never know who you might network with. A *Film Fest* supplement to *Variety*'s 26 August–1 September 2002 issue listed over 370 international film festivals and film markets that would take place over the following year – and there are many more, from 'African American Women in Cinema Film Festival' in Hollywood to the 'ZoieFest!' in Atlanta. The American Film Market takes place in Santa Monica, California in February and there is also a Miami Film Market. In America the big one has been the Sundance Festival, which takes place in Utah in January and which has given a leg-up to many beginning filmmakers. But they are by no means only in America. Whatever the location, gender, genre, or format you favour, there's surely a festival to suit you for networking. I am listing some of the more notable, and you might find one near you. Be sure to check the Internet for latest correct details.

In the UK there are two major festivals: the Edinburgh International Film Festival in August (www.edfilmfest.org.uk) and the London Film Festival in November (www.lff.org.uk/). These are aimed at the public, not distributors and exhibitors. They do not have markets attached but they preview the best new cinema from around the world. In late November or December there is also the Cinemagic Festival in Belfast (www.cinemagic.org.uk/), which includes screenwriting

workshops. Other major festivals include Berlin in February, Cannes in May, Toronto and Venice in September, and the Mercato Internazionale Film e Documentario (MIFED) in Milan in October.

Apart from Open, General, Independent, International, Features, and Shorts, diverse categories are catered for. Certain festivals specialize in films by women or specific ethnic groups, or focus on particular film formats (such as experimental shorts, short videos, silent films), genres (documentary, science fiction, horror, romantic comedies), or themes (human rights, current affairs, non-violent conflict resolution).

The following sections list festivals that web searches have connected with the particular focus mentioned (though that is not necessarily the primary focus of the festival). The time of year given was the most recent at the time of writing.

Festivals Featuring 'Screenplay'

Ajijic, Mexico. *International de Cine* – six days in November, features Animation, Documentary, TV Commercials, Short Subjects, Feature Films, and Screenplays. www.ajijicfest.org

Havana, Cuba. *International Festival* – eleven days in December, favours Latin American Films, Videos, and Screenplays. www.habanafilmfestival.com

Houston, USA. *International Film Festival* – ten days in April, lists Features, Shorts, Docus, TV Commercials, Experimental, Student and MusicVideo as well as Screenplays. www.worldfest.org

Nantucket, USA. *Nantucket Film Festival* – www.nantucketfilmfestival.org

Reno, USA. Along with the three-day November Film Festival is a Blockbuster Screenwriting Conference. www.renofilmfestival.com.

Rome, Italy. *Independent Film Festival* – four days in February covers Documentaries, Shorts, Animation, and Screenplays. www.riff.it

Santa Clarita (California), USA. *International Family Film Festival* – nine days in April, Short and Feature Screenplays. www.sciff.org

Telluride (Colorado), USA. *IndieFest* – Four days beginning late August, alongside the Film Festival covers Independent Films and Screenplays. www.tellurideindiefest.com

Festivals Featuring 'Student' or 'Teens'

Aberystwyth, UK. FFRESH: *The Student Moving Image Festival Of Wales* – in October. Screenings, meeting people, awards, masterclasses, and seminars. www.ffresh.com

Big Bear Lake (California), USA. *Big Bear Lake Film Festival* – three-day festival in September. www.bigbearlakefilmfestival.com

Houston, USA. *Houston International Film Festival* – ten days in April, www.worldfest.org

Kiev, Ukraine. *Kiev International Film Festival Molodist* – eight days October, www.molodist.com

Lake Placid, USA. *Film Forum* – five days in June, www.LakePlacidFilmForum.com

Miami, Florida, USA. *Made in Miami Film & Video Festival* – ten days in January, www.madeinmiami.org

Sarasota (Florida), USA. *Cine World Film Festival* – ten days in November, www.filmsociety.org

Stamford, Greenwich & Norwalk (Connecticut) USA. *Directors View Film Festival* – five days in February, www.dff.org

Tallinn, Tartu & Viljandi, Estonia. *Black Nights Film Festival* – seventeen days beginning late November, www.poff.ee

Festivals Featuring 'Experimental'

Albany, USA. *Empire State Film Festival* – nine days in September, www.empirefilm.com

Dallas, USA. *Deep Ellum Film Festival* – five days in November, www.def2.org

London, UK. *Raindance Film Festival* – ten days in late October, www.raindance.co.uk/festival

Madison (Wisconsin), USA. *Wisconsin Film Festival* – four days at the end of March, www.wifilmfest.org

Memphis, USA. *Memphis International Film Festival* – four days at the end of March, www.MemphisFilmForum.org

Szolnok, Hungary. *International Film Festival of Fine Arts* – six days in October, www.tiszamozi.hu

Toronto, Canada. *Planet In Focus: Toronto International Environmental Film & Video Festival* – six days at the end of September, www.planetinfocus.org

Festivals Featuring 'Debut' and 'First Time'

Ann Arbor, USA. *Ann Arbor Film Festival* – six days in March, www.aafilmfest.org

Berlin, Germany. *International Forum of New Cinema* - ten days in February, www.fdk-berlin.de Bogota, Colombia.

Bogota, Colombia. *Bogota Film Festival* – nine days in October, www.bogocine.com

Bratislava, Slovakia. *Bratislava International Film Festival* – ten days starting late November, www.iffbratislava.sk

Hamilton, Bermuda. *Bermuda International Film Festival* – seven days in April, www.bermudafilmfest.com

Kiev, Ukraine. *Kiev International Film Festival Molodist* - nine days in October. www.molodist.com

Locarno, Switzerland. *Locarno International Film Festival* – August, www.pardo.ch

Mannheim, Germany. *Mannheim International Film Festival* – nine days in November, www.mannheim-filmfestival.com

Nodance (Utah), USA. *Nodance Film Festival* – six days in January, www.nodance.com

Torun, Poland. *Young European Cinema Film Festival* – March–April, www.mke.pl

You can check out www.variety.com/filmfest2002 on the web to find a festival near you (subscription needed – free trial available).

APPENDIX 4 | WRITERS' GROUPS AND COURSES

Canada: Victoria Motion Picture School Ltd., Suite 101, 775 Topaz Ave., Victoria, British Columbia, V8T 4Z7, Canada Tel: +1 250 381 3032 / Toll Free +1 888 522 FILM. The Victoria Motion Picture School (VMPS) Professional training for the motion picture industry.

Denmark: National Film School of Denmark, Theodor Christensens Plads 1, 1437 Copenhagen K, Denmark. Tel: +45 32 68 64 00 Fax: +45 32 68 64 10. www.filmskolen.dk.

North by Northwest, one-week residential script workshops for professional European screenwriters and script editors. Between May and November. Script editing and script analysis sessions developing scripts for introduction to the European market. North By Northwest c/o Danish Film Institute, Vognmagergade 10, 1120 Copenhagen K, Denmark. www.n-nw.com/eng/content/programme_content.html. Tel: +45 33 74 35 28 Fax: 45 33 74 36 04.

Ireland: Vanessa Gildea Training and Information Officer Film Base, Irish Film Centre, 6 Eustace St., Dublin 2, Ireland.

Israel: Department of Film and Television, Yolanda and David Katz Faculty of the Arts, Mexico Building, Tel-Aviv University, 69978 Tel-Aviv, Israel. Tel: +972 3 6408403 or +972 3 6409483 Fax: +972 3 6409935

United Kingdom: Euroscript, development of 20 scripts selected from an open competition. Distance training (story analysis and lines, genres and script editing). 1–8 Whitfield Place, London W1T 5JU. Tel/Fax: +44 020 7387 5511.

The Moonstone, international script labs. Moonstone was founded by the late John McGrath in consultation with the Sundance Institute, operating three workshops per year for writers and directors. www.moonstone.org.uk

University of Wales, Aberystwyth. Richard Gough, Senior Research Fellow in the Department of Theatre Film and Television Studies, teaches the MA, Theatre and the World. Contact Antony Pickthall, Marketing & Development Director, Centre for Performance Research (CPR), 6 Science Park, Aberystwyth, SY23 3AH. Tel: +44 (0)1970 621571 Fax: +44 (0)1970 622132 www.thecpr.org.uk

International Film School Wales, School of Media & Design, University of Wales College, Newport, Caerleon Campus, PO Box 179, Newport, NP18 3YG

United States: University of Southern California (USC) School of Cinema and Television (Los Angeles, California).

University of California at Los Angeles (UCLA) AFI Conservatory (Los Angeles, California). Participants earn a Master of Fine Arts degree or Certificate in Directing, Cinematography, Producing, Editing, Screenwriting, or Production Design.

College of Santa Fe (Santa Fe, New Mexico). The Moving Image Arts Department at the College of Santa Fe gives film, video, and multimedia students access to one of the finest undergraduate production/post-production facilities in the country.

University of New Orleans Film School (New Orleans, Louisiana). For future producers, actors, directors, editors, animators, cinematographers, storytellers, production designers, message designers and historians of theatre and film.

International Film Seminars, New York. 198 Broadway Suite #1206, New York, NY 10038 Tel: +1 212 608 3224 Fax: +1 212 608 3242.

New York Film Academy. Hands-on Filmmaking. One Year or eight weeks, six weeks or four weeks. www.nyfa.com

You may find these sponsored links helpful: NY Film Academy: Learn Filmmaking From: www.screenplay.com

American Screenwriters Association. For beginners to seasoned professionals, offering script competitions, conferences, pitch meetings.

Some International Writers' Guilds

Belgium AVA. E. Limbourglaan 11, 1070 Bruxelles Netverk Vlaamse Scenarioschrijvers. Koninklijke Prinsstraat 87, 1050 Bruxelles

Denmark Danske Dramatikeres Forbund. Klosterstræde 24, 1157 Copenhagen K. Tel: +45 33 45 40 35

Danish Film Institute, Vognmagergade 10. 1120 Copenhagen K, Denmark. Tel: +45 33 74 35 28. Fax: +45 33 74 36 04

Finland The Finnish Dramatists' Union. Vironkatu 12b, 00170 Helsinki 17. Tel: 90 628 191

France Union Des Scenaristes. Rue de Bagnolet 34, 75020 Paris

Germany Verband Deutscher Drehbuchautoren. Rosenthaler Strasse 39, 10178 Berlin

Greece Screenwriters Union Greece. c/o 18 Kodriftonos Str., GR-11257 Athens

Iceland Writers Union Of Iceland. Hafnarstratei 9, Box 949, IS-121 Reykjavik. Tel: +354 1 131 90 Fax: +354 1 61 31 90

Italy SACT. Via A. Gramsci 20, 00107 Rome

Netherlands Netverk Scenarioschrijvers Vsv. Singel 464, 1017 Aw Amsterdam

New Zealand New Zealand Writers Foundation. PO Box 47, 886 Ponsonby, Auckland. Tel: (09) 360 1408 Fax: (09) 360 1409. www.nzwritersguild.org.nz/foundation

Norway Norske Dramatikeres Forbund. Postboks 579 Sentrum, 0105 Oslo, Tel: +47 22 20 16 28. Fax: +47 22 42 03 56

Spain Guionistes Associats De Catalunya. Passeig Colom, No 6 (Desptatx No 3) Barcelona 08002. Tel/Fax: 93 319 71 35

Sweden Sveriges Dramatikerforbund. Bla Tornet, Drottninggatan 85, S-11160 Stockholm

United Kingdom The Writers Guild of Great Britain. 15 Britannia Street, London WC1X 9JN. Tel: +44 (0)20 7833 0777 Fax: +44 (0)20 7833 4777 www.writersguild.org.uk

| NOTES

Chapter 1
1. See Lasky Sr's autobiography, *I Blow My Own Horn* (Doubleday, 1957)
2. See *Whatever Happened to Hollywood?* by Jesse Lasky, Jr. (New York: Funk & Wagnall, 1975)
3. *'Funny Money'*, episode from *The Naked Hollywood* (BBC, 1991)
4. *Hollywood Reporter*, 30 October–5 November 2001

Chapter 2
1. *British Academy of Film and Television Arts*, 22 April, 2002
2. *Sunday Times*, July 8, 2001
3. Such as *Danger Man*, *The Avengers*, *The Saint*, *The Baron*, and *Philip Marlowe*.

Chapter 4
1. BAFTA interview, 1 December, 2002
2. See *The Dark Side of Genius* by Donald Spoto (1983) and François Truffaut's *Hitchcock* by Truffaut (1978)
3. Interview in *Paris Review*.

Chapter 5
1. See The Theory of Illumination, Henry James.

Chapter 9
1. Private correspondence.
2. Q & A session at BAFTA, 24 September

Chapter 12

1. 'The One to Watch', Sunday Times, 3 November 2002.

Chapter 13
1. See *The Writer's Journey, Mythic Structure for Writers* by Christopher Vogler, 1992.

Chapter 14
1. BAFTA interview, 4 September 2002.
2. BAFTA interview, 1 December 2002.
3. BAFTA invertiew, 10 December 2002.

Chapter 15
1. *Sunday Times Magazine*, 30 June 2002.

Chapter 16
1. *Writing Comedy: A Guide to Scriptwriting for TV, Radio, Film* and Stage, by Ronald Wolfe (revised edition, London: Robert Hale, 2003)

Chapter 17
1. Interview with Sandy George, *Screen International*, 12 January 2001

Chapter 19
1. *Guide to UK Distribution*, Film Distributors' Association, 2002 edition

Chapter 20
1. *Variety*, 27 May–2 June 2002
2. Interview, 'Culture' supplement, Sunday Times 11 November 2001
3. Screen International 22 February 2002

FILM INDEX

NAMES INDEX

SUBJECT INDEX